INSIDE DATA SCIENCE

INSIDE DATA SCIENCE

HACKERS AND THE MAKING
OF A NEW PROFESSION

PHILIPP BRANDT

Columbia University Press   *New York*

Columbia University Press
Publishers Since 1893
New York   Chichester, West Sussex

Copyright © 2026 Columbia University Press
All rights reserved

Library of Congress Cataloging-in-Publication Data
Cataloging-in-Publication Data is available from the Library of Congress.
ISBN 9780231214087 (hardback)
ISBN 9780231214094 (trade paperback)
ISBN 9780231560184 (e-book)

LCCN 2025021631

Cover design: Noah Arlow

GPSR Authorized Representative: Easy Access System Europe,
Mustamäe tee 50, 10621 Tallinn, Estonia, gpsr.requests@easproject.com

CONTENTS

PREFACE

D ata science has come of age quickly. College campuses, corporate offices, and the pages of the daily paper are among the many places that are hard to imagine without data scientists today, a group that barely existed a decade ago. How could that happen?

The answer is complicated. Rapid social changes, including data science's rise, are iceberg-like objects. We see only the tip. The sudden appearances of new political movements, art forms, or technological niches help some, worry others, and give everyone else something to watch or discuss. But the vividness is also deceptive. For one, it distracts from the continuities that still dominate social life. Even as far as the underlying changes matter, their outer shine hides the internal workings. Although sociologists have spent decades building methods for tracking social processes without falsely factoring in the future, formal methods work best for problems where appearance plays no role. In data science, however, the certainty and uncertainty about its place in the world of quantitative expertise was the defining challenge. Analysts and observers, who discern and interpret patterns from formal or informal procedures, cannot just forget how things turned out when thinking about their beginnings.

This complication undermines research projects studying emergence, including an analysis of data science's rise. To start, they have to name the problem they address, which centers the design on the outcome and not the cause. Capturing emergence without working backward from its manifestation requires a point of departure that precedes the problem's final form. This requirement leaves scholars with a dilemma. Either we have to think twice about studying an emergent process, forgoing possibly important discoveries, or we have to allow our approach to doing research to evolve, which means messing with our core principles. For better or for worse, I was too new to this line of work to understand the situation when data science appeared, and I pursued this problem that had not yet gained broad salience. The lessons that followed structured this book and generated ideas for tackling the next surprising situation.

The solution required more than the combination of methods and styles expressed across the chapters of this book. The entire process of research was involved. The writing took about eight years from the first to the final draft. This followed four years of original research. Twelve years was both too long and not long enough. My research advanced too slowly and demanded that I turn to smaller studies to buy time to finish this one. The additional work and time were just enough to solve the complex problem of data science's emergence as a professional role.

In the meantime, the data science case changed in scope, makeup, and appearance. It has become not only ubiquitous but also different from what it was at the time of its inception. Its integration into academic institutions has solidified data science's place in the world. It also gave established scholars a chance to reimpose their view of quantitative work. The expansion of data science training has made the role more visible and also helped firms regain the upper hand over data scientists. And this quickly forming clarity has attracted a different crop of nerds to data scientist positions.

As a result, the image of data science in this book about data science's early formation is partly at odds with the popular image of the field. Rather than challenging other presentations, however, it complements them to produce a more complete portrayal of this new expert role. This new perspective is rooted in a focus on the fleeting activities of early protagonists instead of the established academic or commercial stakeholders. This switch identifies the foundations of a much larger historical process. Both the people and the processes are hard to see. But data science's rapid rise to public salience is an invitation to cultivate a sensitivity to the interplay of popular and technical issues. Such a view is crucial in an era when digital technologies continue to penetrate our private, professional, and collective lives.

Part of the payoff is intellectual. The new perspective provides insights into data science and the modern technological world and enlarges the scope of the problems that sociologists can consider. The practical payoff is evident for the work of students or scholars near data science. While they can follow existing footsteps, those are still fresh and, crucially, don't capture the experiences of the predecessors who left them. This book brings the older experiences to the fore to open the set of possible solutions for the remaining challenges. After all, even the initial accomplishment was far from a solid foundation for a new line of work. Professions and occupations operate through associations. There were ideas for similar initiatives in data science, and some went further than others, but none as far as those before them. However, just like the pioneers first defined the role, their successors can still define the organization of this new line of work. And just like some onlookers piggybacked on the early data science ideas, others can get involved and shape its ongoing development.

This book reveals the social machinery that undergirds the shiny, scary, sorry, or superb developments that data scientists—or hackers, programmers, sociologists, artists, or others with data science skills—may seek to advance, correct, or avoid. It makes some more complex points along the way. For instance, it highlights discipline as a process that organizes social life next to more rigid and familiar forms of coordination. It also discusses reflections on one's social surroundings as a systematic activity whereby people navigate the world. Mostly, however, the book surveys data science's early days, the excitement, worries, and struggles of those who were involved in it. New directions look different for all who embark on them. But they always come with experiences of breaking unfamiliar ground, like those the following pages present.

INTRODUCTION

The early 2010s were a pivotal time in the long history of technological change. Those years saw maps of the world rendered from Facebook friendship networks, lives lived via cloud-based services on personal laptops and mobile devices, and vast opportunities provided by newly abundant and accessible server capacities. But as is often the case, such abundance came at a cost. Facebook toyed with its users' emotions, and rogue outsiders used the platform to manipulate political beliefs.[1] Even public services compromised their mission in their rush to adopt data-driven solutions.[2] These developments lacked the elegance of today's artificial intelligence technologies, but they rang in the current era.

Far from seeming like the dawn of a new era, in the early 2010s much of the world was still reeling from the devastating financial crisis that had led to the Great Recession. But while Europe fought for its currency and political union, the US economy was already recovering its momentum.[3] News headlines announced a new gold rush or oil boom, this one fueled by raw materials not buried in the ground but floating in the virtual cloud. In their purest form, the raw materials were ones and zeros, the binary code at the core of all modern information technologies. The invention of the personal computer and the many software packages and applications produced since then had long reduced most operations to users pointing and clicking with a mouse and to libraries of specialized commands for programmers. But just as this routine engagement with information technologies had settled in, cheap broadband connections made coding lessons available to anyone who was curious, growing scattered nerds into a major force.[4]

The technological innovations produced during those years have drawn much scrutiny. Popularizers, critics, and commentators have identified new forms of economic exploitation, cultural creation, and threats to democracy, social life, and personal freedom.[5] Strikingly, accounts that covered these widely different issues sooner or later made the same observation, one unexpected at the time: the presence of *data scientists*, the computer coders whose statistical analyses and machine learning algorithms were reshaping modern life. Some academic researchers were skeptical, explaining that data science was nothing new.[6] And more recent artificial intelligence applications have buried those remaining traces of human involvement in quantitative analyses. For a moment, however, data scientists, novel or not, were the protagonists of the era of big data.

Today, "data scientist" is a household term. The *Oxford Dictionary of English* defines it as "a person employed to analyse and interpret complex digital data, such as the usage statistics of a website, especially in order to assist a business in its decision-making." The Wikipedia entry has a less corporate orientation: "Data science is an interdisciplinary academic field that uses statistics, scientific computing, scientific methods, processing, scientific visualization, algorithms and systems to extract or extrapolate knowledge and insights from potentially noisy, structured, or unstructured data."[7] These definitions mention the same technical areas but differ otherwise, and quite significantly so. The more authoritative *ODE* situates the novel role in a clear spot; the collaborative Wikipedia outlines a more open area of work. Which one is correct? Why is there still so much uncertainty, now over a decade into the role's existence?

Uncertainty is the defining challenge of data science's rise. Questions dominated their reception when data scientists stepped into the spotlight. The public wanted to know who was behind the threats and promises, businesses were looking for untapped revenue opportunities, and first-year college students saw new career prospects. Data scientists also had questions about what was going on with their lives.[8] Several specialists have followed up, studying the fruits of data scientists' work, their place in the professional world, their entanglement with academic sciences, and their sense of self.[9] These studies captured a fascinating moment in which the occupants of a new expert role were on the brink of securing stable professional prospects. As data scientists continued to thrive, however, the question of their inception has remained unanswered and, in the shadows of newer and more advanced data-processing applications, almost slipped out of sight.

Data science's emergence highlights a crucial yet puzzling aspect of our understanding of professions, offers a fascinating moment in the evolution of the world of work, and opens a window onto the onset of the current technological era. Its rise to ubiquity and subsequent retreat to a more muted presence shows that data scientists were not as inevitable as their status suggests. In contrast, their early days show how a group of coders seized a moment and challenged the established division of expert work around quantitative problems. They embraced technological advances in moments when academic traditionalism often looked past their promises. At the same time, they used longstanding scientific expertise to remain on top of economic and techno-logical changes that often obscure the efforts of expert commu-nities. Data scientists' feat contextualizes today's AI-dominated moment and sheds light on entirely different groups in similar situations.

THE PUZZLE OF A NOVEL PROFESSION

An explanation of data science's emergence must build on exist-ing theories and scholarship to get a handle on the problem's scale and scope. While the abundant early attention made data science look unprecedented, the big changes around it are a classical sociological concern. The field's founding figures, from Karl Marx to Emil Durkheim and Max Weber, studied the interplay of technological change and social life and work, developing increasingly nuanced accounts of the organization of tasks and changes in economic conduct. Robert Merton extended those ideas to the interplay of science and society. While the warnings of statisticians and other specialists that data science wasn't new could cast doubt on a dedicated analysis of data sci-ence's emergence, precisely those reservations of an established group underline data science as a sociological puzzle. If anything, the specific arguments questioning data science's legitimacy dovetail with sociological insights into the broad recognition of arcane expertise.[10]

Sure enough, modern social scientists, and by now a more diverse group, have studied many different aspects of data sci-entists. They have shown that data scientists struggled with their role's novelty and ambiguity. They found themselves sited between different institutional fields and often acting as agents of or accomplices to big-tech corporations.[11] Broader writing has assessed the damage data science has done,[12] what it might be able to do,[13] and ideas for getting it right.[14] All these contributions have helped place and understand the role of data scientists in the modern sociotechnical infrastructure and economic order. But the reliance on such specific perspectives has so far left us without an explanation of how the first data scientists found one another and recognized themselves.

When data scientists gained attention, the scientific understanding of expert professions was experiencing a major shakeup. After a decades-long dominance of a view proposed by Andrew Abbott that professions defend their turf in a system of rivaling groups, Gil Eyal argued for "replacing" this understanding with a body of scholarship that had begun to flourish in Abbott's shadow.[15] The alternative view drew attention to the informal underpinning of expertise and its application to lay problems.[16] While some loyalists argued for the continuing pertinence of Abbott's more formal view, the challengers gained ground and have become the default point of departure for much new research.[17] Regardless of which side is right, this internal skirmish underlines the ongoing relevance of the questions that data science's rise raises but also complicates the interpretation of empirical patterns.

This opposition summarizes the main fault line in our understanding of expert work, and I will organize my analysis around it. But contextualizing this tension in the larger literature offers some initial orientation. After all, just as Eyal responded to Abbott, Abbott was critiquing thinking before his, and a plethora of specialized insights have appeared along the way. These evolving ideas clarify the data science case as a sociological problem and a source of novel insights.

Early writing on professions focused on their defining characteristics. Authors like William Goode, Everett C. Hughes, and others listed shared values, the reliance on abstract knowledge, autonomy over training, licensing, and codes of ethics in different combinations.[18] These items turned occupations that stood out intuitively, most clearly in the classic examples of medical doctors, lawyers, architects, and so on, into an analytical category. However, later generations have called out their predecessors for using analytical rhetoric to rationalize positions better seen as being much more ideological.[19] This criticism points to a twofold challenge in understanding expert work. Scholars of professions are part of the problem they study; whatever they conclude about experts reflects back on their own status and legitimacy. And to complicate the problem further, although experts occur widely, their specific appearances and consequences vary across time and space.[20]

Leaving behind the semisuccessful endeavor of defining professions, sociologists have studied the internal functioning and dominance of professions in society. Some of the most productive insights came from careful analyses of how medical doctors dealt with one another and their patients.[21] Challenging earlier expositions, Eliot Freidson, for example, found that neither collegial oversight nor dedicated service orientation were as present in treatments as the definitions of professional status had led one to expect. Interactions between experts and their patients turned out to shape the outcomes more than the content of formalized expertise.[22] Magali S. Larson's influential book elevated the analysis again to the larger professions. She focused on "occupations that we call professions" in an echo of the skepticism toward clear-cut definitions. But she used that cynical view for analytical and theoretical gain. Professions, Larson argued, worked as "collective mobility" projects that monopolized areas of expertise for individual and collective advancement.[23] This scholarship showed that working definitions of professions were enough, and maybe most effective, for shedding light on important social problems around expert work.

Abbott's was the last word on that comprehensive level until Eyal's challenge. In the meantime, a long list of studies shed light on specific problems in the world of expert work. Beth Bechky, for example, has studied the jurisdictional conflicts from Abbott's theory between occupational groups in a technology firm. Dan Menchik analyzed the decision making among physicians; Rebecca Sandefur, the use of legal expertise in courts; Damon Phillips and his coauthors, status orders in legal work; and Wendy Espeland and Michael Sauder, how law schools faced external rankings.[24] These studies addressed important mechanisms that undergird expertise. They are less concerned with a continuous understanding of how expertise fits in the social world.

One issue that links different levels and areas of expert work is professional identity. Identity appeared in the early definitions and in modern research, which has asked how experts acquire, adapt, and refine their professional identity. We understand that it evolves when preconceptions are in conflict with the profession's day-to-day activities,[25] at least among established groups that come with ready-made images like medicine, finance, or consulting. In more inclusive views that consider the growing number of workers with multiple professional affiliations, studies have shown how those affiliations form hierarchies, exist side by side, or get integrated.[26] Which configuration someone adopts has to do with the status society has assigned to their job.[27] These accounts do not fully explain professional identity. But they illustrate how one theme connects individual and collective experiences around expertise. Whatever the definition of professions, experts ask themselves who they are in relation to their work, and part of the answer has to do with what the group thinks (insofar as there is one), who is part of the group, and where the individuals or groups find themselves in the social structure.

Data scientists extend this focus and raise new questions. They neither relied on the imagery of an established profession, nor did they resort to mostly individual solutions to such a conflict. Instead, they constructed their identity together to find footing in the division of expert labor. This process links data scientists to the foundational sociological interests in professions as an evolving system of groups that use abstract knowledge to address concrete problems. Studies of lawyers, doctors, or psychiatrists discerned their development in past socioeconomic regimes and demanded retrospective analyses, but data scientists have assembled their role in the digital era and in front of our eyes.

INSIGHTS FROM DATA SCIENCE

The analysis will show that early data science didn't just fit one or the other theoretical perspective. Data science expertise came as mathematical equations, algorithms, and functions in programming languages, which established degree programs and newer online forums and tutorials taught widely. Besides this institutional infrastructure, the many definitions summarizing the evolving movement's meaning formalized its emergent substance. As Abbott's theory predicts, the new role caused a backlash among established quantitative experts. But, as Eyal's view would lead us to expect, the data science accounts highlighted informal interactions between early protagonists. An anecdote of the first data scientist at LinkedIn included a nod to the first data scientist at Facebook, who himself mentioned conversations with a scientist from Yahoo's research lab. Other protagonists published definitions together.[28] Accordingly, early studies of data scientists have found evidence in support of both sides of the theoretical divide.

The lack of clear fit partly reflected the early stage of data science's emergence. All professions got their start at one point. But although not all professions have survived until today,[29] the lengthy existence of some offers more material to study and theorize, leading accounts to be more accurate for the various forms into which expert groups have matured. They are also more immediately significant for outsiders. However, data science's fit with two supposedly opposing theories may also indicate the consequences of an internal conflict and the reliance on diverging empirical cases at the expense of general sociological insights. The challenge that the formal view overlooked crucial informal dynamics and relations rested on a selection of problems that unfolded below and between the groups of the classic focus. Rather than providing a better understanding of expert work, they fleshed out the nuances of the existing spectrum of sociological thinking. The rise of data scientists, in contrast, highlights distinct social dynamics that demand a new theoretical view.

Looking closely, the early appearances of data scientists question classic professions or academic experts as the relevant reference point. Many data science pioneers introduced themselves as data "hackers," and they returned to that label as popularizers started taking over data science discussions. Public discourse often depicts hackers as malicious programmers who break into computer systems to steal files or disrupt operations. But hackers have a long history of doing good in the tech community. For insiders, the label refers to programmers who improvise solutions, such as creating applications and systems with a collective orientation and outside of large corporations.[30] Early data scientists placed themselves in this lineage when introducing themselves as data hackers. The problem of the rise of the data scientist role is, thus, at least partly a question of how hackers with statistics skills defined a distinct professional identity.

The focus on data analysis sets the hackers who started calling themselves data scientists apart from other programmers. For most, the idea of data comes with charts of vertical bars or horizontal lines in newscasts showing election results or market dynamics. These graphics display aggregate information of hundreds, thousands, or millions of data points, which occasional data analysts are familiar with from spreadsheets in standard calculation and computation software packages. The most recent trends around big data, machine learning, and artificial intelligence stack layers of complexity around and on top of those rows and columns, making them larger, combining different types of records, and finding more complex associations between them. Whereas these images initially invoke ideas of rationality, precision, and truth, a long list of studies has shown how culture, politics, and economics shape the meaning of data and how formalized data shapes those social processes.[31] The ubiquity of datasets gave data scientists a platform while also tying their emergence to bigger social dynamics.

Even before data scientists, experts haven't been far from datasets and their consequences. While merchants, engineers, and administrators used and spread datasets early on, the most significant changes started in science. Scholars have rendered unseen worlds visible through data analysis, building procedures that have then diffused back into practical applications where, eventually, the data scientists found themselves.[32] Data scientists recognized this history in the choice of their profession's title and how they introduced the role. But research that has tracked those legacies has also pointed out changes in science throughout its own development.[33] While some universities are centuries old, the scientists who invented modern data-analytic procedures did not have the same positions as today's academic researchers.[34] Just the last few decades have seen a measurable change in how scientists work.[35] An analysis of data science's emergence needs to consider academic scientists, whatever their complaints about intruding data scientists, as an evolving group itself.

Data science's emergence promises crucial scientific insights into competing theories of expert communities, the ever-changing world of their work, and the iterative process of knowledge production and application. Instead of demonstrating either the formal or informal underpinning of technical expertise or who put two words together first, it sheds light on how scattered hackers first found one another to solve problems together. This puzzle plays into both dominant theories, but it also advances sociological ideas beyond the technical setting. Mature expert groups enjoy benefits and privileges vastly different from most other groups in society. Whether political, cultural, or religious, they, too, first had to form. The specificities of these settings will likely come with their own stories. But with data scientists having gone through those processes so recently and publicly, they offer a unique view into the dynamics of a profession's collective emergence.

DATA SCIENCE IN NEW YORK CITY

Insights into data science's formation require observations of data scientists first finding one another. The most common research strategy so far has involved interviews with data scientists. These interviews produced important insights, but they missed the moment when data scientists defined themselves as suitable interview candidates. An analysis of data science's emergence needs to capture how data hackers got together and what happened when they did. This book reports such an analysis.

The flavor of data science that's been at the center of the events of the past fifteen years started in Silicon Valley, the home of the tech startups and the place where a few lost souls first described this new role. But while data science is unimaginable without the Bay Area, the region's long history as the engine of technological change undermines an analysis of data science's emergence. No design could untangle the effect of the local ecosystem and the collective dynamics among early data scientists. A sharper analytical lens requires a place that stands enough on its own that it doesn't just follow Silicon Valley—which would introduce a different set of issues—while giving data scientists enough context to come together. New York City in the early 2010s was such a place and serves as the field site for this analysis.

New York had already gone through a phase of trying to emulate the wonders of Silicon Valley, a sorry attempt that ended with the failed "Silicon Alley" during the burst of the dot-com bubble. By the time data scientists appeared, these events were ancient memories, having left the city without a culture and institutional infrastructure conducive to technological advances. But, as ever in New York and particularly following the financial crisis of 2008, ambition was in the air and resources plentiful. Michael Bloomberg, a software entrepreneur with an explicit agenda to strengthen tech activities, was the city's mayor. Google opened a large office in Manhattan, as did Facebook, and funding poured in for data initiatives at existing and new academic institutions. New York even featured in the Silicon Valley–based origin story of data science, with an early member of the Facebook data science team consulting a mentor from a previous New

York–based research experience about the label. Data hackers had much to lean on and put together.

I found myself in New York neither by design nor by chance when data science came around. I had followed tech activities in Silicon Valley like much of the world from a distance before arriving in New York City to pursue a degree in sociology. While the city had plenty to offer for a young sociologist, I was still excited when I caught a whiff of what I suspected had come from out west. The majority of the observations that followed the initial hunch and informed this analysis began in 2012 and lasted until 2015. These were the years when data science was just gaining recognition and spread widely. During this time, I watched data scientists reflect on who they were in firms and research fields, talked to them, looked more broadly at how far they had come and where from, and tried using their techniques and expertise. These impressions captured data scientists in the whirlwind of changes at the time, revealing the situations in which early nerds, coders, and hackers found themselves.

Data scientists sought respite from larger events in a series of focused discussions about their role and work. The most decisive insights into data science's emergence in this analysis come from observations of over seventy public gatherings with over one hundred presentations and discussions. The events were called meetups because the groups that organized them used the online platform meetup.com—founded in New York City—to coordinate, which helped volunteer hosts keep member lists and send emails with information about the date and time, location, and topic of an upcoming event. Several different groups formed to discuss technical topics such as programming languages, database technologies, or analytic techniques. They all centered on presentations of guest speakers—from startups, larger companies, city offices, or academic institutions, either locals or out-of-town visitors—but left time for questions and discussions after the event. These gatherings were where the early data science community came together. Neither speakers nor attendees knew for sure what data science was, but they noticed shared problems that made sense to discuss around that label. These discussions showed the process whereby the participants defined a new expert role and professional identity.

A novel profession does not reveal itself from the outset. I found early data hackers and their gatherings trying to understand what was behind the excitement about the new computational techniques for statistical analyses that I had encountered in more academic settings. I learned that many others were asking themselves that question, if for different reasons, and, curiously, including those to whom we looked for answers, making this incipient movement a striking research problem.

METHODOLOGICAL STRATEGY

Rigorous research requires that problems fit the scientific method, which begins with a theory that informs a research question and hypotheses for empirical tests that lead to retaining or rejecting the hypotheses. Data science quickly looked like a new instance of longstanding sociological concerns with expert work that provided theories for analyzing its emergence. But this was not how data science first appeared. Whereas research of expert work has typically found relevant observations in situations of expertise application and training, data scientists had come together outside the familiar places for those activities. They were still easy to note, but the lack of a clear start, end, and scope of their formation posed unique analytical challenges. An analysis of this process requires different theoretical traditions and hypotheses. While one could sort those out in advance, such an assessment launches the research process before a specific theory could guide its unfolding.

The scientific method is also only a recent invention, a formalization of analytical intuitions that have delivered the insights that defined modern science in the first place.[36] Early generations of scientists worked methodically, like modern scholars, while also having to respond to the research challenges that were still new to them and not yet tightly defined in elaborate debates.[37] The inventors of the equations and measurements that placed us on Earth and Earth in space in the eighteenth century, techniques still in use today, also mobilized "audacity."[38] Scientists could admit when they saw patterns in data points and "suddenly it struck" them.[39] Data science's emergence is more familiar to us now than their problems were to them. But professional formation occurs rarely enough to benefit from those fundamental sensibilities in addition to the rigors of routine research problems.

The challenges that come with data science are not unique, and with the foundational analytical concerns still in sight, contemporary methodologists facing similar problems have started revisiting the modern consensus. They argue that attentiveness to a changing research problem remains crucial for theoretical innovation.[40] Such an analysis still proceeds systematically—observations can only be "striking" if they emerge from a procedure that started with clear expectations. But the research process involves adjustments. The qualitative methodologists Iddo Tavory and Stefan Timmermans reminded modern researchers of "abduction," the creative moment of formulating a new hypothesis in light of existing theories, as the critical step for making discoveries. They built on Charles S. Peirce's original ideas to outline a strategy for contemporary research of "recursively moving back and forth between a set of observations and a theoretical generalization."[41] Researchers had continued to use abductive strategies but often left them implicit amid a focus on modern concerns, undermining a systematic discussion of getting discoveries right.

As surprising discoveries, like data science's emergence, are sudden and rare and, thus, impossible to subject to fully standardized research procedures, analytical "tactics" for analyzing them are the most systematic solution. A key tactic involves "defamiliarization" to bring into view new observations or relations between familiar observations and, with them, new ideas.[42] The new views may take adjustment, but those adjustments generate new hypotheses. Importantly, these ideas must then still hold up to systematic analysis involving the initial observations and new tests. Defamiliarization is, thus, part of the research process, not its end or goal or a rejection of the established scientific method.[43] The gulf in data science between its technical underpinning and broader appearance makes abduction a promising methodological framework for capturing the struggles and dynamics that connect them.

However, the problem's expanse also undermines the defamiliarization tactic, at least initially. The crucial challenge that comes with analyzing the emergence of a highly technical activity such as data science becomes clear in reference to an example of abduction from Tavory and Timmermans's introductory textbook. The example is grocery shopping, a familiar everyday experience they used to show how a series of simple questions reveals important complexity in this familiar experience. For instance, getting groceries is less uniform if we consider it can start with a recipe or an empty fridge. The shopping experience may start on the sidewalk, at the door, or between the aisles. In the end, we discover that we understand such an everyday experience less than we may have thought. Now, data science is no everyday activity. It did not come with intuitive images, making it stand out from the social scientific research situations like the shopping example that is familiar to scholars and their subjects.

Data science requires familiarization before defamiliarization is possible. Such familiarization could start with its history. But this past already has a present in statistics and with computer science on one side and programmer and hacker communities on the other.[44] States and commerce were central throughout science's history. While they shaped data science's formation, too, a focus on this continuity alone would miss those aspects of the profession's emergence that took place outside of those institutions. Instead, familiarization has to start with data science, the situations and discussions of data hackers who first started to consider their work as a new expert role.

Data science's formation challenges even the innovative ideas of the abductive method, resetting the point of departure in the absence of a common understanding or academic writing. This gap puts additional weight on the collection and analysis of empirical observations. Although the social world is readily visible, we may not see all of it, especially when it is in flux and as arcane as quantitative expertise. Parts that look similar may have different underlying dynamics, some of which we already know, while others have remained hidden. Understanding which is which requires going back and forth between what we know and what we see from varying perspectives. A study of data science's emergence has to consider different possible directions with one eye on unfamiliar images as the case becomes more familiar to remain sensitive to the distinct problems in a profession's formation.

ACCOUNTING FOR EMERGENCE

The analytical challenges that come with a research problem like data science's emergence don't stop with the selection of a field-site and the collection and interpretation of observations. They extend to the written account of the research process and the results.

The standard assumption among writers has been "that [readers] want to know what they found," not "the false starts and dead ends" or what the analyst "had read just as they had their idea."[45] And rightly so. The analyst should make a complex problem accessible. But the conclusion that the solution is an idealized version of the research process is misleading as well, not only in an era where the social sciences increasingly commit to transparency of their research process. The standard reaction for accounting for additional complexity has seen calls for increasing documentation of the research process and adherence to rules for communicating hypotheses and analytic strategies. But the analysis of an emergent process such as data science's formation puts additional demands on these new strategies.

The abductive approach offers a methodological solution for generating systematic observations of an emergent process, but it comes with writing challenges. A rethinking of the cultural form of academic writing took a scholar of the caliber of Pulitzer nominee Diane Vaughan over a decade of reflection.[46] But her accomplishment inspired new thinking for conducting and communicating discovery-oriented research.[47] Instead of narrating the analytic steps following formal rhetoric, which couldn't accommodate unexpected turns of an emergent process, it needs to expose those turns to the reader. The reporting of the analytic insights must account for the researcher's decisions that led to them. This book follows up on Vaughan's proposal.

Data science only started to take shape at the outset of the analysis. For an accurate picture, the analysis has to account for the initial openness of data science's future. The first three chapters of this book remain close to my experience of pinning down this moving target. Since data science hadn't announced its emergence in advance or declared its successful completion, I couldn't define a precise outcome of interest from the outset. The discussion documents how data science became traceable and suitable for a systematic study. This reflective strategy adds unique insights. Since data scientists didn't know what lay ahead either, these disclosures capture a crucial part of their experience. The tone changes to a more familiar external perspective for the remaining chapters, which report an analysis from when data science had grown enough into itself to locate its underlying dynamics. However, they remain "hunches" in the abductive framework and reveal the presence of some central sociological concerns in data science's emergence.

ARGUMENT AND OUTLINE

The striking appearance of data scientists in New York City, the academic debate's stalemate, and the iterative methodological approach make for an original account of a professional role's collective construction. Technical competencies and digital tools were necessary, but they did not define a new expert identity. Scattered nerds and coders recognized themselves as data hackers and presented themselves as data scientists. They followed no strategic plan and faced questions from established sciences about what they did and who they were. While training helped clarifications of their work, they had no expertise in seeing and justifying themselves as a new professional role. This book demonstrates that they defined data science in creative interpretations of the social dynamics around their work. Their shared concern with seeing the world through datasets disciplined their reflexive hunches into an increasingly robust professional narrative.[48]

The book develops this argument in two main steps. The first step, which consists of chapters 1 to 3, proceeds abductively in peeling back data science's outer layers. It moves from the myriad traces of early data science activities to committed discussions in New York City's tech community, the intricacies of technical data science work, and its historical roots. These observations constitute the backdrop of data science's collective definition. The second step consists of chapters 4 to 6 and returns to the dominant theories about expert work to look inside data science's emergence. It scrutinizes early presentations of data nerds and hackers at after-work gatherings. The chapters move from curious turns in those technical talks to new ideas that data scientists had for positioning themselves in the modern division of labor.

Chapter 1, "Encounters," begins where many serious encounters with data science began, in a lecture hall, and then New York City's tech scene during the early 2010s. Nerds and coders had started to discuss their jobs, problems, and ideas during regular get-togethers. They coordinated through digital tools but met in person, where they still faced challenges similar to those faced by other collective activities. In return, their openness set these groups apart from academic fields that had traditionally controlled quantitative expertise. These meetings became the social spaces of data science's collective definition.

Data science's first impressions were abundant but also hard to place. Chapter 2, "The Work," takes a bird's-eye perspective to locate the data scientist's role in the labor market. Data scientist jobs were numerous early on, and their descriptions overlapped with popular discussions while adding specificity. For dual analytic leverage, the chapter adopts a data science approach, including code, database technologies, and machine-learning techniques, to analyze a large swath of data scientist job descriptions. The quantitative analysis finds skills that coalesced in data scientist jobs developed across separate specializations. The procedure situates data science work in its sociotechnical contexts, capturing how new data-analytic approaches spread through an open and increasingly dense digital infrastructure. However, neither new technologies nor firms explain the assemblage of data science expertise.

The first set of analyses ends in chapter 3, "Science and Data," with a journey to data science's scientific roots. Vocal specialists—applied mathematicians and statisticians among them—rejected any distinct novelty in the then-new calls for data science. History supports their pushback, but it also reveals a more profound puzzle. The chapter shows recurring skirmishes between experts in quantitative analyses throughout two centuries of scholarly debates. Each iteration saw one side drawing attention to practical challenges in data-analytic work—now central in data science—and established colleagues who stopped them. The practical concerns remained underdeveloped. Rather than relabeling established academic ideas, data scientists revived and embraced problems that earlier generations tried to hide. Their seemingly naïve insistence on these problems revealed a massive hole in the stock of scientific knowledge.

The first analytic phase locates data science's emergent dynamics in a loose community of data nerds and hackers who linked old techniques with new tools and technologies. How did they recognize and articulate their work as a new professional role? Whereas the initial chapters surveyed data science's contours, phase two turns to field observations of over seventy public events and discerns the presentations and discussions to uncover the collective construction of data science in light of existing theories of expert work.

Chapter 4, "Interactions," enters the events where the data community met. Numerous groups with loose and overlapping memberships formed around different data topics. Hosts organized meetings in startup spaces, corporate meeting rooms, and university lecture halls for which speakers joined to present their work. Participants asked questions that showed different backgrounds and interests and sometimes led to more confusion than clarification. But speakers consistently presented data science as an analytic process that involved reflections on technical ideas in response to practical concerns. Their commitment to their problems and audiences led presenters to describe obscure procedures in imaginative terms as distinct data science practices.

Chapter 5, "Relations," continues following these inside observations. It focuses on surprising but crucial topics of data science discussions: relations with colleagues, clients, and established scientists. Speakers paused their talks about machine learning techniques or database systems to share stories of encounters with others at their work. Curiously, they described their personal experiences analytically, which externalized and generalized conflicts, misunderstandings, and other odd interactions as social dynamics. The details differed, but their conclusions from these observations were that their data-analytic ideas and activities had to be understood as a new expert role. Reflexivity turned individual experiences around modern data work into a shared professional narrative.

Data science was not only a question of new takes on data-analytic procedures or professional relations. The construction of this new role was also deeply personal. Chapter 6, "Identity," concludes the argument that qualitative reflections among data scientists were crucial for their definition of a novel expert role. The analysis shows how presenters reconciled new situations as data scientists with earlier setbacks, anxieties, and misguided aspirations. They shared feelings of loneliness and how those feelings passed once they identified others with similar skills and ideas. Talking on stage, speakers went as far as tracing their work today to obscure thinkers and familiar scholars with an eye toward the intellectual processes behind well-known ideas. Those self-reflections cast curiosity about systematic observations of the social, natural, and technical world as a core value of the data scientist identity.

The analysis ends before data scientists sorted out their professional prospects. University programs have continued to grow, and data scientists have continued to staff workplaces worldwide.[49] But new artificial intelligence technologies have significantly shifted the discourse and likely affected their fate. The book's insights into their early days are crucial for understanding the interplay of science and society as artificial intelligence is on the rise and cracks in ancient institutions create new uncertainties.

1

ENCOUNTERS

Anyone who paid attention to tech in the early 2010s eventually heard about data science. It didn't start as a big event, and there was no major announcement. It came up in everyday situations. Twitter timelines were likely places, but so were coffee chats, the daily paper, or TV shows. The name made intuitive sense—data and science were essential parts of technological progress—but the sound of them as a union still had a surprising ring to it. Observers asked themselves what was behind the buzz, while quantitative analysts wondered if they were now data scientists.

Clarity came in 2012 when the *Harvard Business Review* introduced the data scientist role as "The Sexiest Job of the 21st Century." The article, coauthored by Thomas Davenport and DJ Patil, an academic and the founder of the data science team at LinkedIn, the professional networking platform, explained that a data scientist was "a high-ranking professional with the training and curiosity to make discoveries in the world of big data."[1] They told the story of LinkedIn's first data scientist as an example, complete with some potentially enlightening details—he was a physicist by training—and a story involving disagreements over the data scientist's say over data processing priorities. The "sexiest job" line stuck and joined a list of catchy definitions, which included a Venn diagram showing data science in the intersecting skill sets of "math and statistics knowledge," "hacker skills," and "substantive expertise," and a silly tweet that placed data scientists between software engineers and statisticians.[2] No one believed that these tag lines explained data science, but they put the ongoing changes in context and gave them meaning.

Such general ideas of data science offered comfort but raised more questions than they answered. A fuller picture emerged as data scientists soon became associated with shocking news stories of election manipulation and state surveillance. Even though it was unclear what could have prevented those incidents, commentators quickly proposed technical solutions to rein in the new developments.[3] Their insights into the mechanics that caused the damage also shifted the view of data science that outsiders got to see. They highlighted concrete technical issues ripe for fixing, but their perspectives missed the full process of the arrival of data science. This chapter starts on the sidelines, as the early protagonists did, and finds its way into what was beginning to become data science. It traces data science's emergence while it was unfolding. This dynamic view can capture the simultaneous sense of familiarity and surprise and, ultimately, the twists and turns along the way.

The analysis starts where data scientists started their stories: an account of the situation. But whereas they found themselves in the weeds of big-data analyses, I found myself between them, processing those experiences. The first data scientists I met had come to my campus to prepare students for what was ahead in data science jobs. This training was only the start of a process that invited those who wanted to learn more to follow along and see data science in practice. I followed those who did to find businesses that were adopting data science. But the practicing data scientists there found themselves scattered too widely to make sense of their role. I followed them further when they found one another, not only in classrooms but in casual after-work get-togethers, where they discussed the technical intricacies of data science and its place in the world.

The chapter's account of that journey through data science's early days follows the abductive method. After recovering the popular presentations of data science on the ground in New York City, the chapter contextualizes those occurrences in the social scientific understanding of expert work and collective action. References to familiar professions give some orientation, but the theories they informed stumble over data scientists' early meeting grounds. Closer inspection and a different set of references transform that obstacle into a key window into data science's origins. Although data science is a case of expert work, it's also an outgrowth of everyday social interactions.

DATA SCIENTISTS' POPULAR IMAGE

There was no escaping from popular data science definitions. Data hackers who shared their early impressions found themselves dealing with ideas others had proposed when talking about the role. Those of us just catching up had to negotiate between what we saw and what we heard or knew. Different motivations would draw attention to different sides of the early definitions. Excitement and enthusiasm spread quickly, feeding on the crisp and clever lines describing this new technical role. However, their authors were also insiders and offered details that said more about the experiences behind the newly popular images.

Popular data science proposals admitted complications right after offering a basic definition. In the perhaps earliest published introduction,[4] Jeff Hammerbacher, among the first Facebook hires, recalled how he and his team set up a data processing system and implemented some rudimentary and then more complicated analyses. Throughout the story, he stressed that their approach followed no guidelines, remembering how he "later learned" or "didn't realize it at the time" but that "it turns out."[5] The inevitable point came when they "were all surprised" about the duration of data processing operations as the database grew larger, only to then see the analyses, together with the system, collapse.[6]

By itself, the account could be mistaken for a naive admission of the project's lack of a clear structure and strategy. But the stories of others who designed large-scale quantitative analyses mirrored it. DJ Patil, the data scientist coauthor of the *Harvard Business Review* "sexiest job" article, reported a standoff between engineers and a data scientist even in his more polished presentation. The data scientist had just joined and begun "forming theories, testing hunches, and finding patterns,"[7] which led to an idea that would put demands on the technical system other than the sheer expansion that was the engineers' concern. No one knew whose ideas to follow, Patil told his readers, until LinkedIn's CEO intervened and sided with the data scientist.

The details differ, but both stories acknowledge moments of uncertainty. The situations were more specific and fleeting than the big-picture opposition between enthusiasts and critics around data science's overall emergence. And Hammerbacher and Patil had linked the catchphrases that gained traction to these more complicated reflections. Together, they show there was no concerted campaign for establishing the data scientist role,[8] just attempts to make sense of early data analytic work. Data science is rooted in struggles with uncertainty.

This view of data science summarizes this book's research problem. The problem sits deeper than questions of who said what and when to make arcane knowledge publicly visible and whether that's new or not or only reflecting larger technological changes. The question is how those who supposedly said these things recognized and assembled an area of expertise to talk about in the first place. This problem is not obvious from the beginning. Data scientists know coding and statistics, giving them the technical skills that undergird the larger discussion. They are difficult enough to understand. Articulating expertise that integrates those skills is an entirely separate problem. While signs of their struggle with this dual challenge were all over their most visible stories, more vivid themes—new technologies, big businesses, and scientific entanglements—kept those signs in their shadows. A systematic analysis of data science's emergence needs to uncover that deeper level.

DATA SCIENCE 101

The way I encountered data science followed a strategic decision, as is standard scientific procedure, but my choice did not have an analysis of data science as its goal. This approach turned out to be a shortcut that avoided the impressions of data scientists in a formal position either in popular discussions or the interview situations that other researchers experienced. However, it involved learning the problem I sought to explain from scratch.

The undertaking began in 2012. I was two years into my graduate program in sociology at Columbia University in New York City. I had completed the required coursework and started looking for a dissertation topic. I explored questions concerning small manufacturing firms and others concerning foreign exchange students in rural communities. Both were issues close to my sociological interests but far away from the data science discussions, which started at this time only outside of my purview. As I couldn't decide between these options, I learned about a class that could supposedly help me improve my methodological skills. It was new, had the curious name "Introduction to Data Science," and looked like a welcome and possibly productive distraction from the daunting choice of a research topic.

Today, universities offer comprehensive data science programs, which students can pick even before arriving on campus, leading to different experiences from mine but also from those of the early data hackers. The lecture I stumbled into was the first of its kind at our institution. This situation reflects the entanglement between data science and established disciplines and how universities featured in early data science accounts. The data scientist in the *Harvard Business Review* story had just completed a PhD in physics before joining LinkedIn. The creator of the famous Venn diagram defining data science, Drew Conway, was a graduate student in political science. None of them or their peers who had already held jobs had studied explicitly to be data scientists. My choice of the course out of curiosity more than strategy introduced features of the experiences of those who first defined data science. Ironically, my naïveté set me up for a research design that was quite close for an outside analyst to the inside perspectives that defined data science's earliest days.[9]

My initial concern when registering for the class was how the content could help me with my ongoing and new research projects. The syllabus promised a comprehensive survey of methodological approaches, including causal modeling and machine learning techniques, solutions for processing large-scale datasets, and some specialized techniques, such as network analysis. It introduced this technical material around concrete examples, ranging from purchasing patterns to global social media discourse. But the technical side dominated. Depending on their prior training, students could attend regular tutorials teaching the mathematics behind statistical tests and another sequence for the programming skills necessary for analyzing datasets. The instructor also organized a two-day workshop that covered specialized programming languages and software tools that were not part of the lectures but were critical for data science work.

This content responded to my original hopes for the class. It gave me new ideas for handling datasets and setting up statistical analyses. But the purely technical side and the setup were a misleading start for insights into data science's emergence. All of this took place on a university campus, and the material could have been part of many other courses without data science in the title. The lead instructor, Rachel Schutt, had a PhD in statistics. Data science, meanwhile, was gaining attention for its entrance into workplaces where it addressed practical problems.[10]

The lectures introduced me to the applied side, too. Most meetings featured guest speakers who described their data science work in tech companies, startups, consultancies, or industry research labs. Rachel herself came to teach in the evenings after finishing her day job at Google. She led the course together with a writer and activist, Cathy O'Neil, who had moved from a faculty position in a math department to a quantitative analyst role in finance and then a data science position in advertising. Rachel told us at the beginning that she had noticed the increasing attention to data science but also a disconnect between the use of the title and the skills of those who explored this emerging area. Cathy had seen much of the dark side of data science applications in her industry positions. The class was their attempt to ensure that those interested in data science jobs knew how to do the work and be sensitive to its harm. The lectures and tutorials did what I hoped and improved my technical skills. I became a more confident programmer and more literate in machine learning techniques. But it was the larger situation that "struck me" as a sociological observation.[11]

My prior understanding had led me to expect technical insights. I encountered a collective movement. The two outside instructors who were data science insiders, the tutorials, the workshop, and the guest speakers made the experience stand out from the many courses I had taken. Even the students were different, coming from a variety of programs and in numbers uncommon for graduate courses. Seen through an abduction-oriented methodological lens, the class defamiliarized my understanding of quantitative expertise in a university setting. It changed from a tool that I had to learn for my research to a research problem, a social object and collective experience undergoing change. As a sociologist, that change caught my attention. Understanding its origins required tracking down the ongoing discussions, and that required leaving campus.

THE STAKE-OUT

Like in much of social science research, my initial ideas to study education or the economy built on existing writing and benefited from the salience of those areas. The class did what existing research and everyday life could not provide for data science. It exposed me to a corner of the social world where something curious was going on that seemed worth investigating. But a research project needs a research design, which begins with the selection of a case or definition of a boundary for making systematic observations. I had to locate the relevant data science actors and activities in the larger process of technological change; I needed to find my equivalent of the introduction's textbook case of a run to the supermarket.

My theoretical point of departure built on data science's early signs of a profession with abstract knowledge. Existing scholarship covered related cases in workplaces such as startups and corporate offices, like those from where speakers visited Rachel's lecture or those that employed the data scientists quoted in the news and published in trade magazines. Rachel herself was a working data scientist. And so my first cautious step into the field beyond the syllabus involved signing up for one of the office-hour appointments she offered to her students. I told Rachel that my questions were not only clarifications of topics from class. She agreed to discuss data science more broadly. I was nervous about the prospect of talking to a specialist as an outsider.

Rachel sent me the address of a coffee shop near her office in New York City's Meatpacking District, which she had selected as her office-hour location. It was also the kind of place where she met with peers and where the idea for the class had started during breakfast chats with Cathy. Our conversation moved between exploring data science from my perspective as a novice and observations I was making as a sociologist listening to a data scientist. Rachel shared different takes on data science that circulated at the time, many of which did not fit the type of data scientist she thought could do the work. Her reflection was a first observation for me that supported the research strategy in light of the established literature on professions, where conflicts were a longstanding insight.[12] Before I had fully mapped out the case, the social dynamics others had seen in related cases started to appear. But most importantly, for launching a study, Rachel promised to make introductions to other insiders.

Our conversation was my first step into the field outside the university. Others that followed and the experiences from the class became a multipronged strategy for specifying the case's boundaries. As these initial impressions settled in and new conversations, many of which Rachel brokered, began, I searched for different signs, signals, occurrences, and instantiations of data science. My reading into the social scientific field of science and technology studies made me sensitive to the techniques that were part of data science. In class, we covered a new one each week as a solution to a quantitative problem. I became interested in linking those techniques to consequences in the social world, for instance, understanding if travel, culture, or health-related data science applications use the same or different methods and to what effects. I started pursuing these questions in a spreadsheet listing techniques and algorithms I could identify and their fields of applications. This research contextualized the conversations with Rachel and others.

Following some recent concerns in studies of newer professions, I also tracked companies and other initiatives in New York City that said they used data analysis. I made a long list in a second spreadsheet that recorded their activities and how central data analysis seemed in them. The list included the workplaces of the guests who visited the Introduction to Data Science class, but they only made up a small fraction of the hundred-plus entries. I started developing a broader view that moved away from the lecture that had first defined my understanding of data science.

The diverse applications of data science were impressive and increased my nascent confidence that this exploration could become a systematic study. But the overview did not do justice to the social processes that the broader literature on expert work discussed. To find them and determine their role in data science's formation, I made a plan for getting into the workplaces of data scientists. This plan identified several establishments that used data analysis as research sites. One was a platform called kaggle .com, which coordinated data science competitions, allowing sponsors who sought solutions or simply exposure to the community to present a problem that competing data scientists could solve for a reward. While this was a standard reference in the community and promised a good overview of the case, it was also too unique for a full understanding of data science.

I planned to complement the platform case with a company that developed a recommendation system for nearby leisure activities, a firm in real estate, and one working on fraud detection. In addition, I identified a city office for data analysis, a state-level criminal justice initiative, and a nonprofit startup that helps other nonprofit initiatives or public services pro bono to use their data. Anyone with more experience than I had at the time can tell that choosing so many sites would overwhelm a sole researcher. However, the plan shows how I enlarged my sense of the case from the snapshot that the course that got me started could offer.

As I compiled my lists and talked to data scientists, I also followed those I already knew into their world. Rachel's coinstructor, Jared, who led the programming tutorial meetings, organized a group that met regularly to discuss problems around the implementation of statistical analyses in computational procedures. As in the data science lecture, the main part was a technical presentation of a visitor or member of the group. But the meetings took place in the city, not on campus, usually in common spaces of startups or other professional meeting venues, and they started after regular working hours. Access was not limited to students but was open to whoever had signed up on a free online platform. The only cost was a voluntary contribution to the collective pizza order. These events, which started as a nerdy pastime, turned out to be a launchpad into the heart of data science's formation.

This multipronged approach led me to several familiar impressions and revealed surprising places. The hints of tension in and around data science that I noticed in the initial conversations fit with what I had read in the literature on expert work.[13] So did the specialized techniques I started to associate with data science.[14] I hoped to find more of both in specific workplaces and applications. Then I discovered cheery get-togethers where data scientists shared geeky jokes, exchanged notes, and reflected on their professional experiences. While most of the other strategies sketched out a rounded picture of data science, these impressions did not fit existing theories and required a closer look.

THE NERD PROFESSION

Situations like the data science gatherings, a sight that deviates from what's familiar, are the goal of the abductive approach. Methodologists acknowledge that those situations are messy and assure users and critics of the approach that this is only an intermediary step, one requiring additional work to address a research problem.[15] But there is no standard way out. Because surprising situations come suddenly, the best researchers can do is proceed tactically.

Researchers can continue by revisiting the situation's start.[16] In my case, the bewilderment began in the fall of 2012 when Rachel's office hours helped me stake out the problem I considered studying. My notes included a telling entry. One follow-up email I sent to Rachel started with me reporting that "I went to a meetup today." The remark is not yet special. It referred to one of the after-work events to which I had followed Jared and other data scientists. Meetup.com was the name of the platform that the organizers used to coordinate the activities. "A meetup" had seemed like such a standard reference in the conversations around data science that I was sure Rachel knew what I meant. Instead of telling Rachel about the content, I added, "*unbelievable* how many there are related to data, and attended by data scientists" in parenthesis (emphasis added). Clearly, something I saw had "struck me."

My disbelief had several reasons. One was the sheer number of events I mentioned in my note. But the enthusiasm among data scientists for getting together often spread into the rooms where they met. The crowds radiated an excitement that seemed odd to an outsider who had only read the technical topics of these events in advance. Imagine a bunch of nerds, some stereotypically quiet and just waiting or writing code on their laptops, and others chatting in small groups, enjoying the camaraderie and anticipating something exciting. There was no music or special effects but nevertheless an almost electrifying energy; several events were so well attended that latecomers were left standing in the back. Walking from the streets of New York through anonymous corridors into this social atmosphere was a striking experience.

The curious appearance of meetups extended into their proceedings. Technically, these were professional events held in workplaces to discuss work problems. But no one wore standard business attire, rarely name tags, let alone corporate logos, or tried to sell something. Even recruitment pitches were restricted to the first few minutes and to regular participants or whoever had made their space available for the group. Presenters often worked for companies, but they rarely presented what their technical work did as a product. They focused on the problems they encountered and how they solved them or failed. One presentation that came close to a sales pitch ignited an intense email discussion that criticized the format and led to an apology from the organizer. In all these ways, the data science meetups were vastly different from typical professional events.

The meetings were odd, too, from a technical perspective. Existing accounts of professions, old and new, and whatever dynamics they find tend to focus on professionals in their workplaces, occasionally their associations and governing bodies, or during their training. Meetups or similarly casual events had not appeared in those accounts.[17] Historical research has traced the origins of modern sciences to similar meetings in Paris and London two hundred years ago. But those associations positioned themselves as the gatekeepers, granting the privilege of participating in the technical discussions of the time to a select few and excluding others.[18] Meetups were open to everyone. And yet, meetup presentations were about the core issue in the writing on expert work: technical expertise.

The settings where existing accounts have placed their discussions tend to mirror the familiar formality of expert work, if sometimes only indirectly, through interactions with established groups. The analytical work of social scientists then reveals the social dynamics behind those façades. Meetups, in contrast, were informal places where data scientists came together to escape professional formalism. Their conduct there didn't match the seriousness that social scientists typically have to see through to get at what makes lawyers, doctors, or consultants who or what they are. Anthropologists who have studied the underground programmer community have reported similarly casual dynamics around technical work, but those informal activities explicitly sought to undermine corporate or professional formalism.[19] I saw upbeat excitement, instead, without a clear goal other than the discussion of shared problems and accomplishments around data analysis activities.

The meetups were striking experiences and unusual in light of the existing understanding of expert work. In a departure from standard procedure, where these discoveries follow an initial round of careful analysis, here it came before the analysis had formally begun. In line with the abductive approach, one of the attempts of the multipronged strategy for mapping out the data science case brought into view a new avenue. And questions about the standard views of professions follow. The methodological approach still works for this slight departure. But instead of motivating additional scrutiny of the research problem, that is, data science's formation, this situation demands stepping back and revising the design in a way that accounts for meetups as a social object.

GETTING TOGETHER IN THE 2010S

As baffling as the meetups seemed when I first went, my regular participation quickly made them familiar experiences. Such familiarity can undermine the analytic process, and the abductive method requires that researchers question their intuitive sense of a research situation, even in the textbook's case of grocery shopping.[20] The researcher must view their case in a larger context,[21] an exercise that raises several questions for the data science gatherings: What are meetups other than the places where data scientists end their days? Where did they start? How far did they go? What were they to data science? And what was data science to meetups?

Meetup.com began as a startup in the early 2000s, about a decade before I turned to them to see what data scientists were up to.[22] The idea started as a big vision and solution for practical problems. Its founder, Scott Heiferman, linked its inception to the 9/11 World Trade Center attacks, after which he noticed New Yorkers talking to one another, a sight he had missed when first arriving in the city. He connected this phenomenon of shared isolation, of being alone in a crowd, to the systemic problem that the political scientist Robert Putnam had diagnosed in his famous book *Bowling Alone*.[23] Putnam's survey of the involvement of Americans in various types of collective activities showed on a large scale what Heiferman had experienced personally. He cited these big issues next to much more practical problems that he noticed when, for instance, he failed to get friends to accompany him to a concert of a band that only he liked but they didn't. He was aware, of course, that there were many people out there that he did not know but who liked the band as well, but he didn't know how to reach them.

Heiferman's idea to use the internet to connect people gained momentum, but the startup's early uses had little to do with data science. For example, Meetup.com featured in the 2004 presidential campaign for the Democrat Howard Dean as a strategy for gathering supporters. This innovative campaign tool caught the attention of researchers, who found more involvement in the political campaign for meetup attendees who had attended more meetups.[24] Meetups did not change the nation's political landscape—Dean rarely came in higher than third and stopped campaigning before the end of the primaries—but this example gives a first idea of what meetups were doing in spheres other than professional ones.

The political meetings were visible but far from typical meetup themes. In the 2010s, large US cities might have thousands of active groups,[25] including groups for dog walking, wine tasting, reading, writing, photography, motorcycles, feminist discussions, athletics, and many more. This diversity and prominence are no conclusive evidence of whether Heiferman had realized his dreams and helped Americans reconnect.[26] But it starts to show what the meetups to which I followed the data scientists were. They assembled people around shared interests. Data science was one interest among many.

The meetups I saw ran smoothly, almost like a show. They may not have always started on time (my notes for one meetup documented a "first sound through the speakers at 6.57pm" when the "start was scheduled for 6.15pm"), a microphone may not have worked at first, and once a speaker even disappeared. (In fact, he hadn't actually left, which I knew because he sat next to me in the audience and only waited for a later slot.) But these glitches understate the challenges that are part of collective activities, including meetups. The platform required each group to have a designated organizer. It didn't impose extensive guidelines on that role, such as a minimum number of meetings, length, a keeping of minutes, or any kind of reporting. But a study has shown that in practice, leaders take the initiative and plan meetings and see them through, reserving restaurant tables or bowling alleys, finding bars or hiking trails, or simply deciding on a time and place and reliably showing up to make sure all is as planned so that members can engage in an activity.[27] The tasks are all voluntary and, with the occasional questions and requests from members, could take up enough time that groups made them team efforts.[28] Finally, the endearing images of strangers becoming friends over shared interests often came with caveats: Members pitched ideas but then did not follow through, or old members were unsure about their new peers.[29] The online invitations may have been new, but the rest was not.

This resemblance of meetups and social life outside of an online platform extends to larger collective dynamics when groups grow in size. In a women's hiking group, for example, a participant remembered that when they had over a thousand members, the organizer sought help in doing events.[30] A technology-related group in New York City had grown to over sixty thousand members, attracting the interest of two sociologists, who implemented a computational analysis that detected shifts in how members exchanged messages from broad to specialized conversations as the group grew.[31] Meetup groups have not only gotten bigger but also became so numerous in the 2010s that researchers were able to observe larger social dynamics taking place between them. One study analyzed almost fifty thousand groups in three major US cities to ask how new ones form.[32] They showed that members who leave a group to form a new group bring members from the initial group with them.[33] And in a similarly macroscopic view, another team of scientists tried to discern the success of meetup groups in terms of group size and event frequency and identified the alignment of new members with a group's profile as an essential factor.[34]

These different perspectives on meetups reveal data science events next to everyday collective activities, concerts, religious ceremonies, or athletic events, all with the troubles and excitement that come with them. The setup as an online platform gives them a formal look, but it started with one person's search for peers. They have become social settings with familiar tensions, struggles, and larger processes. Groups form, grow, fight, split, and collapse on meetup.com as elsewhere. The links I clicked to find data scientists sent me into a social world with full experiences.

These insights complicate the impressions from the initial meetup visits, which had quickly become familiar affairs. I was partly wrong when telling Rachel that the meetups were "unbelievable." The millions of events and participants on the platform that come into view when looking from a distance make them utterly common. This recognition amplifies the odd appearance of data science meetups as professional events. While the existing understanding of expert work had no clear place for them, the larger context revealed meetups as meaningful collective activities. But the plausible existence of meetups for data scientists does not make them relevant events for formal knowledge production or definition of boundaries for data science. What effect can those meetings have other than letting data scientists hang out after work?

FERTILE GROUNDS

Meetups were a common way of socializing when data scientists found them for their purposes, but they still look odd next to standard images of expert venues and, thus, as a basis for a new profession. The traditional view of professions stressed their client-service orientation and authoritative expertise,[35] which early sociological writing took as an explanation of professional status.[36] Recent discussions agree that such talk is more a description than an explanation of what professions are in the social world. They have found conflict, competition, institutional entrepreneurship, or informal relations to be more convincing explanations.[37] But the analyses have still presented those insights in the context of familiar professional settings, hospitals, consultancies, or engineering offices. Cultural imagery has imprinted itself on empirical research on expert work.

A profession's appearance is partly a question of perspective. Although dazzlingly specific from up close, more distance reveals professions as just one of a series of social settings with general features, such as outsized status, repositories of knowledge, and sources of identity. Expert work also produces effects similar to those of other social processes. It is one mechanism of many, for instance, that makes different areas of a society more alike or one of several bearers of formal signals we accept as guarantors of our trust.[38] This view of professions as part of a spectrum of social objects makes meetups, with their many collective activities, meaningful places for data science's emergence.

One of sociology's defining insights is that small groups can have consequences much larger than their size or status would suggest.[39] Most immediately, they expose us to others, and others expose us to information, resources, support, and advice.[40] These benefits are personal and, thus, different from the collective accomplishment of a new profession.[41] But groups may also generate forces that upturn or redefine larger structures. The clearest examples are social movements or other forms of collective action that aim to achieve some change.[42] Learned societies in the history of quantitative expertise exemplify this insight in the arcane world of technical expertise.[43] However, these movements, scientific, political, or otherwise, don't capture the data scientists who came to meetups to hang out and learn, not plot a revolution.

Larger changes can also come as unintended consequences from small groups' regular activities.[44] The best example is the United States itself, when, in its creation, the thirteen colonies' residents replaced British rule with a governance system unlike any other at the time. The French intellectual Alexis de Tocqueville came to visit the United States in the early 1830s, leaving after a few months with enough new impressions for his two-volume account *Democracy in America*. The political system was not what impressed Tocqueville most. His central takeaway came from having "met with several kinds of associations in America."[45] The scene Tocqueville saw is hard to imagine today. But whoever has been part of a team, a band, or a church group has experienced the power of collective activities. A lasting impression that the groups that Tocqueville saw left on him was the "extreme skill with which the inhabitants of the United States succeed in proposing a common object to the exertions of a great many [participants]."[46] The groups and their skills became his key insight and made *Democracy in America* an instant success and a classic.

While Tocqueville's reflections on those groups have entered the social science canon, initially felt he needed to "confess I had no previous notion" about them. He was embarrassed that his knowledge of governance systems from years of elite education had not prepared him for what he discovered as their foundation. If such a concern was Tocqueville's reaction, I have to worry about my email to Rachel about the supposedly "unbelievable" meetups.[47] But surprises like these are an integral part of the research process. In sociology, they are crucial when consequences that are widely visible turn out to have roots that require looking closer and from different angles. Tocqueville made the trip from France to the United States before he could see the groups. He was on the right track when going to an unfamiliar place to look behind what seemed clear from afar.

With its rules for elections and governance structures, democracy is salient to everyone.[48] Mature professions come with images of office spaces, technical writing, and professional associations. A governance system is a much bigger accomplishment than the formation of data science. But if voluntary groups of everyday citizens could pull that off back then, a new profession seems like an easy feat for nerds at modern-day events. The Dean campaign's usage of meetup.com draws an illustrative link between the two eras and modes of coming together. Politics may happen elsewhere today, but an emergent profession can still get something out of those informal groups.

The conceptual analogy puts images of the United States in the 1830s next to New York City during the 2010s, revealing another stretch, but one that works with the data science case in mind.[49] The first popular stories of data science began in Silicon Valley with Jeff Hammerbacher at a very young Facebook and DJ Patil at an equally young LinkedIn. The origin of data science here indicates a new chapter of the familiar narrative of technological innovation over the last forty-some years.[50] New York, in contrast, is better known for its attempt to emulate that success, a project that managed to create "Silicon Alley," which quickly ended with the burst of the dot-com bubble.

New York lacked existing infrastructure, but change was in the air when data science entered the scene. The mayor was Michael Bloomberg, a technology entrepreneur with an explicit agenda to strengthen tech activities in the city. Google opened a large office, as did Facebook, and funding poured in for data initiatives at existing and new academic institutions. While San Francisco had more meetup groups per capita across all themes by an order of magnitude,[51] a meetup called New York Tech Meetup still attracted sixty thousand members.[52] Another data-related group celebrated itself as the largest of its kind and inspired offshoots abroad. New York even featured in the Silicon Valley–based origin story of data science, with an early member of the Facebook data science team consulting a mentor from a previous New York–based research experience about the label.

In 2012, when I started to attend these events, data scientists at New Yorker meetups lacked the ecosystem of Silicon Valley's local institutions. They came together because they sought out one another, finding spaces to populate and in which they imported and developed customs that might have made Tocqueville take notice. Without the legacy in technology but fresh interests and commitments, New York offered a unique opportunity for watching data scientists negotiate their early days.[53]

The link to Tocqueville's story illustrated what everyday gatherings can do when they have the space. It also recalls a key obstacle in that Tocqueville did not make the trip to understand democracy or find the groups that created its defining customs. His trip was official government business to study the prison system, on which he published a report soon after his return. *Democracy in America* followed on his own account years later. On a much smaller scale, I had enrolled in the data science class to learn technical skills that I applied in my ongoing research but not to study data science's formation. Tocqueville wrote a classic. I almost missed meetups as a key site, and, in any event, today, such a switch of direction demands more justification than an apologetic note, like Tocqueville's, can provide. What did the accident, even though fortunate, lead me to miss?

SOCIAL EMBEDDEDNESS

I found the meetups because of Rachel's lectures, and I was in Rachel's lectures because I was a student, and enrolling in classes was my job. What I saw was different from what I expected, but

I liked it and sensed an interesting research problem. This hunch got me out of the university's confines and into the world of data scientists. But I missed how everyone had gotten there, including, ironically, myself.

My path to meetups was less smooth than I had first thought. The class was not an obvious choice. I entered my third year of graduate school and had fulfilled my course requirements. I worked on research projects on other issues and explored promising dissertation topics. Only an email from a professor of statistics to one of his colleagues in my department that then reached me and a few of my peers alerted us to this and another course.[54] Introduction to Data Science caught my interest because the description promised it might help solve some technical problems in my ongoing projects.

This encounter with data science showed entanglements in science that indicate an analytically productive path into data science. There is the university with a history in innovative quantitative thinking, the crossing of disciplinary boundaries, here around a course offering, and the workings of science's less visible sides, like the emails that led me to the course. But this initial scrutiny does not show much of the uncertainty that defined the early data science activities outside of university campuses. Maybe the lecture, which gave me a full view of data science once I got there, had put me on the wrong track.

Another beginning of the path intersects with one of my first activities after arriving in New York for graduate school, long before thinking about my own project and knowing data scientists or even the idea of them. I attended an event where someone whom I knew from my incipient research activities was scheduled to give a presentation. The gathering was a meetup, and the speaker was Drew Conway, the data science pioneer who invented the Venn diagram. I didn't know what meetups were, and I knew Drew only as a PhD student in political science at New York University. He had generously responded to emails a few months before to answer questions about social network analysis, a research technique I was teaching myself at the time, after an online search for answers led me to his blog and the code he made available there, about which I emailed him questions. With that experience in mind, and by then in New York, I was excited to see a tweet he posted about his meetup presentation.

Little at that event, held in the backroom of a bar in the early evening, anticipated the profile Drew would gain over the next few years or my note to Rachel about the "unbelievably" active meetup scene. Drew became known for his Venn diagram, which I would see in many presentations in the coming years as a quick definition of data science, sometimes with this or that tweak. Although he had written the blog post with his definition around the time when I met him, the purpose of the event was to demonstrate a set of techniques, a "package" or "library," in programmer speak, for the analysis of networks, a special problem in quantitative data analysis. This moment was tightly embedded in data science's early days without any of the markers, like a lecture title, that would soon define its appearance and make it broadly accessible.

I kept bumping into data science's subtler underpinning in the years between that first encounter and Rachel's lecture. I spent a week during the following summer in day-long sessions of a program teaching a coding package called "networkx." The training took place in Ann Arbor, Michigan, far away from either New York City or San Francisco, where data science started to thrive. Every summer, social scientists from across the country and beyond congregate in Ann Arbor to participate in rigorous summer training sessions in research methodology. The research case I used as an exercise during the course was the interpretation of the Bible in early modern England, a fascinating social scientific problem but far away from data science or what it started to stand for.[55]

This detour added to my connections to the data science world that started to form outside my view. The programming package I learned was the same one I had seen Drew present at the New York City meetup the previous year. And Python, the programming language I needed to learn to use the package, featured in summaries as an essential tool for data scientists. My instructor in Michigan went on to lead a data science program at Harvard University. That was not clear at the time when we met, when he was a postdoctoral researcher in a political scientist's lab, although he had a PhD in mathematics. But his skills and expertise anticipated that transition, again, missing only the potentially deceiving popular appearance.

Not only did I learn skills that later became associated with data science from people who became data scientists, but I also used them as a data scientist would. A friend in my graduate program studied Turkish politics, and I helped him obtain datasets for different provinces over several decades and get that data into shape for statistical analyses. Another friend was interested in the art world, and together she and I obtained the dataset, involved a computer scientist whom I knew from another programming class, and then implemented social scientific analyses.[56] These were not my research topics in sociology, but I understood them enough to apply my technical skills to advance the projects.

I did not conceive of these activities as data science, but neither had anyone else who did some data hacking before it was widely visible. Jeff Hammerbacher noted that he had "found that grad students in many scientific domains are playing the role of the Data Scientist" and called for "further definition for the role of the Data Scientist."[57] We did not know that we played that role. Now, data science comes with abundant popular images. And their appearance makes it an interesting research problem. But the early markers were no clearer than an emerging profession could provide. The popular images don't depict data science's early unfolding.

This unpacking of the first few times I crossed paths with data science brings the first iteration of the abductive analysis full circle. The Introduction to Data Science class offered a comprehensive picture of data science and a surprising collective experience. However, my first meetings with Drew and with the program instructor in Michigan, the work with my friends, and Jeff Hammerbacher's observations captured pivotal moments of encounters with data science without the label and a dedicated discussion. They caught the underpinning of data science's popular rise when those who engaged with it did work, work they would eventually describe as data science, before that description was in use. I went to the meetups to watch data scientists as data science started becoming what everyone eventually saw it to be. Over the next few years, I followed over seventy of these gatherings, watching over a hundred presentations. But, like those who went there to create that image, that was not the beginning, and traces of those trajectories would be important to detect in what they had to say. They and I thought about and discussed issues tied to data science before and without any concern in those moments for data science. The meetups were where we found one another again.

The meetups were not only a promising site because they were widespread and potentially consequential forms of socializing that data scientists used for technical discussions. They were also tied into a broader community and conversation around the issues that make up data science. I did not identify them strategically in the way I tried to map out places where data scientists worked and the techniques and technologies they used. But it wasn't pure chance, either. The path that led me to them intersected with those of dedicated data scientists before they or I knew where we were heading. I did not help define data science or use what they did as one of them. These intersecting trajectories created a situation allowing me as a "sociologist [to] scientifically describe a world that includes as problematical phenomena not only the other person's actions but the other person's knowledge of the world."[58] This was a crucial position in data science's emergence where no one could know anything for sure, creating an uncertainty impossible to capture in retrospect.

CONCLUSION

Data science is not as self-evident as its ubiquity or the affinity of data and science suggest. This much even the most basic definitions were quick to admit. This recognition implies a special course of action for understanding data science's emergence. If data science's meaning was in flux, an analysis of its formation must consider the situation at the time of its definition. It must start before the future is clear and not move backward from the current situation.[59]

This chapter outlined an empirical solution to that problem involving observations from when data scientists had just started to define their role and line of work and outsiders had started to pay attention. The time was full of uncertainty that challenged systematic observations. Where was the right place to look? Rather than imposing order on the uncertainty, this chapter reported an abductive approach designed to iterate between familiar and unfamiliar observations to track its contours.

Popular observations around data science echo images of expert work in offices and other workplaces or professional settings. While many existing accounts have made observations of activities deviating from formal protocols and procedures, little of the giddy interactions of data scientists at meetups have been described. Yet revisiting those observations in a broader context of social scientific writing made them plausible places for the formation of data science.

This discovery revealed the stage and backdrop for data science's collective definition. What happened in those rooms once everyone settled in? What ideas did the presenters share? How did audiences react? How did those groups overcome the problem of turning diverse skills into a distinct area of expertise and then articulate that area of expertise? And how do these groups, still scattered across time, space, and different specializations, form a coherent account of their work?

Those questions are crucial for understanding data science's emergence. But just as the data scientists went to those meetups because of their work, an analysis of their formation can only discern their dynamics once it has covered data science tasks. The following chapter will consider what data science skills are and how they came together when data science formed as a new role. It peeks into the machinery of computational analyses of large-scale datasets to ask: Where do they fit in the world of work? What was left to discuss at meetups a decade ago? And what did that do for what everyone got to see eventually?

2

THE WORK

What is happening?" I asked myself as the impressions from the lectures, workshops, and meetups were sinking in. I didn't know yet that this was how the community was coming together and that there were hundreds of gatherings to come, dozens of which I would attend over multiple years. I also still didn't know how participants would use them, what they would say and show, and how. Data science's first traces were striking even before they settled into a new routine, but I wasn't sure that were they were worth following scientifically.

The signs were all but clear. The get-togethers were fueled by a professional workforce willing to spend after-work hours talking data. Alternatives were abundant, and the commitment could shift or wear out any day. Rachel taught the class to train competent future colleagues and peers. She still had a day job and could decide that that was enough of a headache. Meetup hosts organized groups for camaraderie, attention, and clarifications, all needs that could yield to others or be satisfied otherwise. And I was only seeing all this in New York. We had regular visitors from other cities and even from abroad, but their appearances didn't say much about how data science fared in those places. These impressions, which made data science fascinating and puzzling, could vanish as quickly as they appeared. I needed to capture data science in a stable frame to better see if sociology could shed light on it and if an analysis of it could advance sociological knowledge.

The foundation of the learned professions, which data science intuitively resembled, is the performance of tasks that require technical expertise. This is work that takes place in specialized jobs. In the scholarship on professions, sociologists not only study who gets what job or not but also the entanglement of positions and the professions and occupations staffing them.[1] Jobs were a topic among data scientists, too. DJ Patil's programmatic article on data science was titled "The Sexiest Job of the 21st Century." Much of the excitement at the time cited a consulting firm's research report that predicted an imminent shortage of data scientists.[2] These scattered observations pointed in a promising direction. For data science to have a future that makes its origins worth understanding, I reasoned, it should manifest itself in the world of work.

This chapter analyzes descriptions of data scientist positions across the United States when they first appeared in the early 2010s and in the years leading up to that time. Initial glimpses substantiate more fleeting traces of data science's emergence but add little more and fail to capture its intellectual and technological underpinning. A bird's-eye perspective on data science job vacancies injects new momentum into the analysis. It mobilizes data science techniques, which have no history in the scholarship of professions, to bring the tools and procedures that are part of data science's emergence into the analysis.[3] The analysis captures the interplay of the internet, open-source software, mathematical models, and databases in data science's formation. Much scholarship has documented similar processes in specialized expert communities.[4] This implementation produces a more complete picture by turning the community's expertise on itself and capturing its internal functioning and expanse. This dual set of outside and inside insights reflects the position of data scientists between the world of technology and everything in the social and material world suitable for observations at scale. Data scientists bring these two sides together. Scholars of various organizational processes have discovered how solutions to such complex problems have followed surprisingly messy paths. They drew on pragmatist philosophy to explain that phenomenon.[5] These processes unfold around "problem situations," which are "ambiguous" or involve "conflicting tendencies" but lead to new accomplishments.[6] This chapter recovers such situations in the technical steps of assembling a data analytic strategy. Early data science discussions and existing technical ideas offer points of departure, but some go further than others, and their implementation requires specialized adjustments. Together, the analysis then shows how far and through what channels this work spread and how those connections came together.[7]

START

Data scientist vacancies were a number-one topic in tech conversations in the early 2010s. At the meetups, attendees routinely advertised openings in their teams before the evening's main act, speakers shared amusing stories of the offers they were getting daily, and organizers excluded recruiters to let attendees enjoy the time among peers, making the abundant demand for data scientists part of an event's story. These were clear signals, and with their informal occurrences, data science showed evidence of one of the most important discoveries in modern sociology: the informal underpinning of labor markets. But these impressions were still only incidental and did little to capture data science's reach.

Labor markets also have a more formal side, which would indicate a more solid base and, analytically, offer a broader picture of data science. This side operates through job posts,[8] which were as easy to search online in standard job portals for data scientist vacancies. Just a quick check gave me long lists of results for my geographic area and elsewhere. They described vibrant work environments and listed technical skills and fields of training as requirements. But these were only short online entries. Did they mean that data science was a serious development? Did they offer any insight into that development? What should I be looking for?

As the good student that I tried to be, I turned to methods that I was just learning in my sociology program to deal with these questions. I downloaded about a dozen job postings to look more carefully at what they said and asked, and I used a text-analysis software package called NVivo. The software can open documents, like standard text processing programs, and offers functionalities for highlighting passages in those documents and assigning labels to them for subsequent analyses. Qualitative researchers use this setup to uncover deeper meaning in what they have seen people do or heard them say or in what a person, organization, or institution has written or published, such as job ads. A researcher can go back and ask the software to display all the passages with the same label assigned to them. I applied this procedure to a set of data scientist job posts I found online.

NVivo helped organize the diffuse impressions I had gleaned from the descriptions. Like other job posts, those for data scientists asked for skills, experiences, and qualifications. They mentioned programming skills, for instance, "proficiency in the R computing language," and data processing technologies, such as when asking for "strong SQL command skills." They also sketched out challenges that successful candidates would have to master, such as "take research questions and construct analysis to answer them with little input." And they mentioned the degrees that applicants should have and in what fields, often "in a technical or research field."

These steps also highlighted differences in ways that pointed at new puzzles. One listed "R, Python, and Matplotlib," whereas another asked for "Matlab, R, SAS, or SPSS and SQL" or "C, C++, Java, or Python." The R programming language appeared in many of them, but where one paired it with Python, a more widely used language in software engineering, another linked it to Matlab, a more abstract language. Python could also appear together with C++, again, a more arcane language, as well as Java, a more practical language often used for web programming. This variability extended to the tasks that the posts described and the degree requirements they listed. These similarities and differences were still interesting and fleshed out what data science meant. What did they say about data science's emergence?

Although job posts included details about data scientist positions that popular discussions omitted, this approach to discerning them offered limited analytic traction. The promise of qualitative research is to find meaning in detailed descriptions and accounts. Job post texts were short and cryptic. A richness only revealed itself in their abundance and the differences between them. While single posts didn't say much, a larger corpus could make them an intriguing lens into the novel data scientist role. My reading and markups were too slow and imprecise to take advantage of the large number of data science job ads. I needed to look at many posts while still paying close attention to the specific skills, techniques, and technologies they mentioned. Such a strategy could then capture the spectrum of this new role, maybe even from before the positions that were open when data science revealed itself as an interesting sociological puzzle. These tasks were impossible for me but easy for a computer to do. And my early impressions of data science were giving me ideas for letting a computer perform these tasks.

TOOLS AND MATERIALS

One of the first data science applications we discussed in Rachel's class was a filter that recognized spam emails. Emails were not job posts, and I only had a basic understanding of how those examples worked, but there were enough parallels to make me wonder if my data scientist job post problem was a data science problem. The payoff would be a shift from single texts to many texts and from reading to measurement.

Whatever the technique, the first task is to acquire many job posts in computer-readable format. This was easy, at least at the outset. For my initial selection, I went to job platforms, entered "data scientist" in the query field, and then scrolled through the results of posts with descriptions like the ones I quoted earlier. I opened an empty document into which I copy-pasted the different pieces of information and then saved the file to my hard drive for future use and analysis. These steps were too cumbersome for setting up a formal analysis. But the many repetitions necessary to collect many such posts lent themselves to a data science–style analysis.

Data scientists look for ways to use code that automates manual tasks and scales them up. For example, code can "scrape" websites and extract information, such as those in job posts.

Basic scraping tasks involve attaching a search term to a website's URL, calling up the website, and obtaining snippets of information from the website's content. These steps only take a few commands, and scraping examples were abundant in the coder community. They were a rite of passage, a display of technical savviness and expression of personal curiosities as data hackers culled information on sports leagues, farmer's markets, or pizza places. Coders documented their exploits for the community in blog posts and during presentations. These stories had first led me to data science, and I had scraped my share of websites by the time I scrolled through the endless lists of job posts.

Those early activities taught me useful lessons for this new exercise. There were often issues with specific formatting solutions on websites, for instance, that led to unwanted or incomplete content extraction. This was no serious problem for job posts, which appeared as entries in the same website design. But platforms like these had started to integrate content from databases into their websites. Regular users wouldn't notice any difference, but basic commands for scraping websites found nothing to record in those places. While hackers came up with tricks around this problem, adjustments created problems in the data-gathering process. They require manual checks that become prohibitively costly with larger datasets and undermine the point of the whole exercise.[9]

Nevertheless, scraping introduced me to new ways of using a computer. Data science started in an era when the computer mouse and drop-down menus had long been the standard means of navigating software applications. For scraping, the fields on which users usually click become part of the code that decides what content to keep. This makes websites a good problem for novice computer programmers who haven't learned those skills from textbooks. A coder can use the browser to organize the otherwise abstract tools and techniques, looking at the website in one window, the code in a second, and then what that code scrapes in a third.

The first step was moving from user-friendly software to a programming language. Python was a go-to choice in the data science community. It comes with intuitive commands, similar to self-explanatory dropdown menus in common computer interactions. But programming requires further reorientation. For example, an operation as basic as making the computer show something involves a specific command. It's a simple one, "print," but details like this set programming apart from user-oriented software applications. Not all solutions have to start from scratch. Python comes with a host of packages, called libraries, with commands that call up specialized functions for specialized operations, including those related to website scraping or data processing.[10] But, while convenient, one still has to know what the packages do. Workshops like the one I took in Michigan during my first summer of graduate school introduced me to the basics of using Python and understanding how to use a package or find the right one. The scraping exercises helped me practice those abstract skills by translating what I did as a website user into code for automated data extraction. All those lessons gave me new ideas for approaching the data science case.

As I was figuring out how to scrape job posts to catch up with data hackers, the digital world was catching up with me and making scraping unnecessary. One of the platforms from which I obtained my first batch of data scientist job posts was Linke-dIn. LinkedIn had launched a so-called application programming interface, or API, for the developer community. APIs offer access to computer systems and databases. In contrast to code that pretended to be a regular user for extracting information, APIs allowed one to query databases directly. System and website operators charged for these services or offered free access, hoping it would motivate developers to create applications that would generate additional users. The control website operators retained in these setups could create problems. For example, I could not have accessed LinkedIn members' connections to see if data scientists had connections to other data scientists. But I was already hanging out with data scientists in person. Here, I was interested in the broader understanding of the data scientist's role and could take advantage of the API's permissions.

So I discarded my initial scraping operation, signed up for a LinkedIn Developer account, and registered an API. In return, I received a set of letter-number combinations, which I had to integrate into my code. The API then let me send queries and returned content from LinkedIn's database. It included query fields for job titles and for specifying the information it would return. My implementation wasn't clean or sleek, but it worked, and it was an exciting opportunity to obtain large numbers of data scientist job posts with tasks and skills.

The API ensured much higher-quality records than scraping could extract, but it came with new technical challenges, specialized commands for building a connection to a system or database. I wasn't a software engineer and didn't know many commands or how to program sophisticated functions. However, following the temporary setback of a useless web scraper, luck was back on my side, and someone or some group in the coder community had already written a Python library with functions for using LinkedIn's API and made it available for others to use. The pains of learning Python for scraping paid off, even though this was no longer a scraping exercise. I understood the basics and could look up the rest.

The API still didn't solve all the problems. Quantitative research in social sciences had familiarized me with datasets that came in one piece and were mostly ready for statistical analyses. But data science was still emerging, and I needed to track its progress, which a single dataset could not capture, since new data scientist posts appeared daily. A software engineer would have had no problem setting a timer to activate the API and obtain a new batch. But I was glad I got any at all. Instead of getting deeper into software engineering, I stuck to what I had started to pick up in data science and used a hack, a less elegant trick that still solved the problem.[11]

I set myself a calendar reminder. Once a month, a notification appeared on my laptop, and I ran the Python code that connected to LinkedIn's API, queried the latest posts, and saved them in a folder. The file names included the date and time to organize this growing set of records. I repeated this exercise a few times to obtain almost two thousand job ads for data scientists from different types of organizations in various industries and of different sizes. This was a lot of new material to work with.

With basic skills, some tricks, and a community of coders sharing advice online, I managed to get the API going. In the end, a few lines of code were enough for me to obtain job postings for data scientist positions that appeared on LinkedIn. The job posts streamed as texts straight onto my laptop. One more line of code saved them as a file on my hard drive. The amount I gathered confirmed the phenomenon's presence in the job market. Figure 2.1 shows the locations of vacant positions I started to collect, connecting the digital records that came out of the computational procedure to real places.[12] This exercise also started to put my impressions from events in New York into a new perspective. All the excited conversations, cheeky tweets and blog posts, wide-eyed students, and nerds who were happy to hang out with someone were part of a much larger process.

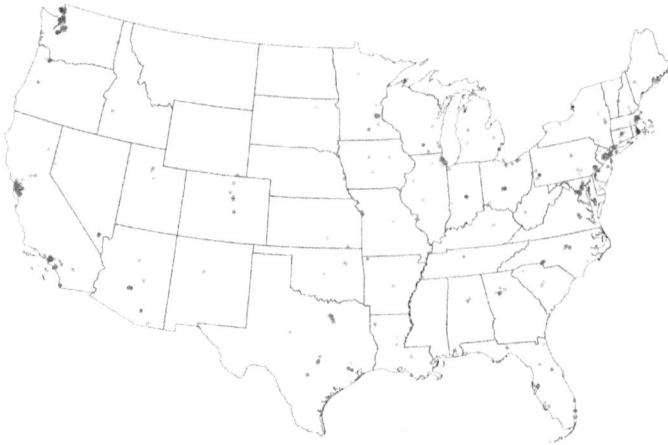

FIGURE 2.1 Map of the contiguous United States that shows the locations of establishments that hired data scientists (dark dots) and more established professions (light spots).

This process extended to the labor market, indicating significant commitment that impacts people's lives. But what else do the job posts say about data science's formation?

DATA MANAGEMENT

As pragmatist philosophy predicts, the new solution brought with it new problems. The monthly API retrievals offered a way of tracking the emergence of data science. But I didn't understand what I was seeing when I first looked at the dataset, aside from the sheer number of records. Datasets, I knew from my quantitative methods training, came as spreadsheets with rows and columns. Excel used this structure as its standard format, and even specialized software packages for statistical analysis offered similar display options.

The API didn't output the familiar rows and columns. The entries had an identifying number or label, like those often at the beginning of rows in spreadsheets, but without the neat sequence of cells following it and with the same information for the entries in all other rows unless they are missing. The files I got from the database came with a series of entries on a level below and indented from the main entry, each with its own label and information, and all in curly brackets. They were like column names with single entries below, except that each entry could have the same, some, or entirely different information from the previous main entry. Each subordinate entry to a main entry could have multiple subordinate entries, and so on. After having struggled for years to deal with spreadsheets, I was lost in this maze.

I learned from the available documentation that these were so-called .json files, a format for storing large-scale datasets. Data storage formats help organize digital records according to rules that aid the display of the content and operations on the content. Excel has proprietary formats, indicated by the file name suffixes .xls or .xlsx. They organize information in rows and columns while also remembering colors a user may have added to cells or formulae. The nonproprietary versions are .csv or .txt formats, with the same basic logic but fewer functionalities. JSON was another format with special functionalities for large-scale datasets.

While cumbersome to learn, the job post records reveal the benefits of the JSON format. Each job ad came from an employer with basic information job seekers may want to know and a main contact person who was overseeing the hiring process. The organization came with an industry affiliation, the location, and even its year of founding. Just the location required two specifications, one for the longitude and one for the latitude, while the age information only included one entry, the year of founding. The nested storage format could easily accommodate these specificities.

The main elements of a job post for this analysis of data science's definition were the tasks and requirements, which had their own entries next to the workplace that posted the information but above the level of the workplace information. They came as two fields of textual descriptions.[13] Overall, each entry started with a job ad identifier, which then branched out into more information about the workplace on one side and more information about the specific job on the other. Figure 2.2 shows a few blurred entries to highlight the structure of the information. There is a clear pattern of longer and shorter entries for the descriptions and more formalized pieces of information. But they are still complex structures.

The JSON format helped with handling the data, but I still needed to analyze the posts, and new problems came up. As my collection routine vacuumed up new posts, I skimmed through them, checking for technical problems and eyeballing the content for substantive patterns. Each new batch of entries increased my confidence that data science's formation was a problem that could be a social scientific research project. But as I wanted to check how consistent the emerging patterns were, which was the main point of implementing the computational analysis, I quickly got stuck. Spreadsheet programs had functionalities for selecting rows based on characteristics to better see how many and what entries shared features. The tree-like structure of .json files was good for organizing job ad content, but they didn't come with functionalities for analyzing them quickly.

The problem was that this was "unstructured" data, which was, again luckily, or just corresponding to pragmatist predictions, a

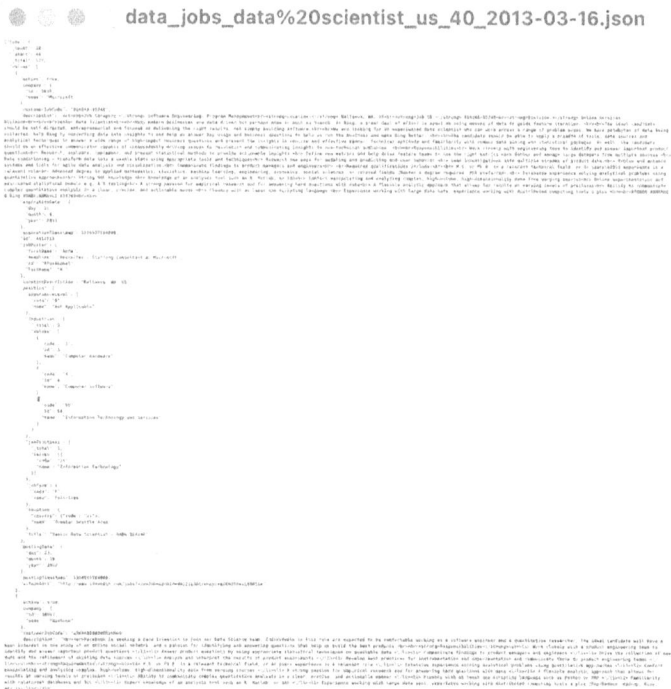

data_jobs_data%20scientist_us_40_2013-03-16.json

FIGURE 2.2 Screenshot of a text editor displaying schematic job posts (entries blurred) in the JSON format.

favorite topic in the data science community. I had learned by then that the term "unstructured" was used for datasets that didn't fit the row-column format, such as my job posts. They often still have a structure to them, a regularity, but entries may vary between and within each main record. The more datasets I started to see, the more intuitive sense I could make of the distinction. And the discussions in the community pointed out solutions for dealing with unstructured records like job posts.

Specialized database software solutions are available for facilitating the storage, accessing, and processing of these records. Individual users or consumers rarely deal with database software. Only large organizations, government institutions, universities, and businesses deal with problems that require database solutions, and those solutions can get expensive quickly. But even commercial providers couldn't escape the open-source movement that has shaped modern programming and was responsible for so many data science technologies. They often offered free versions that included the basic features for small-scale problems and without the support that paying customers would receive. This was good enough for me.

I downloaded MongoDB, one of the solutions I had seen the community discuss, and integrated it into my process. In contrast to standard data storage files, Word documents, spreadsheets, or even .json files, databases find their dedicated space on the hard drive. I had to load the records I had already assembled and simply saved in a dedicated folder into Python and then insert them into the new MongoDB infrastructure. And I updated the monthly downloading routine to send the new records into the database instead of creating yet another file in my folder. With this software addition, the slightly erratic steps that had led to it turned into a comprehensive and systematic data collection procedure.

The database setup further delayed the analysis. But it built a basis for more effective analytical work, leveraging earlier detours. My use of Python had deviated from the usual packages for social scientific analyses, but it paid off here because a Python library was available for using the MongoDB database. I could write a query in Python to obtain subsets of job posts from the first few batches to see if they were similar or different from the last few batches, for example. I could look at those from one industry and then from another or those assigned to different functional divisions. These steps were possible before, but the database technology made iterations between data collection steps and data analysis easier and, thus, close to the original aim of understanding aspects of data science's emergence outside of the lecture hall and meetups.

MEASUREMENT

This analysis took time and effort to assemble, but it started to look productive. After a few months, I had gathered almost two thousand job posts for data scientist positions.[14] Their numbers and consistency increasingly revealed data science as worthy of research. Could they also offer insights into its emergence? The existing scholarship on expert work had much to say about skills, knowledge, and technologies in the fates of occupations. But job posts differed significantly from the historical or ethnographic analyses this research typically used. None of the many technical steps that helped obtain, organize, and store the job descriptions extracted patterns of specialized or abstract expertise, the relevant dimensions for understanding data science sociologically.

Textbox 1 shows an excerpt from a description posted in 2013. It echoes the catchy data science definitions from the introduction and the discussions I started seeing in New York City from the previous chapter. It is also more technical and specific, listing concrete skills—analytical, technical, communication, and collaborative—as well as educational degrees. For example, algorithm testing falls into computer science, and "R" refers to a statistical programming language. The post asks for communication skills, which correspond to the interpretation and domain knowledge references in those definitions. Even the vaguer reference to the ability to find structure in unstructured data appears in this post in its warning about "ambiguous areas." The similarity between the definitions of prominent data science promoters and a detailed job description serves as the first indication of a shared data science understanding.

This is only a first impression, of course, gleaned while the extent of the problem of analyzing posts like this revealed itself.

Excerpt of Job Posting for a Data Scientist Position

You will handle data exploration, hypothesis creation (from both business and product goals), testing algorithms, scaling to large data-sets and validating results. We have a broad set of technologies with which the Senior Data Scientist will work: Hadoop/HDFS; Shark/Spark; NoSQL databases, and numerous charting, graphing and analysis applications such as: Gephi, Google Charts, etc. . . . We'd like to see good coding skills covering some procedural as well as statistical or data oriented languages. (Such as: Java, Scala, Python as well as R, SQL, etc.). Good communication skills and an awareness of how to communicate data effectively is a must. This individual must be comfortable working in newly forming ambiguous areas where learning and adaptability are key skills. Required Education: MS or higher in the field of Statistics or Computer Science or Applied Mathematics.

The initial set of excerpts showed their promise, with references to programming languages, database technologies, and statistical modeling, all indicating references to technical expertise. But they were written for people to read one by one, not for comprehensive analyses, while conventional analytical procedures centered on tables with rows and columns, not texts. Standard cells either have numbers in them or other countable information, such as records of persons, with information on their age, income, or marital status. Excel and other software packages put the techniques for calculating averages for age or income, or the percentage of those married, at users' fingertips. These techniques for analyzing numbers in spreadsheets don't work for texts and their meaning.

Data science once again promised a way out. I had seen data scientists identifying patterns in emails to detect spam or in financial statements to find market trends. The Python programming language came with libraries and functions for text processing thanks to the contributions of the wider programmer and academic community. An alliance of computer scientists and linguists in universities created an enormous toolbox for natural language processing, or NLP, for short. Plenty of presentations and websites showed me how to use the libraries and procedures for specific problems.[15] But the emergence of a new profession wasn't another annoying email that a filter had to catch. They were pieces in the larger puzzle of data science's emergence. How could these tools reveal the technical expertise undergirding the data scientist's role and its contours?

Data science tricks wouldn't solve the problem of an emergent profession; I needed social scientific ideas for guidance. And social scientists were at the data scientists' heels, with many working on the measurement of meaning in texts at that time.[16]

Their theoretically informed solutions were not yet available,[17] but a curious collaboration between an economist and an information scientist had published some ideas as part of an analysis of professional correspondence.[18] Like some of the data scientists I saw present, they used emails as their dataset, but they were interested in themes and topics in those messages, not just separating spam from regular messages.[19] These concerns seemed like a possible bridge from job posts back to the ideas for understanding professional emergence.

Some more practical tasks were now necessary. I learned that I had to chop texts into words and put letters into lowercase, operations that required little more than single Python commands. I had to remove articles, conjunctions, prepositions, and what linguists call stop words, which was a bit more complicated but no real problem, thanks to NLP packages written by computational linguists. Another look at the separate words showed that other forms of text had come along with the job posts. I noticed cryptic letter combinations between less-than and greater-than signs. This was markup code, such as for setting words in boldface font. There could be meaning behind these stylistic choices but also idiosyncratic preferences; at this point, I just wanted the words. Deleting these markup commands was a bit more tedious—I added a function to the code for recognizing nonletter text fragments and replacing them with nothing—but, at this point, it too was no significant obstacle.

These steps turned LinkedIn job posts into a dataset of lists of words. Word lists may sound simplistic, but pioneering research has found them sufficient for identifying laws governing our use of language.[20] They should shed light on the much smaller problem of data science's emergence. However, the initial impressions from data scientist posts showed that I had to take one more step from simple counts to word combinations for capturing skill, task, and expertise arrangements. The email exchange study offered guidance not only for practical steps but also for such a conceptually more meaningful analysis. Its authors wanted to understand themes, which they identified as representative and distinctive words.[21] Their reasoning to find words that "distinguish topics from one another" seemed smart,[22] and the similarities between emails and job postings—both relatively short pieces of text with a conventional structure—encouraged me to try their approach.

This measurement strategy involved two analytic steps for finding words that belonged to different topics. While the study defined topics as emails with similar language,[23] here, data scientist posts defined the focal topic, and the question was whether and what words distinguished them from other positions. To adopt this logic, I matched the data scientist posts with a random array of positions as a general professional work topic, which I obtained again through the API with queries that picked job posts at random. This added over thirty thousand posts to the database. I could now adopt a strategy from the publication for finding "words that tend to appear in the same topic clusters often and in other clusters relatively infrequently" and "words that are consistently used across a large number of the e-mails [or job posts] in a given topic cluster," or job ad cluster.[24]

These measures promised significant analytic progress, but I had to integrate mathematical equations from the article into my analysis. The technical steps so far all used functions available online and in Python libraries. I just had to write code that organized those functions in a sequence around the processing of the job post. In contrast, these analytic ideas from the email analysis only appeared as equations in a published manuscript. Instead of relying on available functions, I had to program my own, translating the different components of the mathematical equations into Python commands. The Greek letter sigma, for sum, in mathematical notation became a command for summation, a horizontal bar indicating division became a forward slash, and so on. I could then apply these new functions to the job post texts.

The result was impressive. Once I let the code run on the word lists from the job posts for data scientist positions and the reference set of random positions, each word received two scores. One score indicated how representative it was of the data scientist posts and the other how much it distinguished data scientist posts from the average professional job post. Figure 2.3 shows each word as a dot according to the two measures on the x-axis and the y-axis. I learned from the email study that I had to pick words from the lower-right-hand corner.

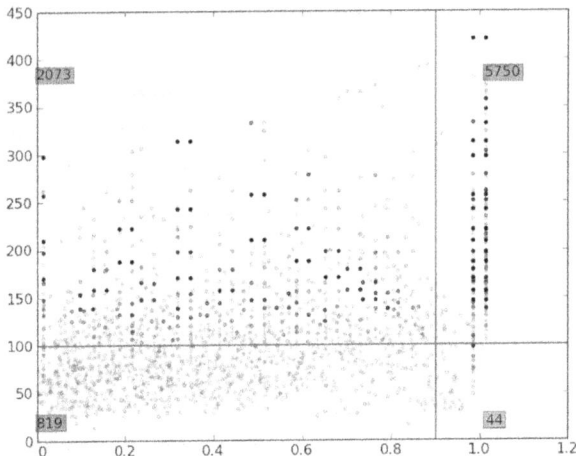

FIGURE 2.3. Check distribution of representativeness indicators for ds of size 8686. Figure showing how distinctive words (dots) were of a topic (y-axis) and how much they represented a topic (x-axis).

The initial measurement step revealed a list of words that included:

nlp	weka	phd
findings	nosql	unstructured
predictive	graph	ensuring
predict	hadoop	hypothesis
consistent	mahout	bayesian
pig	machine	datasets
analytics	matlab	cybercoders
statistical	scientists	unsupervised
hbase	mathematics	economics
spss	multivariate	mapreduce
extract	mining	hive
econometrics	theory	prototypes
millions	visualization	algorithms
huge	python	logistic
statistics	trees	

Suddenly, this analysis had revealed the first collectively generated definition of data science. Much of the list was familiar from the popular definitions, such as *Python*, *statistics*, and *NLP*. *Python* and *NLP* had even helped create this list. *SPSS* is a proprietary statistical software package. *NoSQL* refers to a class of database systems that offers flexibility for unconventional data structures, such as MongoDB, which I used to get a handle on the job descriptions. Other words look more conventional even though they may not make immediate sense. *Extract* refers to dataset operations, such as extracting measures from otherwise complex records, such as distinctive words from job descriptions. *Predictive* refers to a type of machine learning, for instance, the statistical model data scientists use to determine whether an email may be spam. *Unsupervised*, another word on the list, refers to another form of machine learning.

Some words were more specific. *Econometrics* refers to a class of statistical techniques that economists have refined around the analysis of datasets from markets, in contrast to, say, applications of statistics to problems in biology. *Bayesian* refers to a specialized and sophisticated approach to quantitative analysis, which has old roots but gained new momentum around the time of data science's rise. *Logistic* refers to logistic regression, a statistical technique that overlaps most clearly with machine learning. It was the first technique that many data science novices learned about. *Hypothesis* is a philosophical concept and a staple in scientific knowledge production, but more in statistics than in computer science and machine learning, fields that deal more with *algorithms*, another word on the list.

Finally, *Pig* refers to a platform and programming language for fast analyses of large-scale datasets, and *visualization* to graphical representations of quantitative information, such as in figure 2.3. These are more practical concerns than concerns of pure science, which the inclusion of *huge* among the words rounds off. *Huge* referred to large-scale datasets, but it was clearly just a casual term. The casualness signals that it was a form of distinction from otherwise highly formalized expertise.

Although mostly convincing, the list included some concerning surprises. *Statistics* makes sense; it is the scientific field that largely informs data science, but there's also *statistical* as another reference to it. This repetition indicates I should implement a step called stemming, which converts full words as they appear in texts to their common stem by removing suffixes. I came across solutions for these problems as I got deeper into NLP techniques. Another problem was the *cybercoders* reference, a recruitment agency that had to do with data science but didn't indicate its underlying skills and expertise. I also needed an additional step to double-check the results of these initial distinctiveness measures. While these issues showed that more work was necessary, the list looked promising for a start.

The words all fit the evolving discussion around data science. They provided a definition generated from almost two thousand views on the data scientist role—one in each of the job posts that were the basis of this analysis—and not the idiosyncratic ideas of some vocal proponents and popularizers. The definition was consistent with the popular discussion. However, it also showed a greater coverage and balance of different branches of quantitative expertise and their conceptual, practical, and technological sides. A systematic picture of the data scientist role started to form, integrating different perspectives of data science work and expertise.

TESTING

The implementation of this data science exercise continues to fit the expectations of pragmatist theories. Initial ideas run into smaller and larger setbacks that were not in sight before, but, once there, new solutions and entirely new possibilities for moving the analysis forward come into view. The successful extraction of three dozen data science words that followed the scraping and storage problems led to a new challenge. How well could some words that came from just two scores and a stack of job posts define an emerging professional role?

The previous step, which benefited from social scientific thinking, led to a situation that once again resembled the spam detection problem I had seen data scientists discuss. They explained that spam detection systems started out with information on when users of email programs flagged some emails as spam. The data scientists then used machine learning techniques to pull out incoming emails that looked statistically similar, considering scores assigned to words, to flagged emails. This logic translated to this new version of the job post problem. Its core is a specific statistical procedure that associates input factors, or, more technically, features, with a binary outcome of whether an event occurs or not. The words the previous step had already selected served as features. Instead of determining whether a text was spam, this problem required finding out if a job post looked like a data science job post or not. I didn't know much about machine learning yet, but I knew one technique that the data science lecture and textbooks had introduced as the most basic machine learning exercise. This was the so-called logistic classifier, an alternative take on one of the bread-and-butter analytic techniques that sociologists used as well. Whereas I learned as a social scientist to focus on the associations between input factors and the outcome, watching data scientists, I learned to focus on how well the statistical procedure predicted the outcome.

The data science setup required some further adjustment from what I had learned in my social science methods classes. They taught me to analyze full datasets. In contrast, the data science version required two steps: training and testing. Training refers to estimating the statistical relationships between input information and the outcome. Testing refers to exposing the classifier to new records and letting an algorithm assign labels to those records depending on the input factors and the statistical associations from the first step, such as whether emails were spam or job posts asked for data scientists. This split ensures that the classifier works not only for the one dataset in which it first determines associations. The data scientist then checks how many correct predictions the model made to determine its use for entirely new records.

The examples I saw showed me what I needed to do, but my analysis came with a complication. The standard procedure assumes that the dataset includes all input features. In the job post application, I devised a separate procedure that extracted words from texts to capture their joint meaning. I retained this initial step as part of the procedure by extending the two-way split to a three-way split. Classifying data scientist job posts required a step for identifying features, one for classifier training, and one for classifier testing. Practically, I first paired the collection of almost two thousand data scientist jobs with twice that number of a random set of job titles. The classifier should identify those entries with a data scientist title.

The setup worked. The classifier successfully recognized data scientist posts on the basis of their distinctive skills according to two key metrics: The test step indicated about 95 percent precision and over 90 percent recall rates. Precision specifies the share of job posts the model said were data scientist job posts that really had data scientist in their title. Recall specifies the share of data scientist posts hidden in the test dataset that the model found. In other words, the classifier got the vast majority of those it should have gotten, and almost all those it got were correct, all on the basis of the distinctive skills the procedure had formally identified. This exercise showed that a systematic definition of data science existed beyond what specific popularizers said.

While intriguing, this data science exercise reduced what I could see of data science to two metrics in a table. To gain more confidence in this approach, I first repeated the extraction, training, and testing steps multiple times, each time throwing all job posts back together, dividing them randomly into three new subsets, and starting with the word selection, training, and testing all over again. Each of the classifiers was able to identify data scientist posts. The result was comforting and added meaning. Each of these iterations basically used what some posts said about data scientist positions, double-checked with what others said, and then checked again whether that was consistent with the rest. The agreement wasn't uniform, but it was consistent and distinctive of a broad set of data science positions.

The interpretation still relied more on code and models than substance. It followed from techniques I had seen in analyses of email communication rather than of jobs and work. In another return from data science thinking to social scientific thinking, I wanted to anchor the results in the larger world of expert work that had first cast data science's emergence as an interesting sociological problem.[25] There, established professions dominate many areas of social life. Lawyers and medical doctors are the standard examples. While medical doctors have too little in common with data scientists to make a useful comparison, lawyers share with them a reliance on formalisms in their work, if of different kinds. Technical areas of work offer some clearer reference points. Software engineers also use computer coding in their jobs, and financial advisors and risk analysts are groups that deal with numbers. These occupations are not equally prominent, but they highlight some key dimensions for contextualizing data scientist positions.[26]

The comparative cases have histories and characteristics that inform the interpretation of formal measures. Lawyers are the classic example of a profession claiming abstract knowledge as the basis of their work. They have lost some of their mystique,[27] but the classifier should still recognize them.[28] Risk analysts and financial advisors are so-called organizational professions,[29] which means less autonomy, but their reliance on general standards and analytic procedures should make them recognizable for the skill-based classifier, too. Software engineers are a slightly different story. While their training involves highly technical expertise, history has seen them lose out to management soon after their emergence, which led to a fragmentation of their stock of knowledge as individual software engineers specialize in the systems and infrastructure of their workplaces.[30] The skill-based recognition should work less well for them.

This comparative exercise made all the code I had prepared for the initial data science analysis pay off. The code functions that queried the data scientist job posts worked for the other titles just as well (see table 2.1). After identifying those cases, I obtained job posts for them, as I had for data scientists, to put them through the same analytic sequence. I paired the new

TABLE 2.1 SAMPLE STRUCTURE

Title	Analytical purpose	N (in 1,000)
Attorney	Classic profession	2.9
Data scientist	Focal case	1.8
Risk analyst	Occupation/quant	1.2
Software engineer	Occupation/tech	8.4
Financial advisor	Occupation/ bureaucratic	1.8
Random	Common skills/ trajectories	~40

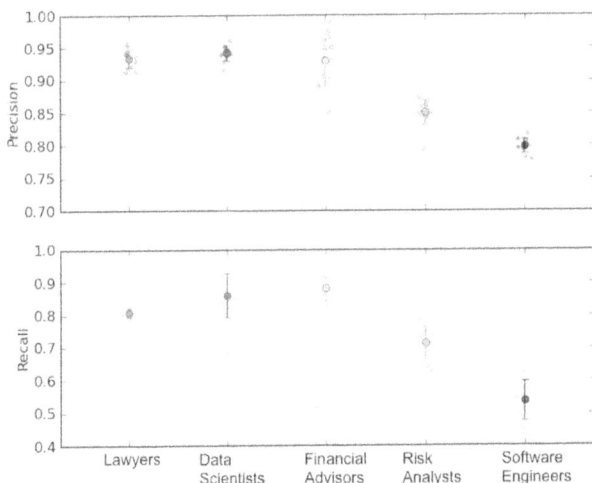

FIGURE 2.4 Classifier performance for job descriptions of five expert groups. Distributions of model performance scores for multiple iterations for five positions. The horizontal variation comes from a random number to enhance the legibility of the scores.

records again with random sets of job descriptions, identified words that were distinctive and representative in one subset, trained logistic classifiers on the second subset, and tested them on the third, iterating through this analytic sequence many times for each job title for different internal perspectives. Figure 2.4 shows the precision (a) and recall (b) performance scores for data scientist positions and the comparative cases. The skill overlap of several of the positions resembles that of data scientist positions. Most importantly, it works well for attorney positions as the classic case and casts no severe doubt on the organizational professions.

The precision result drops more for software engineers but remains still close to the other cases and quite high in absolute terms. More concerning is the low recall rate of barely over 50 percent. This result is surprising compared to the other results and casts some doubt on the analytic strategy. At the same time, however, it is consistent with the research into the history of software engineers, which has seen them fragment in the face of managerial control. The much lower recall scores reflect the reported focus on specialized problems.[31] Rather than questioning the analytic strategy, this set of results next to those for data scientist positions offers support and adds meaning.

The comparisons provide a more complete and meaningful picture. The descriptions of data scientist positions so early in its emergence already resembled the descriptions of some of the most established professions. However, the definition of data science still reveals itself more in the process that has produced the results than in the formal scores. The API, Python code, and mathematical equations in academic articles started to show the interplay of available resources and their specialized application to this problem. This interplay became tighter as the problems became more specific. With the addition of a logistic classifier, the analysis integrated the accomplishments of the centuries-long history of statistical thinking. These tools, techniques, and technologies are not the solution. And even the simple listing of each step would have led to a much easier reading. Their joint application as part of a data science solution to specific problems, some of which only move into view following an earlier solution, is the answer.

MODELING

How did the tools, techniques, and expertise in data scientist posts place data scientists in the world of work? Existing theories of expert work have linked the prospects of professions to their underlying stocks of knowledge.[32] They have discussed expertise as either uniformly specialized and vulnerable to external control or more diffuse, applying to a range of problems, and conducive to autonomous work. The analytic steps so far showed some variation in how skills applied in different positions, but their structure got lost in the percentages, and the focus on formal titles possibly cut off parts of underlying expertise. The theories in the literature on expert work, however, indicated how concrete skill arrangements in positions could indicate if data science was simply a new specialization or a distinct combination of expertise.

The API gave access to LinkedIn's full job post database. The limitation to active posts for title-based queries became irrelevant for this new step of loosening that formal scope. I obtained about fifty thousand posts to find positions that included skills distinctive of data scientists and those for comparative cases. The technical setup was already in place. The previous step's classifiers could identify data scientist posts from a larger collection of job posts. I could apply this classifier to the corpus of over thirty thousand older job descriptions and have it find jobs that looked like focal positions. Technically, these were false positive classifications—their title was not data scientist. In this context, however, they captured positions that required the skills that were consistently associated with the formal label in analyses that focused on the label. They were the skills that went on to gain recognition under the new data scientist positions.

The repurposing trick worked. The classifier found several hundred job posts that resembled data scientist posts in terms of the skills they mentioned in the years right before the title appeared. This collection offered a lens into data science's origins and underlying expertise beyond the title's formal recognition.

The specific numbers don't say much, given LinkedIn's growth as a platform at the time.[33] But the relative frequencies between these posts were insightful. For a first check, figure 2.5 shows a slightly cryptic early visualization in which I checked whether the posts were in plausible organizational functions, listed on the y-axis. It shows a predominance of IT (dark gray patches indicate a high proportion of all posts) and, to a lesser degree, engineering (eng). Both made sense and gave me some confidence in this application of the classifiers. Something interesting was going on with a switch from quality assurance (qa), customer service (cust), and education (edu) to analysis and research (rsch), as well as some consistency in product management (prdm). But these occurrences were hardly noticeable next to the main ones, and they still fit into the broader image of data science.

The links to established functions revealed more of data science's context in workplaces but still didn't say anything about the expertise that constituted data science. And data science alone could once again not solve this problem. Expertise is a sociological problem, and sociological writing conceives of knowledge as a set of relations between insights, concepts, and ideas. Popular measures of knowledge in modern research consider citations between scientists' publications, their linking of chemicals or other objects in their work, and the themes of their work according to co-occurring words.[34] This relational view of knowledge translates to applied expertise, with links and relations between publications and concepts featuring as links between job posts through skills and other keywords.

The problem of data science's emergence becomes a question of how positions group together and whether they use separate or overlapping skills, indicating singularly specialized and integrated expertise.[35] Such a relational understanding of knowledge

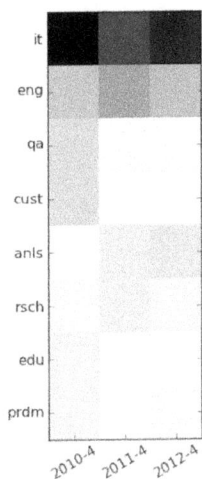

FIGURE 2.5 Functions with a prevalence ≥ 0,05 among data scientists.
Figure showing the relative prevalence of retained job posts based on
skills across formal functional affiliations.

lends itself to techniques from social network analysis, which
reveal structural patterns from relational datasets. Job posts had
connections through shared words translated into a so-called
bipartite network, which projects to the level of the positions to
reveal links through shared words. To capture a structure's patterns, I used a machine learning technique that clusters positions according to their interconnections in what specialists call
community detection.[36] The clusters then served as a basis for
organizing the posts in simple visualizations that highlight
overlaps between clusters to index expertise fragmentation and
integration.[37]

Figure 2.6 shows the graphical displays of the job post
structures in two versions: raw matrices (top row) and aggregate
models (bottom row). Rows and columns represent job postings.

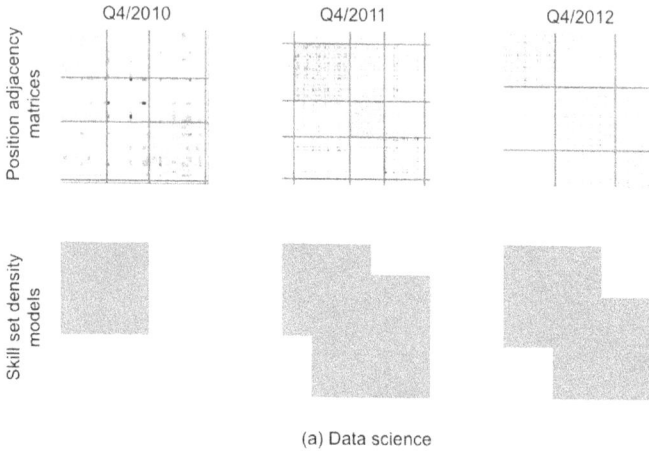

FIGURE 2.6 Matrix visualizations of data scientist–like job posts (rows and columns as nodes) with co-occurring skills (ties/cells) in raw format (top row) and aggregate representations (bottom row) for three temporal snapshots.

Dark spots in the cells represent connections between them through shared skills. In the top row of raw images, the single rows and columns follow a horizontal and vertical order in which positions of particularly dense areas of overlap appear next to each other. The bottom row of models shows simplified versions of the raw matrices, with blocks of posts as gray or blank patches if they have many or only a few interconnections. Gray areas on either side of the main diagonal indicate overlap between positions that are part of different skill specializations. These images are not immediately meaningful on their own, but the similarities and differences between them finally reveal key features of data science's underlying stock of knowledge.

The positions initially overlapped in some skill combinations but not in others, as the 2010 images show. Positions increasingly overlapped in 2011 and 2012 while retaining considerable fragmentation. The specific arrangement of blank and gray patches is unimportant. Instead, their mere combination along the diagonal and on either side of it indicates the relevant patterns. The images show that the skills that data science has come to combine previously applied to separate but overlapping specializations.[38] The characteristics of the workplaces that posted these job descriptions contextualize the structural patterns around skills. Organizations that looked for data science skills tended to be young, small, and were often privately held, all characteristics that facilitated the combination of otherwise usual skill sets.[39] And they had different industry specializations. This evidence shows how the data scientist role came to use expertise that integrated established skills but was previously applied to disconnected problems. The distinct expertise required for those connections has become evident through the documentation of this data science procedure that involved specialized data storage technologies, machine learning techniques, and sociological theories.

Sociological thinking motivates one last return to comparative cases to interpret these patterns and ask how this process aids an emergent expert role. I repeated the relational analysis for the positions resembling attorneys and financial advisors.[40] Their patterns were mostly stable, and figure 2.7 focuses on the most recent period to contextualize the images for data scientists.[41] For attorneys, the images show job descriptions overlapping through skills such that they form distinct yet overlapping areas, indicated by the pattern of blank and gray regions. This image resembles the structure in the most recent image for the data scientist posts. For financial advisors, the organizational profession, the overlap looks different. There is a uniformly dense structure that results from the overlap of all clusters and

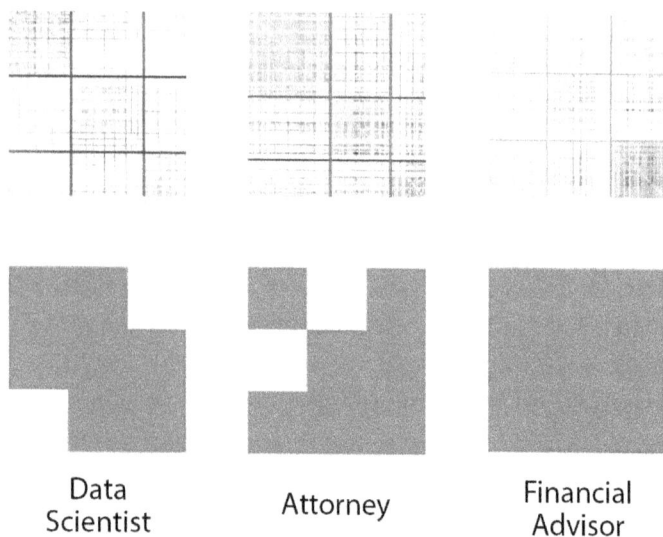

FIGURE 2.7. Matrix visualizations of job posts (rows and columns as nodes) with co-occurring skills (ties/cells) in raw format (top row) and aggregate representations (bottom row) of results for data scientist models, attorney models, and financial advisor models for 2012.

lacks differentiation. Data science emerges as a case that's more similar to an established profession than newer professional roles with close connections to their workplaces.

This analysis has led to a new insight into data science's formation. The tens of thousands of job posts that went into this analysis have come down to only three data points, five if we consider the temporal slices for data science skill structures, or twelve if we consider all the slices for each of the four cases. This small number of observations doesn't undermine the analysis's utility. It is the inevitable compromise of modeling exercises. The necessary guidance came from the vast debate that has informed the case comparisons of expertise structures and the techniques for implementing them.[42] The similarities and differences along key variables revealed data science's expertise as a decisive factor. Data scientists have stitched together a stock of knowledge built around analogical applications of expertise, allowing them to move from job to job and, ultimately, escape external control.

THE SOLUTION

This exercise tracked the scattered traces of data science's inception down to a single site: the labor market. The consistent appearance of new data scientist job posts was comforting but offered no deep insight, especially in retrospect. Everything else would have ended or at least significantly altered the project. The challenge became handling and analyzing those posts. Today, textbooks and teaching materials explain the procedures and techniques for processing textual records. I turned to the ideas I could find when data science started to form and filled the remaining gaps with solutions I was picking up in the data science scene. This approach was clumsy and involved setbacks, but it also produced striking results. It revealed a shared understanding of data science, showed how clear it was, contextualized the understanding of data science, and revealed the emergence of its contours in workplaces, again, in context.

The analytical process that produced these insights was consistent with expectations from pragmatist theories of practice. It involved a tedious back and forth between bigger and smaller obstacles and solutions that didn't fully overcome them but opened new directions. Figure 2.8 gives a schematic summary

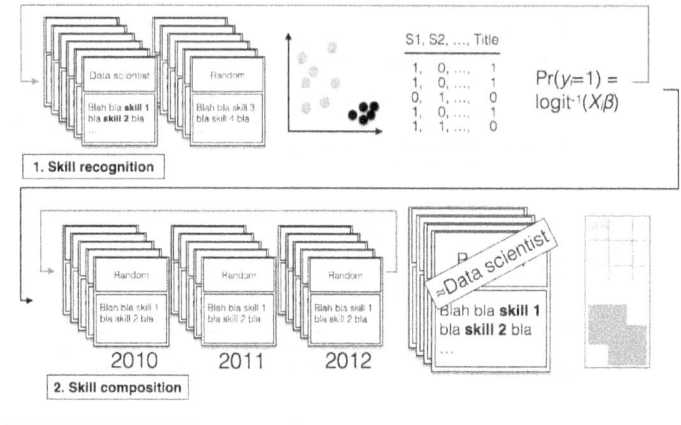

FIGURE 2.8. Schematic summary of the process for
analyzing job posts.

of the steps. There were the stacks of posts with words that
turned into scores for an initial selection to then turn the texts
into tables and train and test logistic regression classifiers, here
at the end of the first row as the most basic equation. I used the
prediction model from these steps to iterate through additional
stacks of job descriptions from previous years and identify those
that looked like data scientist posts even though they did not yet
have the label. They became the basis of a network representation to reveal the emerging structure of this area of expertise.

Why was figure 2.8 not figure 2.1 in this chapter's introduction to serve as a roadmap for the rest? The first section could
have motivated the chapter with the theory of types of knowledge instead of just jobs as signals that would indicate professional emergence. The texts in job posts would have then featured
as a unique lens into professional dynamics and the clumsy processing steps as sophisticated technical solutions for longstanding

social scientific problems. The presentation could have easily skipped over the struggle of connecting the different pieces instead of stressing it. Such a chapter might have been a more pleasant reading experience, and the insights into data science's emergence might have seemed more authoritative.

However, such a version would have been false. Figure 2.8 leaves out some key details. It doesn't show the API, JSON, MongoDB, or the Python code, for example, or the equations from the email analysis. While I could have added some or all of those details, omissions are inevitable in formal representations that serve as summaries. More significantly, such an account would have misrepresented the data analytic process. The choice of a cleaner presentation would still have been used had the topic been something other than data science's emergence. An analysis of, say, diary entries, pamphlets, or letters has nothing to do with APIs, Python, and so on, and available theories and protocols would have steered the analysis clear of dead ends. But data science has connections to those techniques and technologies. And since this analysis tries to shed light on data science's emergence, the technical steps and their unfolding offer crucial insights.

Whatever data scientists said about themselves, journalists wrote, critics warned, and followers imagined, these were the things data scientists did. I wasn't a data scientist, and many, if not most or all data scientists would have taken different turns, adopted different techniques, or produced different kinds of results. Whatever their specific choices, there is no getting around the technical complications of retrieving and organizing records, altering their format, making them compatible with statistical procedures, and selecting suitable procedures. And for any new problem, the data scientists had to pick their path through the vast set of options that the coder community, the academic community, and state and corporate-sponsored projects have provided. This was data science when it all started.

CONCLUSION

The whirlwind of impressions from the previous chapter has subsided in this chapter, giving the analytical floor to grayscale images of data science's emergence. Data science wasn't a hallucination, the vast underlying records showed, but it wasn't a sudden explosion of a few breakthrough ideas, either. Its basis formed in workplaces over several years and involved much older ideas, but it quickly formed a shared understanding comparable to that of established professions. These conclusions undermine some popular impressions and support some more sober views, albeit from a new perspective that reveals a shift instead of a straightforward extension of established work.

The images hardly captured data science in full. I barely had the skills for implementing a sophisticated machine learning–based text analysis, and job posts, a signal for professional prospects, captured little of what one could call serious intellectual roots. I tried to make up for some of these deficits in additional analyses. I turned to the first academic programs and specializations in data science as a starting point. To avoid more problems from questionable technical decisions, I manually collected information on all instructors with a focus on their publications and then detailed information on those publications, including their bibliographies. I did the same for two comparison cases, law, again, and systems biology as another emergent case, and then identified the structural makeup of the reference networks. The idea was similar to the idea for the job post structures, but the process and the material were different, geared toward revealing the intellectual foundation of this new role. The results were consistent with the results of this analysis, placing data science between systems biology and law, less insular than the former but more distinctively specialized than the latter.

These additional results were encouraging. They showed that not only workplaces but also academic institutions recognized data scientists. But this recognition only leads back to the main questions: How did data science form to become recognizable? Where did the label come from that firms assigned to positions and universities to programs? Was what I had first started to see in New York City's data community the cause or the consequence of these developments?

To answer these questions, the following chapter takes another step back to consider data science's intellectual origins before the era of dedicated data science programs. It anchors applied analyses like this one of job posts and discussions of them like those I followed at data science events in the city. The remaining chapters will then unpack what happened at those events, who came, what they said, and how they discussed, to unpack the construction of this new professional role.

3

SCIENCE AND DATA

Data science made its entrance in newspaper headlines, office chatter, and, soon, dedicated training programs, job profiles, and after-work gatherings. But jobs using data science skills had existed before the label appeared, and the skills themselves had roots in established academic disciplines. Between general skepticism and specific worries, the most incisive critiques came from the modern heirs of classical thinkers. Statisticians and applied mathematicians called out data science for grounding its attention and legitimacy on false claims of novelty that leveraged technological changes and the deep pockets of Big Tech to create a new look for old ideas.[1] They had a point. But while those changes played into data science's ascent, the underlying work still involved specific technical ideas. For data science to come about, its protagonists had to make their arcane knowledge, whether new, old, or a mix, broadly salient.

Insider complaints about data science's rise built on intuition more than systematic analysis. They brushed over the motives and activities that shaped data science's emergence and missed social and historical contexts. Those dimensions, less vivid perhaps, involve a crucial side of its rise, namely, the mechanisms that make complex events appear inevitable in hindsight.[2] This chapter traces the ideas that motivated and defined calls for data science throughout the scholarly world from where they came, providing a backdrop to the striking events of recent times. Data scientists who wrote and talked about their role acknowledged upfront their reliance on established academic fields, mostly statistics and computer science. In line with complaints in those fields about data scientists' cavalier recognition of these roots, the chapter finds earlier calls for data science long before modern proposals. But they have no direct connection to data science's recent formation. Instead, they point to a longer chain of disarray and division in technical discussions of quantitative analyses.

Evidence is both in plain sight and more hidden. The chapter considers some of the earliest accounts where academics used the "data science" label to describe their ideas, some of which have entered the most popular discussions of data science and some that haven't. It then goes beyond these obvious indicators and traces the debates that academics who discussed data science cited in their support, even though they did not propose data science as a label. The chapter pushes this logic further and uses the topics and contours of that debate to revisit pivotal moments that existing research has identified in the history of quantitative thought. The two dominant theoretical frameworks for understanding expert work, the more formal one involving a system of competing groups and the one stressing expert groups' informal underpinnings, guide the interpretation.

This analytic strategy assembles a curious cast of characters. The debates directly linked to data science's emergence a decade ago brought together professional academics active in the 1990s and early 2000s, such as Chikio Hayashi, Bill Cleveland, and Jeff Wu, whom I will introduce on the following pages. The debates that preceded data science proposals involved some famous names in statistics—Karl Pearson, George Udny Yule, and, a notch below those, Franklin H. Giddings. There are also Tobias Mayer, Adrien Marie Legendre, and Adam Sedgwick, less familiar figures, even to some specialists, but ones who have shaped the history of quantitative thought in ways that inform our understanding of data science today. Across these groups, no single image of a scholar applies. Hayashi, Cleveland, and Wu were scientists in the contemporary sense, with faculty positions at research institutions and professional recognition through awards. Mayer, Legendre, and Sedgwick were active before modern academic institutions organized scientific inquiry, but they helped create them. Pearson, Yule, and Giddings used those maturing institutional spaces and scattered technical ideas to create fields of knowledge.

The problem of data science's roots in academic research demands a unique analytic lens to account for the external appearance and internal workings of technical expertise. However, once in place, the step into history in this analysis of data science's emergence offers a crucial insight. Data science's rise was not a case where novel applications benefited from a definite set of existing ideas. It started as one of many moments where dedicated users of available knowledge encountered limitations and where, in the course of adjustments, different sides positioned themselves relative to the ideas as strategically as their sense of the situation and concerns with a problem allowed. This entanglement with more longstanding social dynamics transforms data science from a curiosity of the digital era into a lens into the evolution of quantitative expertise and the production of technical knowledge. Data science emerges as a response to an ongoing struggle between ideas about scientific purity and the practical problems of empirical data analysis.

TWO SIDES OF SCIENCE

Starting with the title, data science's relation to science can seem straightforward. Everyone knows that scientists use charts and equations to manipulate, analyze, and interpret numerical data. They have developed those procedures together with statisticians to study problems in biology, chemistry, physics, or economics. Data scientists found distinct problems with data-analytic procedures across those areas and applications outside of academic fields. The name recognizes their background and the new twists while raising questions at the same time.[3] But does this connection imply the status of a scientific discipline for this work or merely the use of the scientific method? What would either one mean or imply? And what does change in science look like?

These questions require moving from data science's etymology to its empirical ties to science. But science is hard to observe, let alone see through analytically: It is vast and arcane, requiring years of specialized training in the confines of labs, offices, or archives, and even researchers don't always understand what their colleagues say or do. A lot is also at stake. The work of scientists has produced life-saving medical treatments, deadly weapons, and new materials and views of the world. To understand those transformative and contradictory accomplishments, generations of social scientists have watched other scientists do their work. Their accounts contextualize data science's connections to established sciences.

One key insight from research on scientists unlocks a series of related ideas. The insight is that science has two sides, one that outsiders see and one that insiders see.[4] Outsiders see rigor and purity and assign high status to those who do scientific research. They may also find them arrogant and detached. Insiders, those who do science as a job, may see a significance in their work worthy of distinct commitment but also hostile colleagues and risky career prospects. What's more, neither side is uniform or polished, and the two don't align.

Science is, then, partly a question of one's position, with the additional complication that views vary for whoever is looking. For example, for outsiders, someone's social background shapes their sense of science and of scientists.[5] And depending on where scientists find themselves, in what country, but also what discipline and even institution, they will have different ideas of what science is or should be compared to a scientist in another country, discipline, or intellectual tradition.[6] While outsiders may differ in what they think of science or take from it, scientists differ in how they practice science and do so in different ways across countries and disciplines and so on. Importantly, what is an occasional and passing issue for the former defines the lives of the latter.

These basic insights mean that science's appearance obscures a clear view of data science's link to science.[7] Outsiders have to look beyond the popular image of science. Science is more than people in lab coats making statements that seemingly, to outsiders, miss the main issues. It's a community of people with passions and fears and worksites inducing excitement, anxiety, and frustrations. Insiders, in turn, have to recall that science unfolds in slightly different ways in different fields, groups, and moments. Their experience of entering the academic world, in what field or discipline, at what point in time, and under whose supervision will have shaped how they understand science. Of course, there are ideas all share, and longer tenure in the profession likely fosters sensitivity to the different takes. But established scholars are sometimes also more skeptical of new ideas. Either way, insiders have to consider their personal involvement to see the links between data science and established sciences.

This kind of reflection on one's perspective is not only a nuisance for observers. It was the defining challenge for data scientists. The ambiguous connection between their selves and their surroundings was the setting of data science's construction, whether they knew it or not. These challenges are common in science, with its core activities revolving around observations and interpretations. The data science case draws attention to different ways of addressing those challenges in specific historical contexts.

FIRST CALLS AND FALSE STARTS

Data science's entanglement in science's complex makeup is evident in how outsiders and insiders greeted its emergence. Outsiders were curious and sometimes concerned but had no strong personal feelings about data science. After all, the name may have been new, but it made sense, with its graphs and statistical models as familiar images of science, and its details remained opaque, just like for other specialized areas of work. Insiders were mostly uninterested and sometimes distinctly unhappy. Data science made much less sense for them as a new idea precisely because it used techniques and expertise from existing scientific fields.[8] The two reactions capture different projections of firmly held ideas on data science. Outsiders sensed something exciting, new breakthroughs and possibilities, the usual reasons for science's appearance in public discourse. Scientists sensed a threat to a set of problems they claimed, whether credible or not, from an intruder.

These reactions are at odds with each other but consistent in making the same easy mistake: They view science as uniform and definite. And some of science's most salient features support such a coherent image. This starts, for instance, with the principles and techniques on which it rests, dating back over two thousand years to Greek philosophy.[9] Ideas and principles have survived in evolving institutions, starting in ancient Mesopotamia and then medieval Italy, creating a centuries-long cultural lineage.[10] Today's global presence of universities and academic degrees, their interconnections, standardized positions and procedures, and images of them in the media, all manifest that image.[11] Older than nation-states, economic systems, and even some religions, and cutting across all of them, science is one of modern society's major institutions. What could be ambiguous?

The high-level view overlooks the twists and turns in science's history and the differences across the disciplines. Universities, as we know them today, have a much shorter history than their ancient roots suggest. In the United States, they adopted their modern form just over a century ago. They started only a bit earlier in the European countries where they first appeared at scale. To be sure, there are several older academic institutions. The universities of Bologna, Cambridge, and Oxford are famous examples. However, for long stretches, they remained singular establishments rather than elements in a system of research and training institutions, such as those that are the main venues of modern science. Particularities often persist, and the system itself varies greatly across different countries, creating a range of experiences for those inside or just watching. If science is less uniform than it first seems, data science's appearance may be neither the plausible development outsiders see nor the cheap trick inside cynics suspect. It is more likely an emergent activity, a collective response to concrete issues and larger changes.

The puzzle of data science's seemingly sudden emergence is easy to debunk. Even a simple query of scientific publications reveals data science proposals as early as the late 1990s and early 2000s.[12] One of the first records of data science in an academic context is from 1996, about a decade and a half before today's version of data science gained wide recognition. Back then, Chikio Hayashi, a Japanese mathematician, shared reflections on his scientific field. He told an audience at an academic conference that, in his view, "mathematical statistics has devoted itself only to the problems of statistical inference" and "have been . . . removed from reality."[13] The analytical tone and language hid a harsh accusation. Hayashi criticized an entire established academic field for having made itself irrelevant. Pushing this point further, he proposed a new approach involving "design for data, collection of data, and analysis on data," complete with a new name, "Data Science."

Hayashi had the same basic ideas as the data science calls from the last decade and used the same title to describe them. The much more muted response he received may partly reflect the attack on his peers that his remarks contained. But he also made his pitch in a specific setting, an international conference on statistical classification techniques. This was a good place for a technical proposal; it didn't help its spread. Was this the first step toward data science's spread a decade later, or was this an instance of similar forces coming together that would return with more strength?

This early sighting comes with its own questions about placing data science. The scene was the meeting of an international scientific association dealing with problems in numerical data analysis. International debates like these are a core feature of science, and the theme sounds like it would attract an audience for technical ideas like Hayashi's. But international associations lack power and influence. Research funding more commonly comes from national agencies or foundations. The specific meeting took place in Japan, which has major research institutions but is far from the center of the global scientific system. At least scholars from several academic disciplines may have something to say about the conference's topic. The attention that interdisciplinary projects often get makes this first look like a feature.[14] But day-to-day scientific work typically observes disciplinary boundaries wherein interdisciplinary activities find little support.[15] These common characteristics of science likely did what they often do and muted Hayashi's call for a new direction.

Despite the obstacles, data science made other early appearances in science, such as in a lecture in 1997 and at another conference in 1999.[16] Those instances had no clear connections, and the proposals made no reference to each other, making the disconnect of the popular discussion during recent years less surprising right away. However, data science's early persistence indicates a more complex process than direct diffusion from some pioneers to early adopters.[17] The separate small-scale occurrences early on may offer insights into the specific dynamics of the later occurrences that gained broad attention.

The 1999 proposal resembled Hayashi's from a few years before. It was part of a scientific meeting in Finland, which is, like Japan, far from the center of the global academic world. The presenter was Bill Cleveland, a statistician at Bell Labs, a research institution in the United States with a long tradition but no university affiliation; this, similar to an interdisciplinary setting, may rub academic peers the wrong way.[18] He, too, started with a critique, arguing that the field of statistics needed "enlargement," and he envisioned an academic field with departments that would combine several areas, multidisciplinary investigations, models and methods of data, theory, and more.[19] There was more open frustration with the prevailing situation in science that motivated the turn to data science and some of the same but also new obstacles to keep it quiet.

These were not the ideas of bitter researchers rationalizing their exclusion from a central elite. Frustrations among academics and alternative proposals flare up regularly, as research has shown for science,[20] and a third appearance from 1997 for data science reveals more of its motivations and the features of science silencing them. It involved another academic, a statistician named Jeff Wu, who gave a lecture with the provocative title "Statistics = Data Science?" Wu was more diplomatic than Hayashi and Cleveland, but his proposal made similar points as theirs when he addressed an audience at an elite institution in the United States, the heart of the global academic community. More than locating data science's origins, next to the other instances, this situation reveals more of the conditions and ideas of early data science occurrences as possible reference points for data science's recent rise.

Wu used a rhetorical trick for his critique. Rather than saying what he thought, he showed his peers how the public viewed statistics. His slides included general definitions that limited statistics to an accounting-like activity. Wu then asked, "Do statistics and statisticians deserve this public image or stereotype?" It wasn't wrong, he acknowledged, but it didn't do justice to the expertise and activities of statisticians. Wu listed a range of opportunities in connection to then-emerging artificial intelligence techniques and new datasets for enhancing the significance of statistics. He echoed his more outspoken peers in terms of substance, proposing a "balanced curriculum," with an emphasis on data collection, modeling, and computing, and "interdisciplinary training" with up to half of courses from outside the department.[21] Wu ended his formal talk with references to "computer science," "cognitive science," and other scientific fields. "'Data Science,'" Wu concluded, "is likely the remaining good name reserved for us,"[22] giving an improvised etymology of the title that matches the attention it would receive a decade later and hinting at an explanation for its disconnected appearances.

The three calls separately made similar points about a narrowness and inward orientation of quantitative academic expertise and the need for an alternative. They revealed data science as an idea that summarized their proposals for advancing science at the end of the twentieth century. They wanted to move the data analytic process into the center. The circumstances illustrate the extent and institutional order of science from the perspective of new ideas.

Do these early anecdotes indicate a firmer grounding of today's data science activities in established sciences, or does the absence of formal references to them suggest the opposite? Insiders and outsiders alike connect ideas in science to those who had them. Many nonscientists know, for example, that Albert Einstein developed the theory of relativity, and scientists give one another awards for their contributions to knowledge or name laws or principles after themselves or colleagues. These features are the foundation of formal theories of expert work.[23] The absence of that recognition for data science sets it apart from other scientific fields and ideas.

But this form of recognition is also far less systematic and more ambiguous than images of Einstein and some others suggest. There are many instances in which different scholars made the same discovery in separate times or places,[24] and there are many ways that recognition for ideas from those who had them can be diverted.[25] Cleveland and Wu still laid claim on their early proposals for data science after it spread widely. As discussions of data science became more systematic, their proponents learned to acknowledge those earlier attempts,[26] showing the direct engagement that theories stressing the informal side of expert work would expect.

The early data science proposals show how recognition and, thus, continuity in science is not necessarily all an informal effort or interplay of formal mechanisms. Today's formation of data science is more deeply embedded in science than its contemporary images capture, indicating the possible significance of abstract quantitative knowledge. It wasn't the sole idea of the coders and hackers who started describing their work as data science a decade ago. But, like these three separate proposals from the late 1990s, they may have had original ideas in relation to existing expertise. Wu documented how easy it was to get to the data science title from existing scientific nomenclature. The same chain of reasoning could have come together in the minds of others as well.

SCIENCE V. DATA

If data science is not self-evident, not even within the confines of scientific disciplines, how did the different proposals all arrive at similar ideas? Where did their frustration come from? And what do these dynamics say about the formation of data science two decades later and outside of science? Although early data science proposals appeared in the seemingly slow-moving world of academic research, their consequences could have been quite significant. The philosopher of science Thomas Kuhn proposed to think of big changes in science as "scientific revolutions," intellectual revolts, though without the terror and bloodshed of political transformations.[27] The image captures the change that scholarly communities can experience. The aftermath of the early data science proposals saw no major transformation, but those who made them were calling for an uprising.

Pursuits of change are hard to track in science. Before researchers can attend meetings and conferences and speak and write about science and ways of doing it, they have to do it. While that is obvious, it's not easy to consider empirically. Outsiders see science mostly via its results, that is, its more or less significant discoveries. Insiders see it through the projects and publications that enable their careers, the administrative duties that slow them down, and shared stories from the professional community. This disconnect between substance and appearance is deeply institutionalized in science. Students beginning their studies learn from methods textbooks, and established researchers debate new standards for evaluating results or finding the truth. But those problems only map crudely on the day-to-day activities of working scientists. Textbook exercises and methodological debates aim for generic presentations. In contrast, any specific research activity that studies a new problem will confront the analyst with unique challenges that may demand adjustments.[28]

Those were the tasks that Hayashi, Wu, and Cleveland wanted to acknowledge when elevating "data" to the level of "science" in their proposals' titles. Their proposals described this work around new computational capabilities, potentially giving the impression that the problem was only one of adjusting old ideas to new technologies. Plenty of scientists have advanced quantitative expertise in their work before, just without the data science label. The relation between data science and ideas from earlier times can show how data science ideas depended on the computational tools from the last few decades or reiterate more longstanding concerns with research work. Without a label that offers a link to those times, I turn to foundational problems for modern quantitative thinking—the analysis of associations and the calculation of errors—to place data science in this longer history of changes in science.

Applied data analysis deals with statistical associations, that is, the question of whether two or more features have something to do with each other. They require observing two sets of values, say, hours of studying and exam scores, for some units, here, students. Studying and scores have an association if, for most units in a set of observations, both values go up or down or one value goes up while the other goes down. If some students who study hard have higher scores while others have lower ones, but quite a few slackers score highly as well, then there is no association. This problem is important because an association can have practical implications, such as that students should study more.

The studying example was a simple illustration for setting up the arguments that practicing scientists often have over getting associations right and drawing the correct conclusions.[29] These ongoing and increasingly intricate debates build on basic technical ideas from over a century ago. But the events from that time reveal concerns that also marked the data science proposals. Here, they appear in a time without today's computational capabilities, uncovering more of data science's roots in science.

Like the proposals by Hayashi and the others, the discussions longer ago saw fierce disagreements, but the focus was more clearly on specific technical solutions. Two key protagonists in England, the leading place of scientific ideas at the time, were themselves leading figures in statistics, which made them an obvious topic for historians of science. They were Karl Pearson and George Udny Yule. The context of their technical ideas highlights some more social features outside of the standard images of science, first, personal experiences, such as that Yule had studied under Pearson before their conflict, and second, entanglement in larger issues, for example, that Pearson was part of a class of rising professionals, while Yule was experiencing downward mobility.[30] Along with the similarities and differences, the more technical ideas for measuring associations reveal more of the link between concrete data-analytic challenges and general ideas for solving them.

Pearson's and Yule's original question was more basic than my school performance example but no less important at the time; they sought to understand the link between vaccination and survival. Today, we know that vaccines save lives. But at the time, vaccines were still new, their effectiveness was unclear, and the question of their association with how bodies dealt with diseases posed a new technical problem. Information on vaccination and survival differs from that on time spent studying and test scores. The former type of information is discrete, or categorical, more like if someone has a high school diploma or not or is employed or not, as opposed to the continuous values of minutes of studying, points received for correct answers, or dollars earned. Yule and Pearson's respective ideas addressed associations of this type of discrete states.

Yule's idea was straightforward. He proposed a measure that counted the number of deceased and living of those vaccinated and not. His technical tool was a table with two rows and two columns for collecting the occurrences of the four possible combinations: unvaccinated and alive, vaccinated and alive, and so on. Yule proposed a mathematical procedure for determining whether the counts were likely due to chance or showed a systematic difference in deaths between the vaccinated and unvaccinated. He reasoned that, besides clear cases, the measure should capture associations where one combination, such as vaccination and death during a pandemic, did not occur.[31]

Pearson had an entirely different solution and questioned the practical focus of Yule's measure. He wanted to understand people beyond such specific issues as illnesses and their prevention. This view considered how vaccination and survival, and other associations, are all interrelated. However, the associations of binary statuses like vaccination and survival are difficult to put in relation to other possible associations in the solution Yule proposed. Pearson introduced a procedure that assumed that the two categories were a special case of the familiar continuous dimensions. From the outside, this assumption is hard to follow, and it was the core tension between the two scholars. Simply put, Pearson proposed mathematical operations that treated vaccination status as if there were degrees of vaccination. This view still seems plausible if he meant how much of a vaccine a person had received. But that was not his idea, and it makes no sense for the question of whether a person survived a disease or not, which Pearson also treated as if a person could have survived somewhat or a lot. He defended that view on the grounds that it allowed him to calculate measures of associations that he could directly compare across dimensions with different characteristics, such as a person's weight, height, wealth, or intelligence, which aligned with Pearson's larger agenda.

Pearson's view has merit at the distance that scientists like to keep from the problems they study. People are part of a world full of complex interrelations that an analysis should be able to capture. But the logic breaks down when it comes to concrete issues like vaccination and survival, which features no less in people's experiences. How can they be part of a continuum, as

Pearson had to assume for his measure to make sense? In Yule's words, "all those who have died of small-pox are equally dead."[32] This recognition does not deny the idea of a broader range of important problems and associations. Yule was as interested in understanding poverty as he was in the effectiveness of vaccination. But he chose to develop tools for each problem specifically. Pearson's willingness to sacrifice the fit between his measure and the problem in the world, even a problem as severe as a deadly disease, highlights an idiosyncratic decision that is part of the work of quantitative analysts. Yule's reaction captures the frustrations that scholars have with one another's ideas with and without pitches for new labels.

This debate has deep implications for statistical thinking, but the relevant insight for understanding data science's roots is more in what happened than in who was right. Two highly established scholars offered two radically different solutions for the same numerical problem. They had different technical ideas in mind, with details mostly invisible to outsiders.[33] But those arcane differences translated into concrete steps for dealing with numbers. One focused on the numbers and how they hang together, happily working on a new solution for another problem. The other tried to fit those numbers into larger ideas about the world's workings, more concerned with those ideas than the numbers and what they stood for.

This split shows a divide in quantitative work of the kind that also marked more recent discussions. The situation was obscure and happened a century ago, but it shared key similarities with the fault line reflected in the calls for data science from two decades ago. Hayashi, Wu, and Cleveland argued against a focus detached from concrete problems and measurement practicalities, like Pearson's, which had become common by then.

Echoing Yule in an era of cheaply available powerful computers, they urged colleagues to remain close to the problems at
hand and assigned that concern with data science a new label.

The long span between the two episodes embeds data science,
so vivid today, in a more longstanding struggle in science. That
struggle unfolds around entirely different concerns than those
tied to today's digitization, Big Tech, or Silicon Valley startup
culture. Instead of exploiting shaky academic foundations for a
new name with corporate appeal, this process involves technical ideas for analyzing numbers and explaining the world's
problems. These ideas are about the importance of observations
behind the numbers or the larger thinking around those observations whenever technical analyses require a tradeoff. Quantitative analyses may look like indistinguishable mathematics from
the outside. From the inside, their machinery and role in the
research process vary substantially. Insiders disagree on how central issues around data analysis should be.

This glimpse into an earlier historical moment has added
depth to the problem of data science's formation. It raises questions about the process that connects them. Quantitative solutions fall into one of two approaches, it seems, and over time, the
general focus has garnered more appeal and legitimacy in science. However, this image can't shake its own specificities
around the fallout between a mentor and his student and members of different groups in British society. While such personal or
social conflicts are a common, informal driver of scientific progress, they are specific to the situation and retain a sense of data
science's rise as a possibly idiosyncratic development. In contrast,
theories that see science as a more formalized endeavor would
highlight the equations that were part of the dispute. The case
offers no basis for untangling these competing interpretations.[34]

PRAGMATISM AND PURITY

The Pearson-Yule conflict has shown more of data science's connection to science. This connection is not in the name or a set of techniques. It is in the tension between quantitatively analyzing specific problems and advancing general scientific ideas. However, the personal links between Pearson and Yule also obscured the view of what is behind that tension. The answer requires looking further into the data-analytic process, where the technical ideas were still part of less comprehensive social arrangements around quantitative expertise. Another century-long step back from the argument between Yule and Pearson, two hundred years from today, can offer such insights.

Earlier times produced the ideas that became the foundation of modern quantitative analyses. Like in Pearson and Yule's day, important problems in the world motivated some of these ideas, if of a different kind. Poverty and sickness were very much around, of course, and a few pioneers had administered the first vaccines. But the developers of quantitative tools were still dealing with more basic problems. They tried to map the world and navigate it systematically. And their work unfolded differently. The scholars exchanged letters, occasionally met one another, and maybe even learned from one another directly, but they worked much more on their own and not yet in a formal professional community. Their situations bring out the core concerns of quantitative analysts and, thus, the backdrop to modern data scientists.

The problems look odd from today's perspective. Before GPS navigation was at our fingertips, one needed a map and directions to find one's way and, after one left a place on the map, a technique for placing oneself on that map again. This wasn't a problem in everyday life, where most knew where to find what they needed, as much it was for larger infrastructure projects, war, or long voyages at sea. Significant investments were necessary to first record geographic features, and then new ideas were needed for organizing and eventually navigating those features. These challenges may seem much less analytical than getting at associations between two dimensions, the problems from Pearson and Yule's time, but they were still tricky to solve at first. Tellingly, similar fault lines emerged as those in later times, unfolding in ways that reveal more of the motivation and context of modern calls for data science.

The core analytical problem was how to place oneself on a map. The solution involved measuring the moon's position relative to Earth. But this step was complicated because the moon's rotation changed ever so slightly, moving possible reference points around. Scholars knew this by then and worked on understanding the moon's movements to map its orbit. The German astronomer Tobias Mayer developed an initial answer using observations of a point on the moon and other known features, such as the moon's pole. He then set up a system of equations to calculate unknown values from his observations. With observations from three days of a specific point on the moon, he could calculate the unknown values, making his problem look like a mostly mathematical one.

The problem's mathematical appearance does not necessarily indicate that a mathematical process will be necessary for reaching the solution. This insight has emerged as the common theme across the early data science proposals and the specific measurement of associations a century before, and it resurfaces here even more clearly. Meyer was exceedingly diligent and produced measures from twenty-seven days, twenty-four more than were necessary for the math to work. But rather than making his problem easier, the additional measures revealed a new problem: inconsistencies. They differed from one another in the way the moon's movements would lead one to expect, but between them, they differed more than that. The effort of gathering additional observations changed his problem into a data problem, a "big data" problem even by the standards of his time. Thus, the first accomplishment of the multiple measures was to show that a single measure was potentially misleading.

This is where the promise of pure mathematics ends and data-analytic ideas start.[35] The naive solution would try to find the three most correct measures for the calculation. But Mayer introduced an intermediary step. Instead of trying to pick the single most accurate measure for each of the three points, he sought the best answer in the combination of the measures. He grouped the equations around his twenty-seven measures into three sets of nine equations. He followed a promising hunch but no evident mathematical logic. The historian Alain Desrosières suspects that Mayer's familiarity with the measurements "gave him the audacity needed to rearrange the equations" and arrive at a solution.[36] The idea around that choice still made a significant leap, moving a quantitative analysis from calculation to estimation.

Audacity is not what outsiders or most insiders commonly associate with scientific work. Mayer's solution recalls features of Yule's technique, both anticipating the ideas behind the early calls for data science. They had a concrete problem, created a systematic setup, and used some math to get to formal measures that addressed the initial problems. In the words of the pragmatist philosophy from the previous chapter, they found new means in the face of problem situations. They put together the analytical procedure in the course of creative tinkering. The much earlier observations reveal these activities outside of the social order that had started to take shape by Yule's time and the digital and corporate context today. At this point, the emerging pattern has two possible implications: data science has either recovered a distinct side of quantitative work, or it has just returned to outdated practices in quantitative analyses.

We already saw that scientists' appreciation of purity is not at all modern, nor are the analytical tricks that respond to quantitative observations but deviate from formal procedures. This second instance from the early period revealed the specific interplay of formalism and pragmatism in quantitative work. This one unfolded just a few decades after Mayer's tinkering and involved the French mathematician Adrien Marie Legendre. Legendre developed a systematic and, thus, seemingly more scientific solution to a problem at a safe distance from deadly diseases or wild landscapes: the orbit of comets. There is no practical relevance like Mayer's lunar measures, but the era's concerns with objects in the sky are still evident.

Legendre, too, had to deal with measurement inconsistencies, but his solution followed principles, not audacity. He developed a procedure for taking inconsistencies into account, proposing to use the "minimum of the sum of the squares" of inconsistencies that followed from the application of mathematical equations to empirical measurements.[37] The implication was significant. Instead of requiring close familiarity with measures that may inform some ad hoc intuition, as it did for Mayer, analysts without that familiarity could now tackle all kinds of measurements and correct for inconsistencies using Legendre's strategy. The principle has lived on in much of quantitative analysis to this day and shows that general solutions are not a distinctly modern concern. But they seem to appear instead of Mayer's pragmatic approach, retaining the

image of opposition and an inevitable technical reason for conflicts over them.

The elegant outcome conceals the process by which Legendre arrived at them. Legendre introduced his principle in a longer essay that said many things about comets and their orbits
before getting, all of a sudden, after seventy-some pages, and
almost in passing, to his groundbreaking idea.[38] This presentation shows all but a deliberate effort. Legendre did not start out
with a general idea or theory and then seek cases for testing, as
much modern science proceeds. Instead, Legendre addressed a
series of problems in different contexts. Pragmatism was again
crucial in this data-analytic exercise, even though its problem
and outcome came much closer to the scientific sense of purity
than those of previous instances.

Only once Legendre had thought of minimizing the sum of
squares did he develop that idea into a general principle. He
moved from the problem of comets back to Earth and a problem he had worked on before. This problem involved "what must
have been the most expensive set of data in France."[39] It consisted
of measures for determining the length of a meter, a much more
practical question than the movement of comets. Before the
meter became the standard unit it is today, it started as an invention of supporters of the French Revolution to detach the definition of distances from aristocratic authorities. Its proponents
had specified the meter in seemingly apolitical terms, as a fraction, a very small one, of the distance between the equator and
the North Pole. But that idea was just an idea until measures
for that distance were available to calculate how long a meter
was. Legendre had helped with obtaining those measures and
still had the data, which he returned to for working out his new
idea for dealing with errors that he had while writing about
comets.

So, rather than strictly working with general ideas in mind, he, too, worked his way from one concrete problem to another concrete problem. He documented his process and reflected on its steps, putting together the general solution along the way. This detail about his process is crucial. Not only did Legendre cover both ends of the spectrum of scientific exercises, but his generalizable solution most likely benefited from the pragmatic ones.[40]

The tension in the early calls for data science runs much deeper than today's impressions would suggest. While Mayer's solution still looked like it may have been from a cruder scientific era, the range of Legendre's solutions showed that early quantitative analysts were after purity, too. However, his flexibility in his own work sidestepped the combative rhetoric of data science's proponents or even Yule and Pearson's professional dispute. This framing shows that different approaches to solving quantitative problems do not have to be tied to separate groups and that a quantitative analyst does not have to pick sides. General ideas imply untenable compromises with data analytic procedures. Others may insist on data analytic technicalities with no interest in more general insights or concerns. Instead, one can inform the other, even if the tension between the two exists. That tension provides the backdrop to data science's formation.

FROM IDEAS TO INSTITUTIONS

These snapshots from the past have reconstructed a much more complex backstory than the contemporary images of data scientists suggested. Scattered calls from a few years before pitched similar ideas with the same label. They also revealed a tension in science with dominant ideas and obstacles for the spread of new ones. Similar technical fault lines appeared a century before on more equal terms, while compatibilities still seemed possible another century ago before enough participants had gotten involved to get defensive about their specific technical choices. How did the productive interplay of pragmatic and purist approaches turn into the hostile struggle for privileged status in recent years?

This outcome is where science most clearly resembles more broadly familiar settings with their more visible social dynamics. We understand quite a bit about the roots of polarization in politics, the adoption of product standards across markets, or the granting of citizenship on one basis and not another.[41] Social processes like these in science are not as easy to see, nor do they have direct implications for the lives and livelihoods of billions of people. But, as Kuhn suggested with his choice of revolutions as an imagery of paradigmatic change in science, those differences in appearance don't deny similar underlying social dynamics. Lessons from the abundant research on the much more vivid settings can shed light on data science's place in science. They reveal how data science has given a social dynamic in science, a double movement,[42] a face that outsiders and insiders can see.

Much research has documented the entanglement of science in social structures and processes. It shapes the academic directions of universities and their organizational setups[43] or how researchers do their work, whether they make new discoveries or confirm old ideas.[44] Elsewhere, developments like these serve as the impetus for social movements to spring up in opposition,[45] and frustration was evident in Hayashi's, Wu's, and Cleveland's calls for data science. We know well what is at stake in society; what about science?

Science is not so different from the rest of society in that it is the result of researchers, like other communities, building institutional protections around themselves. One early, well-documented instance of ideas that motivated such structures in quantitative expertise unfolded in 1833, shortly after Legendre's work on measurement errors. The pivotal event was a meeting of the British Association for the Advancement of Sciences. The BAAS had been founded just two years earlier and was on the rise to become the main organization of scientific discourse in Britain.[46] The issue was not an exchange over substantive or technical ideas, such as those Legendre had just proposed or as Hayashi and Cleveland initiated two centuries later. Instead, the participants discussed whether they might accept statistics into the association as a dedicated section. The whole situation seems odd from today's vantage point. However, at the time, only a few universities in Britain had working statisticians while many did research in other capacities, giving this discussion at the BAAS unique significance. The possible inclusion of statistics was a decision on the scientific status of quantitative expertise.

It is easy to see why some of today's commentators find data science's entanglement in tech applications suspicious, but why would statistics not be part of a general scientific association? When statistics started to spread, many used it to inform political and economic debates. These applications made the BAAS leadership worry about politics distracting from the scientific discussions they sought to foster. The tension became evident when Adam Sedgwick, a geologist, explained his thinking about the issue. "By science," he reasoned, "I understand the consideration of all objects . . . capable of being reduced to measurement and calculation," which meant that applications of statistics would be legitimate "so far as they have to do with matters of fact, with mere abstractions, and with numerical results."[47]

From today's perspective, Sedgwick's condition seems like a warm welcome for quantitative techniques and analyses. Statistics is all about facts and numbers. But in his and his peers' eyes, statistics were not "matters of fact" anymore once they referred to social and political issues and required the analysts' interpretation. In contrast to that position, the examples so far have shown that statistics remain meaningless in many situations without interpretation. In the case of Pearson and Yule's vaccination and survival analysis from a few decades later, the mere counts of the number of deceased and vaccinated could be part of science. But the question of the effectiveness of vaccines, which was the whole point of the counts, would not be, because analysts and others could have political ideas about them. Despite the skepticism, statistics was still included in science when the BAAS created a dedicated section on the condition that it would only focus on facts without political, economic, or social connotations.

The rule that skeptics imposed for deciding what statistics to include and what not didn't work,[48] underlining the ambiguity of Sedgwick's compartmentalization of different steps in quantitative analyses. Such a slip seems odd amid the insistence on precision. But it points to this discussion's political motivation, where ambiguity is common and even a strategic choice.[49] Whereas the earlier discussions were about highly specific questions of how one should go about doing one's quantitative analysis, the issue of accepting statistics into the BAAS involved negotiations over scientific recognition. Social status, privileges, and resources were at stake in a discussion that was seemingly about substantive questions.

The political maneuvering becomes even more evident when it operates in the opposite direction. Sedgwick cast statistics as a potential threat to science because of its entanglement with the social world. The argument worked the other way around a century later in the United States. A few pioneers used it to push for expanding science by including psychology, political science, sociology, and economics, fields that would clearly have worried the BAAS's defenders of scientific purity.[50] These fields are established scientific disciplines today, with professional associations whose members discuss research, teaching, and the implications of their work. When their scientific status was still in question, however, around 1900, the relevant setting for such negotiations had moved from groups like the BAAS to the academic institutions we know today as the main sites of scientific life. This larger change presented opportunities for scholars to steer them in directions favorable to their research agendas.

One of those institutional entrepreneurs was Franklin H. Giddings, whose quest was to establish the field of sociology at Columbia University in New York City. He used the same reasoning about statistics as the BAAS a century before and an ocean away but reversed the logic. Giddings argued that thanks to statistics, "our knowledge of society [will be] up the standards [of] any natural science."[51] Sedgwick had insisted that statistics of the social world lost the resemblance with pure natural sciences and that this combination needed to be excluded. Not long after statistics was fighting for its own scientific acceptance, Giddings used it to convince gatekeepers that these observations, "categories . . . of real or supposed resemblance,"[52] could fit scientific standards, thanks to quantitative analysis. Both arguments hinged on mathematics and numbers as patron saints of scientific abstraction and formalism. They differed in how they could live up to that role when connecting arcane ideas to the world that scientific research seeks to understand. This dual use reveals quantitative analytic techniques as "boundary objects"[53] that those using them mobilized to argue for and against institutional legitimacy. The direction was more about where someone was and where they wanted to get than about the technical idea itself.

Statistics are both an analytic tool and a rhetorical device for securing institutional status. Yule, Pearson, Mayer, and Legendre had ideas for using quantitative analyses in different ways; Sedgwick, Giddings, and others had ideas for positioning them in science. They all benefited from times when larger changes made statistics salient,[54] giving them something to say and getting others to listen, like during the rise of data science at the dawn of the digital era. But the situations of Hayashi and Cleveland at the beginning of this chapter have shown that specific institutional settings may undermine new thinking around quantitative techniques. Having proponents like them and others mobilize technical ideas for institutional gains is only one step toward making them stay.

The field of statistics, the gatekeeper for data science to science, itself had to fight for its position even after the initial success at the BAAS. Its academic journey continued when statisticians sought distinct recognition following World War I, during another wave of quantification. After Giddings and his colleagues already had used statistics to justify dedicated departments for their substantive topics in universities, statisticians still needed to secure that formal status for themselves. They soon succeeded, but only in the United States and, to a lesser extent, in the United Kingdom and Germany, the other larger university systems at the time. These diverging fates point to a crucial barrier to clever arguments. US institutions had taken the older German universities as a template— Giddings was the exception among his colleagues for not having obtained a doctoral degree in Germany[55]—but their interpretation led to a new system. Instead of adopting the hierarchical structure wherein professors held so-called chairs, academic positions dedicated to fields of research that came with several subordinates, US universities created departments of colleagues with more equal status and informal specializations who worked on varying problems in the same academic field.

Statisticians advanced their quest for institutional status further in the United States, where they encountered fewer obstacles in justifying the addition of a new specialized topical focus. The holders of chairs in mathematics in German universities, each formally responsible for an entire field, had a harder time seeing the benefits of statistics to justify devoting the resources to a new chair that would possibly threaten their legitimacy.[56] In contrast, the flexibility of the US department structure did not expose the existing faculty there to similar existential threats.[57] The organizational difference helped statistics succeed in the United States even as it failed to become a distinct field in Germany.

The partial success in different systems says more about the significance of those systems for an emergent expert group than it does to undermine statistics' scientific legitimacy where it couldn't find footing. US institutions may have lagged behind the older German system in terms of scientific sophistication. One indication of this is that many of the statisticians in US universities were new arrivals from Britain, who were leading experts at the time.[58] The difficulties of statisticians in establishing themselves in Germany and the United Kingdom at the time could indicate that their ideas didn't fit those more advanced scientific systems. But the commitment to statistics in the United Kingdom developed its own dynamic toward scientific insight. A large community emerged whose members expanded their focus from concrete problems to include theoretical concerns as well.[59] This shift brought them closer to the idealized image of scientific work, exactly what German academics did not see or did not want to see. That institutionalized stubbornness was their loss.

Statistical ideas featured in arguments over proper ways of doing quantitative work or viewing science as controversial issues even as they often served complementary purposes. Proponents of the different sides mobilized statistics to deny or protect status, resources, and access to others or a community of peers. Statistical work has gained increasing scientific status over time, but this process and the framing of the role of statistics in the research process were not uniform or linear.

Quantitative expertise can work as a switch. In some situations, it serves to address problems in the world; in others, it expresses conceptual ideas in formal terms. Although the latter more directly resembles the scientific idea of purity, these versions are hardly distinct. In this sense, the most recent calls for data science didn't follow linearly on a continuous advancement of quantitative techniques. They followed as another instance in a chain of junctures, of attacks and defenses, of struggles over addressing problems. In the views of the dominant theories of expertise, the history of statisticians shows both the relational construction of technical expertise and the conflicts between institutionalized groups. Data scientists met more rigid boundaries but also drew on a larger community and more elaborate technologies for connecting technical thinking to practical problems.

BETWEEN ACCUSATION
AND INVITATION

This peek into data science's past has turned into quite a trip. The curious encounter of similar ideas linked to the same title

fifteen years before its explosion—without a direct connection—
pointed to yet other occurrences of the same deeper tensions
centuries before, also without the title. The tensions involved
pragmatic ideas for quantitative data analysis and supposedly
more purely scientific ones. This divide turned out not to be the
result of the technicalities of data analysis or the quest for truth.
It was part of a much more common social process of groups
protecting their ideas and status.

The back-and-forth in the development of quantitative
thought changes the puzzle of data science's emergence. Statisticians called data science out on not adequately acknowledging
earlier quantitative thinking. But their own history undermines
that accusation. Instead, contemporary developments are part
of a much larger process involving a series of conflicts that
include statistics but also efforts that statisticians have undermined. Data science may underrecognize some specific older
ideas in statistics. But it still draws attention to concerns in quantitative expertise, including among early statisticians, that purists
have consistently tried to sideline, either on their counts or in
response to the institutions from which they sought recognition.
These tensions are no relics of the past, and they occur much
more widely than the narrow calls for data science from the
chapter's beginning.

Science has come a long way since the earliest ideas for statistical problems. But even that process is still ongoing, because the
dynamics that have shaped quantitative expertise and scientific
institutions have a tendency to revisit old issues in new settings.[60]
For example, new discoveries, science's central aim, have declined
over the last two decades,[61] and, at least in social science, there
is still some frustration with using innovative turns to digital
technologies most effectively, even though earlier adoptions led

to major new insights decades ago.[62] The tensions and struggles that analysts of past incidents could work out so clearly will remain more subtle in these ongoing developments without the benefits of hindsight. They still serve as reference points to identify the driving forces today.

The core scientific concern with systematic knowledge production hasn't changed. Whether someone uses a laptop, typewriter, or pen and paper, scientists are alert and deliberate observers, call out colleagues on findings that don't hold or no longer do, and initiate intricate, if only occasionally reflective, debates on scientific work. In a final lens into data science's links to science, one of these discursive moments captures the wider sense among quantitative researchers that there is merit in the issues that the data science calls raised. This episode unfolded in 2001 and started with Leo Breiman, a professor of statistics at an elite university in the United States. Breiman had written an article on a divide in quantitative research. Some quantitative work, Breiman observed, focuses on models that generate data. Other work focuses on the prediction of scores and specific values in various datasets. He found this divide sufficiently systematic to describe it as the result of "two cultures."[63]

Breiman trained his criticism on the model-oriented approach, which he accused of having "irrelevant theory, questionable conclusions, and [having] kept statisticians from working on a large range of interesting current problems."[64] This puts Breiman in the company of his contemporaries Hayashi, Wu, and Cleveland. While he did not use the data science label, like them, he criticized a purist approach to quantitative expertise, extending the line of reasoning that was at least implicit in Yule, Mayer, and Legendre. Similar to Sedgwick and Giddings, Breiman and his contemporaries argued for reevaluating the organization of quantitative analysis.

The journal in which Breiman's article appeared published a series of his peers' responses. The responses capture the liveliness that marks academic discourse in its most productive phases. Supporters added technical problems that followed and offered possible solutions, while the critics fleshed out the terms of the divide in quantitative thinking today. Focusing on the conceptual implications of Breiman's distinction, one commentator that was generally favorable worried whether Breiman's position was "not to reject the base of much scientific progress."[65] This worry may have partly been in response to Breiman's polemical tone. But it also came surprisingly quickly to the defense of the purist side, reinforcing its perpetual dominance.

The image of two cultures in statistics thinking becomes vivid around the direct defenses. One such statement declared bluntly that "the two goals in analyzing data which Leo [Breiman] calls prediction and information I prefer to describe as 'management' and 'science,'" where "Management seeks profit" and "Science seeks truth."[66] This commentator rejected the worthiness of the second culture in the context of science, connecting the idea of two cultures of technical work to broadly salient segments in the division of labor in modern society. The divide that has emerged in quantitative thought throughout its history is resurfacing today outside of calls for data science. It has come to articulate the implicit distinction between different approaches into two alternatives. Political maneuvering was not explicit around the idea of two cultures, although that framing itself acknowledges another dimension than a purely technical one.

The debate took on a life of its own. Its premise oversimplified the data-analytic process and arguments were made that the critics picked their examples selectively and interpreted them strategically. The opposition was visible between Pearson and

Yule, even for the BAAS, but it was not clear in Legendre's case. Breiman's discussion could have gone differently, for example, had the commentator discussed Yule's attempt to help "manage" public health and poverty instead of reiterating his point about practical concerns around profit seeking, which Yule did not do. Similarly, Breiman could have pitched his two cultures instead as two styles that advance scientific progress at different points, such as in Legendre's work. But a debate like this, where an academic issue becomes political, quickly undermines the key driver of scientific progress in favor of strengthening definite positions as collateral damage.

A direct link of this debate to the deeper divide revealed itself in a small but prominent spot ten years later. Peter Norvig, author of an AI textbook and researcher at Google, referred to the idea of two cultures in a blog post responding to the linguist Noam Chomsky.[67] Chomsky had diagnosed "some successes, but a lot of failures" among applications of "statistical models to various linguistic problems." His skepticism included bewilderment about the definition of "success as approximating unanalyzed data" in this line of research as "novel in the history of science." This conclusion irritated Norvig.

In the post, Norvig first sorted out what Chomsky may have meant and evaluated if the points had merit. He proposed that Chomsky viewed statistics as engineering-style problem solving rather than a source of scientific insights. Norvig saw why but then laid out an argument for the interplay of the two. He explained what a statistical model is and took stock of the success of statistical language models. After concluding that statistics had produced abundant scientific insights, Norvig asked: "What doesn't Chomsky like about statistical models?" The answer involved a deep dive into decades of Chomsky's writing and quotes from a who's-who list of intellectuals, including Charles Darwin and the physicist Richard Feynman.

Norvig landed on Breiman's two-cultures idea to synthesize how all the "distinguished scientists have weighed in." He determined, probably correctly, that "the algorithmic modeling culture is what Chomsky is objecting to most vigorously." But Chomsky included statistics in this characterization, which would place him outside of Breiman's model. Norvig didn't mention this inconsistency, let alone resolve it or finish the line of reasoning. Instead, he added another detour to cast Chomsky as favoring a "mathematical science" over an "empirical science."

Chomsky would have to weigh in on the matter himself for more clarity, but who of the two was right has little relevance for understanding data science's emergence. Norvig's essay itself is telling, however. His chain of reasoning connects the two-cultures idea back to the much earlier arguments for the legitimacy of statistics as a scientific field. The curious cast of characters (at one point, the conservative commentator Bill O'Reilly appeared) he enrolled in this effort illustrates the issue's reach. Norvig's lengthy and winding response to Chomsky's off-the-cuff remarks suggests a personal reaction. It's these long-running and multifaceted tensions around arcane issues that data scientists met when they found one another.

The two-cultures framing and the responses to it show contemporary endorsements of a pragmatic approach to science outside of calls for data science. They echo dynamics from the past two hundred years. This chain of episodes reveals data science as the expression of a deep and vast divide in science around the use of data analysis ideas and techniques for insight. Rather than diminishing the significance of data science's formation in the last decade, it positions the accomplishment more clearly next to technological change and commercial demands in science. Science did not provide the ideas for data science. Much of science has undermined them. But some scientists have also preserved practices important for scientific insights and the raw material for calls for data science. Most curiously, they mix their technical work with talk and negotiations that introduce their own dynamics, sometimes more overtly, as in the case of institutional recognition, and in other instances more covertly, such as in finding new names, whether new cultures or sciences.

CONCLUSION

Science is less and more when looking behind the myth and ceremony of its appearance.[68] It is less pure, elegant, and rational and more lively, cumbersome, and mundane. The same applies to data science. Even this first peek showed it to be less new than the popular discussions from the last decade made it look. But the earlier calls for data science or even instances that anticipated them do not make today's calls less significant. On the contrary, the similarities connected data science to a much longer process of tensions and struggle over ideas about quantitative work and scientific progress.

The historical focus has shifted the puzzle from an arguably new label to data analytic practices. Data science proposed ideas for using computational capabilities for quantitative data analysis; Yule used cross-tabulation and Mayer audacity together with formal equations. The label plays a role insofar as it draws attention to data analytic practices. Sedgwick reserved the label of "science" only to those practices that avoided observations that were too entangled with the social world. Giddings used parallel reasoning to argue for the opposite. The question of quantitative

expertise has always addressed the analysis of numerical observations, but there is never one right answer or a definite solution. The struggles and tensions over answers and solutions, as
well as the social dynamics shaping those struggles, have torn
open a vast gap, an epistemological hole,[69] of issues in statistical
work without dedicated discussions. That hole serves as a fertile ground for data science discussions.

These impressions from the past anchor this book's analysis
of data science's formation. They raise new questions that sur-
round the observations of the nerds and hackers who spent their
after-work hours getting together and discussing quantitative
techniques, wrote about these ideas, and implemented them.
How did those tensions that have marked all these junctures in
science unfold for data science? Where did the modern protagonists draw the line, or which old lines did they try to redraw?
What is the interplay between formal ideas and the social processes that justify them? The following chapters will address
these questions with the images from science in mind to interpret observations of data science.

4

INTERACTIONS

Where and how did data hackers figure out who they were? Their underlying expertise came from science, but by the time of data science's rise, dedicated scientific disciplines were firmly in place and not looking for competition. Jobs were places where coders applied their technical expertise, not where they defined a new profession. After work, however, they met and talked in pairs and small groups and, quickly, in increasingly routine events. The legacy of data science ideas in academic debates and the spread of data science skills across jobs have cast those meetups in a new light. These places let scholars step out of their disciplines and quantitative analysts out of their workplaces. They were the "trading zones" of new perspectives on quantitative problems.[1]

Meetup gatherings promise to reveal deeper social processes in data science's emergence than their casual atmosphere first suggested. They let nerds and hackers with different backgrounds and positions discuss solutions for data-analytic problems. These participants had little patience for popular trends and centered their discussions on code, models, graphs, tables, and schematic figures. The presentations echoed a group's topical orientation, but the specific content and style were up to an evening's speaker's skills, expertise, and experiences. Some presenters kept them as abstract as academic talks, while others made them more lively, like town hall meetings. Many remained between the two and were both technical and broadly accessible. Whatever the specific focus or format, these contributions attached meaning to the still-flimsy idea of data science.

The topics set a broad agenda. Presenters occasionally discussed the role of data scientists in general terms, sometimes citing one of the definitions already in wide circulation, perhaps with a tweak. More often and more extensively, they showed how they worked with data, whether in media, manufacturing, medicine, or, of course, Big Tech. The presenters still focused on technical details and products; client or customer problems usually disappeared between lines of codes and statistical results. When academics spoke, they sometimes mentioned specialized scholarly debates but mostly focused on methodological innovations.

Between the format and content, distinct collective dynamics found room to unfold at meetup events. They looked mostly familiar at the outset, but once events got going, the crowds, sometimes large and often including more than a few unfamiliar faces; changing guests; and the various topics and concerns made their unfolding unpredictable. One speaker told her audience she had "started asking people on Twitter, people whom I knew personally," to suggest what attendees might want to hear. Tellingly, "nobody said the same thing," she reported. Moments like this capture how meetups differed from academic conferences that advance longstanding debates or other clearly defined themes. But this lack of a formal agenda across events does not make them inconsequential.

Scholars of professions and expertise have known for some time that supposedly formal expert work, including in science, involves informal processes.[2] They have shown that discoveries we now see as facts emerged from an interplay of people and their tools, which then turned messy observations into clear indicators and equations. The more formal theoretical view has still shown the significance of science's institutional scaffolding, the universities, professional associations, awards, and so on.[3] In contrast to both, however, data science meetups did not limit themselves to close relations nor to formal markers, thus calling for a new perspective.

Data science meetups first looked curious because of their parallels to Tocqueville's political gatherings, which showed that even small groups could have consequences as grand as governance systems. But those gatherings are themselves the result of collective processes that a different set of conceptual ideas, ideas focused on relations and the interactions constituting them, help discern. The classical theorist Erving Goffman conceived of meetup-like social activities as "social occasions"[4] that induce "involvement" among participants. Goffman stressed the "capacity . . . to give, or withhold from giving, concerted attention."[5] In this view, changes during data science presentations indicate shifts in involvement such that differences in early data science talks reveal the commitment of presenters to the collective events.[6] These are the building blocks of the data scientist role.

Another theoretical idea links small-scale dynamics to much larger outcomes, such as data science's emergence.[7] Randall Collins proposed "interaction ritual chains" to explain what happens when groups come together around a common purpose and experience a shared mood.[8] Data enthusiasts formed groups that met at meetups to discuss quantitative data analysis procedures. Participants went through stages of boredom, bewilderment, and revelatory excitement. According to Collins's thinking, these experiences produce solidarity, symbols, energy, and, critically, new ideas,[9] as those caught up in them encounter and overcome obstacles to their routine activities.

Finally, the contemporary theorist Ivan Ermakoff has developed ideas for tackling the twists and turns of collective events. Most odd moments at meetups went unnoticed because they happened when attendees lost track of the presentations. Occasionally, these internal experiences became public when questions came up that speakers couldn't answer using the set of ideas they presented. Such moments revealed meetups as "indeterminate situations." Ermakoff's theory helps us make sense of when participants were "at a loss to figure out where they collectively stand" as instances that "make their actions conditional on one another's."[10] These contingencies explain outcomes as big as the French Revolution in terms of surprisingly minuscule ruptures in the social fabric.[11]

Like the larger problem of data science's emergence, an analysis of meetups briefly departs from dominant approaches for understanding expert work. The theoretical setup around social occasions, interactions, and contingencies casts meetups next to other collective processes. Empirically, this chapter starts where these experiences started—with finding an event and settling into their buzzing atmosphere—before it unpacks what happened at these events. The main activities were data science presentations, and this chapter starts by showing how speakers managed their time on stage. It spans an arc from the technical foundation that all presentations shared to the collective experiences of following them.

The analysis reveals the meetup dynamics. It discerns how they started with obvious problems but then moved to technical applications and analytic procedures for dealing with them while leaving out details along the way. Meetups were still collective activities, and the chapter shows how listeners identified gaps in presentations and what that said about data science's emergent understanding. Presenters anticipated audiences and went beyond their technical work without losing the connection entirely. Between these moments, the perspectives of presenters and audiences evolved; they aligned, drifted apart, and changed their orientation, adding meaning to the idea of data science along each step.

MEETUPS AS FIELD SITES

I began attending data meetups regularly in New York City in 2012 when I first became aware of data science. This was around the time when data science had started to gain broader attention and when the scene saw existing groups expand and new ones form. I attended my first event when my tutor from the Introduction to Data Science lecture who was the group's organizer mentioned the meeting in class. But invitations were easy to come by. Groups advertised their events on social media, and the meetup.com platform sent regular overviews and recommendations to its users. I had my account, which was free, and clicked a "join" button each time I wanted to follow a group's activities.

On a meetup night, I took the subway from my uptown campus to midtown or downtown stations, from where I walked a few blocks to get to an event. When entering a building, I usually had to provide the event's name and my own to gain access. Then I followed signs or asked for directions to find the other attendees. Some groups had regular locations that became easy to get to. Other attendees often arrived with me, either more lost and turning to me for directions or already more familiar with a location and walking ahead. Mostly in silence and typically in a bit of a rush, we made our way to the event. We passed desks, conference rooms, offices, and the occasional ping-pong table or snack bar. The events were in large rooms, auditoriums, or common areas of open-plan offices. They always had chairs facing a small stage with a laptop, projector, and maybe a lectern and microphone. Once there, most of us quickly found a place and waited for the presentation to start.

Meetups had a welcoming and buzzing atmosphere. They felt a bit like a classroom with students still chatting as they shuffled into their seats, only maybe even more awkward, since we were all fully grown geeks and few were close friends or saw one another regularly. Most arrived straight from work. Many came to see what was behind the hype from a technical perspective, either for new professional orientation or, more commonly, to learn how others were navigating this rapidly changing world. Some of them had to oversee this kind of work, and others implemented it. For me, meetups promised a chance to study the sociological puzzle that I had spotted in data science, even though I would not be able to explain the role that meetups played in this process for a while.

There was a bit of uncertainty about who everyone was and what the procedure and topic would be. In two instances, we went around the room for introductions, but those were exceptions. Some participants chatted, either because they knew one another as regulars, from the wider community, or just because they were sitting next to one another. The equivalent to talking about the weather was comparing notes on R and Python or other programming languages. Many stood around alone, checking their phones to keep up with game scores or eating a slice of the pizza these events occasionally ordered. Sometimes the food was sponsored; other times the organizers collected money online or during the event by passing around a brown paper bag. Many attendees who found their seats opened their laptops to read emails, write code, or prepare to take notes. Others just waited for the presentations to start. A small crowd usually gathered at the front. This group included the organizer, the presenter, and some others they knew or who wanted to introduce themselves, catch up, or help with the equipment. Once the slides were up, the event organizer tried to get everyone's attention. They made some announcements, maybe explained what the group was about for first-time attendees, thanked the pizza sponsor and the host, asked members to share job openings or other news, and mentioned future events. Then they introduced the speaker and left the floor to them. Their job was mostly done.

Participants sometimes had to sit through brief remarks by someone representing the hosting venue about what they did and what positions they needed to fill or by the organizer when they thanked a pizza delivery sponsor or announced future activities. The presenters, who then followed as the main acts, had between fifteen and forty-five minutes, depending on the group. They always took questions at the end. Their topics varied widely, ranging from methods, software, and code to apps and hardware technologies, health databases, and investor and academic perspectives on what was ahead or lessons from the past. These topics and the general agenda were mostly independent of the spaces that organizers secured. The speakers received no compensation. Some were academics, some freelancers, but most worked for companies or in public institutions, in which case they said a few words about what their firm or agency did. Other than in some rare exceptions, they never launched into sales pitches. If they sought attention, it was from potential hires and maybe investors, both of whom would most care about the technical challenges behind a product or service. Some conversations continued after the presentations and Q&A sessions were over. But most participants hurried to the next available elevator and headed home.

Between 2012 and 2015, I followed over seventy of these events, with over one hundred talks and discussions, and saw how they created a sense of community, however fleeting. I noted the same faces returning at one group's events or appearing at the events of another group. We rarely knew one another's names, but we saw a group of individuals with shared interests, and the hosts used brief remarks to foster a sense of connection. One organizer quickly programmed a tool to choose someone from the list of participants to win a group-themed T-shirt. I participated often enough for my name to have appeared—by chance—on the screen on two occasions. I had to get up and collect my award for being a regular attendee. Although fun and engaging, all this mostly set the stage for the main part, a presentation of data-analytic ideas and the technical tricks they entailed.

THE FOUNDATION

At first sight, the presentations looked a bit like lectures, and some speakers taught in their day jobs or as a side hustle. However, meetups were not part of specialized training programs. Speakers presented ideas without trying to teach participants an area of expertise. They shared information and experiences with peers. They tried to help nonspecialists follow and understand their problems and solutions more than link specific steps to larger intellectual contexts. Questions were welcome, but listeners had to understand enough to ask them.

How much did attendees need to know? Everyone could come to a meetup, but only attendees who were familiar with data-analytic tasks could engage. The techniques and applications they used did not have to be identical, just close enough to indicate connections to what presenters said. An initial start was surprisingly easy. For example, a meetup presenter mentioned bipartite networks, which were part of the data-analytic steps described in chapter 2 on data science job posts, this time around the vastly different case of online dating, one of the topics in this chapter. The two applications had no topical or other overt connection, but one analytic setup could serve as a reference for following the other, just like my job post analysis could lean on an analysis of emails. At a time when datasets and open-source analytical software were becoming ubiquitous, some dabbling on a personal laptop around one's own interests could go a long way for following the broader conversation.[12]

A few meetup events were more didactic and taught listeners new approaches to analyzing datasets. Their specific goals say little about data science's larger emergence, but what presenters said during these exceptions illustrates what the organizers, the groups they represented, and the presenters expected from the events and one another. For example, when data scientists discussed the technical foundation of their work, they said things like, "HTML, as you know, is a form of XML," and then that "the tool xml2json, well, as the name implies, converts XML data to JSON data."[13] These statements are cryptic and use acronyms and words that are not part of everyday language. HTML may still be familiar; it stands for HyperText Markup Language, a programming language for displaying information in web browsers. Still close, if less familiar, is XML, which stands for Extensible Markup Language, a programming language for storing and transmitting information for display in web browsers. These basics are not complicated but not enough to really get the presenter's point.

The slides offered some assistance. They showed a Wikipedia page with information about different countries. Like many such pages, the one he showed included a few paragraphs of text and then a table. This table listed countries in the rows and their characteristics across several columns. The specific content didn't matter for the presentation. The speaker wanted to show datasets on the internet that data scientists could extract even though they were hidden between texts, pictures, and so on. He assumed that his audience had some technical background and knew how the two programming languages he mentioned related to each other.

His focus was elsewhere. HTML and XML came up because they organize the texts and the tables in browsers when we surf the web. Both use labels to designate different entry formats, which the presenter did not explain. Instead, he showed on the slides that with just two lines of code he could access the Wikipedia page from his laptop, locate the table on the page, and download the information in the rows and columns, all without ever having to open a browser. The exercise involved no advanced analysis of a large-scale dataset. It drew attention to the concrete steps for processing digitally stored information. And the audience didn't need to know web programming. Some basic curiosity about datasets let them get something out of the presentation.

This whole part was still only the setup for the mysterious xml2json tool, however. The difference between languages like HTML and XML and this tool is that the former are general programming standards, while xml2json is a specialized piece of software that the presenter wrote. Programmers create names that describe what a tool does. In this case, the name refers to the XML language, the two is a word play on "to," and json, or JSON, stands for JavaScript Object Notation, the data storage format I first encountered when accessing LinkedIn's API for the job post analysis described in chapter 2. JSON is similar to XML in that both store information by linking entries to labels for retrieval. But JSON stores information for all sorts of purposes, a bit like an Excel spreadsheet, except that JSON files don't look like tables.[14] In contrast, XML is specifically designed for information on websites with features for navigation, texts, and images. Converting an XML table as a JSON file makes it more compatible with programs for quantitative data analysis. The presenter's illustrations on his slides helped the audience follow along. But even this presentation, which explained more details than most others, skipped much background.

The talk's main point didn't boil down to either the programming languages or the special tool. They were part of a more general approach to quantitative analyses that the presenter introduced. This approach centers on software that integrates different specialized tools and programming languages for automating tasks. In the Wikipedia example, this meant that instead of clicking on different websites and highlighting different values to copy and paste them into a spreadsheet, a user could define those steps for repeat use, for instance, to follow a sports season, political campaign, market activities, or movie or music releases. These were steps others discussed in their presentations as well. But most presenters assumed that listeners understood that those analyses involved the problems around processing datasets. This presentation discussed them directly.

The speaker used a simple illustration to shift the compromise between the scope and the depth of the underlying ideas toward more technical details. He explained his technical steps more than others but less than someone starting from scratch would need to follow. The Wikipedia example here was only a simple problem for illustration, and the presenter could show the code he used to solve it. Other presentations would have skipped the code, which may have easily run up to a few thousand lines, or shown a screenshot of it in passing and just said that they had obtained datasets, where from, and what they did next. Many showed slides with tables or graphics of the type of information that their datasets included. They assumed that listeners would fill in the blanks or ask. But regardless of how much they made explicit, the technical details structured their talks in the background.[15] This presenter spelled them out.

The understanding of what basic knowledge the participants shared remained implicit, letting attendees and speakers occasionally feel the uncertainty and ambiguity of this emergent process. Unfamiliar situations were a constant risk. But they were not only an artifact of the meetup setting. The presenter, who was more explicit than most, admitted that "when I personally use [the code-based approach], I always have to look up how to do stuff with it." This was someone who had spent enough time doing data analytic work this way to write a book about his ideas. His admission shows that missing details were not only a practical choice for presentations, a lack of pedagogical skills, or ill-advised participation. They were an inherent part of data science work, one data scientists learned about and knew they would overcome eventually.

The xml2json problem offers important insights into the undercurrents of data science meetups, but it also remains on the side of data science that receives significant pushback. Data extraction, storage, and processing, the focus of the previous presentation, are the problems in quantitative expertise that repeatedly lost out in the contentious debates discussed in chapter 3, where purists have criticized practical work for distracting from general insights. But those messy issues were not the only topics at data science meetups. The mathematical ideas closer to accepted scientific orientations were just as much in the background of the events. The presenter[16] at another more didactic meetup explained how he "organizes those same data in the same form that you would compute with them mathematically, as an array itself . . . and that leads to all kinds of benefits, especially for scientific and linear algebra applications."[17] Where the technical terms in the previous talk were programming languages, the technical terms here are mathematical. They are abstract concepts, not technologies.

The shift of emphasis reveals more of what other data science discussions took for granted. But the reference to mathematics appearing in passing offers a first signal of a departure from specialized discussions. The more concrete references still do some work for connecting data science to established expertise. An array is a simple storage format in computer science that assumes that values have the same size in terms of how much storage they take up. This format comes with rules for locating specific values next to others. It has a similar purpose as XML or JSON, but rather than supporting flexible data storage for different kinds of records, arrays are at the basis of mathematical data analysis, whether the datasets come from the internet or elsewhere.

The choice between different formats for storing information for quantitative analysis has no direct connection to general knowledge. But linear algebra shifts the focus to the mathematical concepts that underpin statistics and machine learning techniques. Data analysts rarely use linear algebra in their daily work. They enter commands into programming interfaces that call up software functions that initiate algorithms that do the math for the user. The user needs to understand the math to apply the correct functions and interpret the results. While most presenters discussed how they use software functions, this one described a new technology that could apply linear algebra on larger-scale datasets than previously possible on a laptop. The trick was distributing the analysis across many computer processors, a procedure that comes in a variety of solutions today but was still new a decade ago. These few comments from a much longer presentation offered no breakthroughs in statistical thinking, but they illustrate how even practical presentations had links to mainly scientific ideas and issues.

The talk of arrays and linear algebra captures what presenters and audiences were discussing, at least implicitly, when describing whatever applied problems they faced. As the presenter put it, "You all know what this is," referring to another mathematical procedure. Whether everyone did indeed know or not is not important, nor whether the speaker was serious or sarcastic.[18] Those who knew the underlying math better could get more out of the event. And like the other presentations, this speaker illustrated technical ideas with concrete examples. Whereas one speaker discussed Wikipedia pages, this one turned to genomics datasets ("sorry, but I had them lying around"), airplane flights, and bitcoin trades. The presentation explained neither the arrays nor why these examples in particular had been chosen. It showed their interplay and it also emphasized that at meetups the math was never that far away, no matter the problem or style of presentation.

So, data scientists eagerly discussed practical and mathematical themes. The presentation's advanced technical focus did not limit its appeal: A dozen attendees had to stand at the back of the room throughout the event because not enough seats were available. Presenters followed no standard curriculum, as a specialized training program with lectures would offer. They were broadly curious and open to discussing many different technical issues. There were some they did not discuss. Although this was the height of the Big Data hype, for example, presenters kept those references out of their conversations. "I actually prefer not to use this term," one said. Another speaker's audience complained when he talked about "unleashing" data, an idea that had no technical meaning to them. This community had more concrete problems to sort out, as the snippets described here have shown.

Expertise that, as chapters 2 and 3 show, had a long legacy while also remaining distributed across different technical specializations, was coming together at these events. The insights from the earlier chapters capture the challenge data scientists faced at meetups. There is much to say about data analysis work, but there is only so much time to say it, and that was the problem the presenters faced without training or a coherent strategy. They assumed that their audiences had a rough sense of technical ideas. Data science meetups were collective projects advanced by individual presenters and listeners.

The rest of the analysis moves on from these technical details. But they remain crucial for understanding the formation of data science. Technical issues were the routine concerns of data scientists—familiar from their training—and what they faced every day at their work. Data scientists could not resolve each problem right away. That's why they came to meetups and why no one knew how much explaining everyone would need. But the discursive styles, the assumptions that speakers made about existing knowledge, came from the regular engagement with this expertise and its long legacy. With those common grounds to step on, they found the footing to explore other issues.

DATA SCIENCE MEETUP PRESENTATIONS

Data science meetups required the same basic decisions and preparation as other gatherings. Presenters came because they had ideas to share that organizers thought would interest a group. Speakers usually showed material that they had presented before or would show again, but they didn't put on elaborate performances. An invitation signaled their experience or specific accomplishments in solving quantitative problems. Meetup participants would walk up to them and ask questions or try to chat after the official part was over. But public speaking, which was what those coders came to do, still showed itself as a stressful exercise,[19] especially at meetups, where presenters did not know what everyone already knew or wanted to learn.

The technical ideas about programming languages or mathematical procedures structured the talks. But presenters often started with some catchy introduction before they moved on to their technical topics. There was a pattern. They began with a seemingly obvious problem and then identified problems they had discovered as part of their work. Consider Jakub, who came to discuss his data work at a dating website. He started as one might expect and described some basic ideas about appearance, like height or personal pictures. Jakub then mentioned some slightly less obvious details about what culinary preferences might attract each other. The audience chuckled when he explained how much vegetarians were into each other and again when he said the same about fast-food lovers. These statistical insights were intriguing and easy to follow.

Jakub soon turned to more arcane concerns. He explained that the problem for his team was less with helping users find the right person. From pointing out who might like whom, Jakub went on to note how easy it was "to overrun people." He and his team "don't want to dump, 'hey, here's fifty thousand people compatible to you,'" Jakub explained to his audience. The worry made sense; Jakub did not want to be the person who confronted users with fifty thousand options for a date and act like he had done them a service. But he did not say why anyone should get the idea that such a situation was a possible outcome of his data-analytic work. Tellingly, however, his remarks started to come out slightly erratically, even though he was still well within the bounds of his talk. He seemingly switched from prepared points for specialists to direct speech as if he was addressing his users. The indeterminacy of the unfamiliar group and public setting had evidently made an impression.

These turns in Jakub's introduction of his work were not just a result of the meetup setting. They echoed his experiences dealing with romance through a data scientist lens. The insight he shared may seem too obvious for such a dramatic presentation, but Jakub's shifts reflect a accomplishment larger than his casual tone acknowledged. After all, dating was just one of the many parts of our lives that changed with the rise of social media platforms. The more familiar cases of Facebook and YouTube have hundreds of millions of users who post pictures and videos and share personal news and political opinions. They create never-ending streams of information and impressions. Had Jakub worked on those problems, a post with fifty thousand likes or shares, which was the scale he worried about, might have raised eyebrows but would not have caused any concerns.

His and his team's worries about scale were irrelevant from a purely technical perspective; they only made sense in the context of overwhelming a user. Jakub's peers at those other platforms have designed rankings and recommendations to achieve the scaling-up of interactions, which is the goal of social media platforms. Users have made that logic work for themselves by creating communities of followers that reliably produce millions of reactions. These influencers and content creators have become the cultural icons of the digital era. Dating had its stars, too, long before the online world could amplify visibility and with its own nomenclature of "ladykillers" and "man-eaters." Jakub could have worked with fifty thousand matches, just like his colleagues at other social media platforms did. Only a few his users would have thought of the most popular ones as their likely soulmates. As a fellow inhabitant of the social world, Jakub knew that "there is no way you're going to get to know each other, one of them, and decide who is the right person." He faced this cultural specificity when he worked on technical solutions for helping lovers find each other, and the change of tone in his talk reflected that insight.

This challenge with online dating, compared to other social media activities, rarely confronts everyday users of those services. It reveals itself through a data-analytic perspective, not for technical reasons, but because it doesn't make sense as a lived experience. Jakub's presentation had inadvertently shared with the audience how he recognized and responded to the social context of his technical work, a context where the numbers of interactions have a distinct meaning. The clumsy twist captures a moment of reflection between the formal analytic steps in quantitative work. Jakub's acknowledgment of the social world gave data science the kind of odd appearance purists tried to hide and made the role more meaningful for those who were curious.

Jakub's casual introduction was somewhat clumsy, but it gave listeners who had no advanced technical skills signposts for following his technical solution, to which he turned next. He went on to explain that "for the case of heterosexual matching, you have women on one side, men on the other side. You're matching between these two groups. So, basically, it is a bipartite graph, where some of these edges [between women and men] are missing, you know, like some of these edges have been killed by our compatibility system, which says like 'no,' don't introduce these people, because there is not a high enough chance that they will be very happy in a marriage." This was Jakub's approach to coding spaces for romance into the digital-age dating experience. The chuckling in the audience had died out by this point, and worries may have started to spread among those who came for drinks and some celebratory remarks on the power of Big Data.

The basic idea was still clear. Heterosexual dating with the aim of a happy marriage is obvious, if hardly progressive, as a starting point for this work. One step ahead in the process compared to when today's online daters speak of "a match," Jakub used "matching" for instances where a female user might find a male user attractive or vice versa, according to his statistical model, which considered individual partner preferences. Even then this matching was not new at all. There was a time long before he offered his services when professional matchmakers arranged marriages.[20] Of course, Jakub's digital solution could hardly be more different. Rather than considering strategic interests or opportunistic availability, in his world, matches reflect "compatibilities." While the historical, sociological, and hermeneutic considerations and continuities had no place in his technical presentation, the social experience of dating still did as a major concern.

Jakub recognized the experience side to get into his data-analytic setup. He discussed a graph, a bipartite one no less, with some missing edges, and a system that could apparently speak and say "no" to some edges. Details remained scarce again. A graph with edges is a network that consists of two main elements. First, there are nodes, users of a dating website in this case. Then there are edges, ties, or simply connections, such as

Jakub's romantic matches. The more specific version of a bipartite graph has two types of nodes. These networks have the rule that no connections can exist between the same node types, such as among men or women who indicated heterosexual dating preferences. Finally, the idea of a system that supposedly says "no" to some otherwise legitimate connections was a stretch—Jakub referred to an algorithm, and algorithms don't speak, at least not at that time. Maybe Jakub tried to get another chuckle and make his ideas sound accessible; whatever it was, marriage, his main concern, had moved far into the background of the discussion.

Although Jakub's topic was familiar to many listeners, whether they were on a dating app or not, they had to be up for a trip to follow this data science meetup presentation. General ideas about attractiveness and the internet's massive scale gave way to a series of complicated points. Across these turns, Jakub sacrificed details around issues that were broadly accessible. He was a bit more specific when he turned to his technical steps. Even for them, however, he offered no background. Jakub had not come to explain one or the other. His presentation turned the common notion that dating is about people meeting each other on its head. Jakub had come to explain that after taking a data-analytic perspective, the dating problem was reversed, at least if that perspective paid attention to the social experience of dating and its cultural context. Paradoxically, Jakub had to stop users from noticing each other, he learned through his work. This reflective insight organized the presentation of his data science work.

To be sure, some draw of Jakub's presentation came with his topic. He could move between culinary love stories and bipartite networks because those were the themes and tools of his work. The view of data science expertise as the reflective process that connects substantive problems and technical ideas may have mostly echoed Jakub's place amid larger technological changes. To be convincing as part of data science's construction, speakers facing less engaging problems should show similar creativity.

Others presented similar data-analytic reasoning without big cultural gaps amplifying their salience, such as a presenter, Sa'diyya, who worked for a media and information company and gave a finance-focused talk. Unlike love, finance seems as formal and rational as the statistical techniques of data scientists themselves.[21] Even familiar images involve stock charts or spreadsheets of business metrics. However, business indicators and outcomes were not the focus of this presentation. Sa'diyya discussed financial filings, but she did not offer a better model than others who relied on those filings, at least not immediately. Instead, she talked about extracting meaning from their written sections. This idea, she explained further, required assigning numeric values to those texts, which led to the main problem, which involved processing "three terabytes" of "back history." Operational costs, assets, and profits had moved far into the background of the presentation.

Sa'diyya dealt with a vastly different data science project than Jakub's dating analysis.[22] But she, too, framed her work in the presentation in a way that stressed the data-analytic process of tying contextual meaning to quantitative techniques. During the presentation, she mentioned the technical challenges of her dataset's scale without specifying the model she used. The technical details that were the main concerns during her daily work became side notes, at least at this point, to the problem's entanglement in its social context, which was her main challenge to get going. In the end, first dates and finance are not so different when data scientists talk about them during social occasions, indicating the defining challenge of this novel role.

Data science presentations made good on their promise and covered data issues, although in different ways than some listeners may have expected. Instead of dropping Big Data buzzwords, presenters described their data-analytic work. Instead of elaborating on the ins and outs of measures and models, they told stories of the problems they encountered when piecing them together. If there were excessive dating possibilities, data scientists had to design a process for cutting that number. If texts could reveal new information on a company's outlook, but there were too many to consider quickly, data scientists had to design a strategy for looking faster. That reasoning led the presentations to highly specific ideas, a compatibility system for lovers, and a server full of meaning for investors.

The turns of these journeys fit the data science image, but they were not obvious at the outset or stereotypical in their outcome. Speakers introduced them around their professional experiences. Data scientists articulated their expertise in stories about obstacles for data-analytic tasks in light of quantitative and computational techniques for solving them. They struggled with crisp definitions because this work involves professional judgments. The absence of established standards and solutions allows for new directions, but it also makes the data scientist role appear fragile.

ROBUST IDEAS

Although speakers gave their presentations alone, meetup talks were collective activities. Presenters came having thought enough about their work to have something to say, but they had to make sense from the perspectives of their listeners. Participants were attentive and patient during the early parts of the presentation. But they had expectations. Whether they were managers, coders, or academics, they had come to learn about modern data-analytic approaches.

Speakers like Sa'diyya and Jakub counted on listeners to follow the twists and turns between the technical background and contextual embedding. The data hype at the time and the specific topics earned some interest upfront. Who would not want to look inside the sexiest job and learn how lovers found each other online? But the back-and-forth between topics, analytic complications, and technical solutions left gaps for listeners to fill. Practical insights as rewards for attending were rare. Someone had to know what a bipartite graph was or how to process texts to understand the role of data science in online romance or financial investments. Listeners had to be open and curious to get something out of these events. They had to engage with the presentations.

Attendees could ask questions, and they took these opportunities to return to details that presenters had brushed over or contextualize the specific solutions. These situations weren't smooth, as we will see when we follow in more detail Sa'diyya's presentation about texts in financial statements. Her talk about recovering meaning in corporate filings was in full swing when her instinct told her that she was maybe moving too fast for some listeners. Sa'diyya paused her talk, telling her audience, "If you have any questions, feel free to stop me in between. I'd rather have this be a discussion." An attendee took her up on the offer. But what started as a simple clarification quickly turned into a small discussion.

Q: What were you processing it on?
A: On a Hadoop cluster.

Q: Yeah, and in saying that it would take three months?

A: Oh, that was just on a simple machine.

Q: Right, but what were you running?

A: What we were running? The actual process?

Q: I mean, ahm, if it's gonna take three months, are you running Python, running R, or are you running . . .

A: Oh yeah, so we were running Python, with that estimate, that estimate was based on Python and some parsing tools that we have written. But we actually, ahm, I mean, I don't think if we had migrated it to some other language, it would have sped it up much. So, our thinking was, let's put it on Hadoop and try it out that way.

This exchange almost got stuck. Sa'diyya offered to provide details that her presentation may have skipped over. The question seemed easy, but the response did not answer it, at least not at first. Working together, she and the person who had asked resolved their misunderstanding. All he wanted to know was that Sa'diyya used Python for her text analysis.

Although slightly uncomfortable in front of everyone, their trouble understanding and answering the question sheds light on the intricacies of early data science discussions. Sa'diyya understood the question about her data-analytic setup. A "Hadoop cluster," her initial answer, referred to a set of servers with Hadoop installed. Hadoop was a popular software for large-scale data analyses, such as the three terabytes of back history that Sa'diyya had pointed out as her main challenge a few moments earlier. A "simple machine," Sa'diyya's second attempt, referred to a laptop, which she had used for the initial design of her analytic solution. Both answers offered new details that were most relevant for Sa'diyya but, somehow, still left the person who asked for them unhappy.

The person who had asked tried again with a new strategy. He swapped casual terms like "process," "it," and "running" for specific examples of the tools that he guessed Sa'diyya may have used. Python and R, the two examples, have different features, but both were prominent programming languages for data analysis. And Sa'diyya quickly confirmed that she had used Python while insisting that this choice did not resolve her situation. She had tried to explain that her main challenge was processing vast amounts of records, not the specific technique for modeling texts. For her, text analysis and large-scale data processing were part of a data-analytic process, and she stressed expanding the first into the second as her key accomplishment. But for someone less familiar with large-scale data analytic work, like some of her listeners, the technical steps in between were still insightful.

The exchange shows that more of the reflective moments in data science work resurface in tricky situations at meetup presentations. After Sa'diyya defined the problem, the solution involved two main steps: the design of a textual analysis procedure and the implementation of that procedure at scale. She said as much before and then added technical details as part of her answer. She had sensed she was rushing and paused her presentation. The person who asked the question took a few attempts to get his language right. His concern briefly reversed Sa'diyya's focus, shifting it away from the data-analytic process and back to specific techniques. But their exchange eventually revealed that Sa'diyya's casual treatment of technical details was not from a lack of technical expertise. Her accomplishment was to take a new perspective on financial statements for which there was no established description yet. That was its own departure from standard procedure.

Sa'diyya and the person who asked the question both had a point, and they understood each other in the end. These tense interactions during the presentations pushed speakers and listeners to reflect on what they said, heard, and thought. Meetups were fertile grounds for such misunderstandings, which presenters and participants turned into productive exercises. While those moments look like the lucky turnarounds of fragile situations, they follow systematic patterns. The participants responded to mutual cues and followed the relational process of responding to obstacles with new ideas from their expertise and experiences.[23] They repeated the iterative process of the data science work that Jakub and Sa'diyya presented on the level of data science's definition.

This was only a small clarification issue that Sa'diyya resolved easily. Other situations involving speakers and their audiences were more unsettling, as Jakub, the dating data scientist, had experienced. His presentation initially remained less open, with time for questions reserved at the end. Most asked about general issues without mentioning technical details like programming languages. The first question concerned online dating as a business model, noting that a successful match ends the demand for the service. Jakub had not discussed the business side of his work before. He quickly explained that people were slow enough to select a suitable partner. The meetup organizer asked about the data science team's size. Jakub said it had ten members and elaborated that many engineers worked closely with the team. Then there was a question about dating preferences across different countries, which, Jakub explained, varied, and one about the role of conversations between men and women that start after matching. Those conversations were not part of Jakub's focus, he said. The questions all pointed at various specificities and curiosities around Jakub's data work—no problems in sight.

Then, the situation changed. One attendee got up to ask whether Jakub had "done any analyses of the differences between . . . other online matches and offline matches. I mean, isn't there some selection bias?" The tone was as friendly as that of earlier questions, but this one came out a bit choppy, giving a first hint that the issue was potentially more serious. And it asked how we know that Jakub's solution really mattered. After all, those who signed up were likely to stay with someone because they wanted to be hitched. Their commitment was independent of the matches he made. This was a damaging detail, implying that whatever result Jakub attributes to his solution is really a result of who signed up for the service in the first place. While the interaction went more smoothly than Sa'diyya's, the question was potentially much more troubling and put Jakub on the spot.

The language was important again. Sa'diyya's confusing exchange became clearer when the person who had asked the question started referring to Python and R instead of some casual terms. In Jakub's question, "selection bias" was key. It referred to a technical concept that is part of a prominent academic debate about what causes outcomes.[24] Like Sa'diyya, Jakub understood the specific reference. Unlike Sa'diyya, he did not offer a direct response. He could have just dismissed the question; why should he care? He was not an academic involved in those arcane debates, no scholar of love and romance who wanted to explain long-term relationships. He only cared about the people who signed up because they were using his solutions. Jakub still engaged with the question, politely thanking the person who had asked and explaining how they addressed the problem. He also admitted that they had no solution.

The question left him in a corner, and not because of a mis-understanding. With all eyes on him, Jakub became defensive and distanced himself from the evidence he had cited in support of the positive effects of his dating algorithm. As a final and sorry-looking move, Jakub suggested that he was probably not alone with this problem. He proposed the question of whether Harvard graduates earn more because of what they knew or simply because of who they were as an example. "I don't think there are even studies," he wondered out loud in an attempt to diffuse the impression of shortcomings that were specific to his work.

While the response had slowly dissolved, the interaction gained new momentum. As it turned out, the person who had raised the issue did know research that dealt with exactly the problems that Jakub speculated no study had solved. He spoke up again, still with an inflection of excitement in his voice, after Jakub thought he was done with this exchange, to point out research on higher education that had addressed the issue. This new suggestion caught Jakub out and proved his hunch about a lack of research to be wrong, but it also showed that his thinking about the problem resonated with others, including a skeptic.

Jakub saw the constructive idea and intention behind the suggestion. His defensiveness gave way again to enthusiasm. Jakub mentioned higher education to contextualize the problems in his analysis, not advance his problem with online dating statistics. The productive answer shows the effects of Jakub's data-analytic thinking and commitment to the collective situation in a spur-of-the-moment thought. Drawing on his expertise, he had experimented with explaining his thinking about the dating analysis in response to the pushback. The person who asked the question had not brought the solution from the beginning since, for him, too, that knowledge had no direct links. They found common ground in a related problem and the shared stock of quantitative expertise.

The two instances from meetups show that data science presentations could go to surprising places. Both Sa'diyya and Jakub made wild leaps in their presentations. Not all listeners followed each one. But as part of the larger conversation they gave the idea of data science an increasingly solid foundation. Sa'diyya's discussion moved from a specific coding language to a data-analytic process, while Jakub's moved from arcane academic concerns to technical implementations. They made progress and engaged their audiences without starting from scratch or following a uniform path.

The atmosphere at the events fueled these exchanges. The interactions offer more insight than the specific answers. Their back-and-forth undermined polished data science definitions. Like Sa'diyya and her audience, Jakub and the person who had a question tried out different ways of discussing the problem to see where each stood. In line with theoretical expectations for these kinds of situations,[25] the indecision of these meetups revealed itself in occasionally undercooked ideas that caught others off guard. Jakub's experience complemented the practical coding concerns from Sa'diyya's interaction with science's analytic concerns. Together, they capture how an image of distinct data-analytic expertise could emerge from specific accounts. At least, it seems, once someone asked.

SIGHTINGS OF DATA-ANALYTIC WORK

Meetups let data scientists face one another and outsiders. These encounters revealed more from presentations than presenters had planned, but they didn't need questions from listeners to realize that they covered complicated content. Sa'diyya had sensed that she may have lost some of her audience early on and invited a discussion. The question she then got was harmless, and the answer was easy, but even in that situation, the exchange was not. The awkward back-and-forth showed that her commitment to listeners came with its own challenges. She, Jakub, and the other presenters had the attention of their audiences. In return, they took the interests and perspectives of their listeners seriously. This was its own kind of work.

The focus that participants needed during meetups, even if only for listening, is a poor pitch for after-work activities. Retaining it was the key challenge in the construction of a distinct data scientist role. To add to it, speakers did not know the crowds, how many had a technical background, or how many just worked with those who did. One presenter recognized this uncertainty, apologizing to those in the audience "who write checks" because her talk was more for those who "write code." But she also warned that the "hacking" parts may make "traditional academics a bit uncomfortable." Even technical participants were hard to place in a specific field since data science grounded itself on overlaps with computer science and statistics. Finally, the composition shifted between groups and events, leading to unclear expectations on both sides.

Speakers had reason to expect generally sympathetic audiences and interactions. Organizers had invited them to discuss their work, and participants could have decided to stay away until minutes before the start without any consequences. Many still presented their ideas in ways that could help those in the audience who were a bit lost follow along. Jakub, following the initial description of the bipartite network, for example, tried explaining that "you basically imagine this as a series of pipes, and, ah, where these edges have a capacity of two, or whatever is that match limit over there [pointing to a 'node' on the slide], and here the edges between the users have a capacity of one. And then you can just pump water through that, and what you will see is that the matches where there is some water flowing are the matches that you can deliver, given these constraints, right?"

Jakub's tone had changed from the light introduction of his data science work around online dating. Long past seems his talk of who liked whom and the problem of thousands of matches. But this was still the same problem. There were the edges, which constitute graphs, but strangely, pumps, pipes, and water running through them had entered his account. Jakub acknowledged that neither dating nor data analysis had anything to do with these things but asked his audience to "imagine" them. His presentation had already stretched from highly personal and emotional experiences and stone-cold concepts of network science. Here, Jakub acknowledged that scope.

The language was odd, but the move made sense. The problem was still reducing the number of men and women with compatible preferences. Here, Jakub got to the solution, which involved a bipartite graph, a technical concept that only specialists understand. However, any participant, regardless of their data expertise, could imagine water running through pipes and how it finds a way from a large one to several smaller ones. Replace water with people attracted to other people, and out comes a sketch of Jakub's data analytic solution. The technique's details were once again less important than the analytic intuition that led from overwhelming matches in the digital world to possible dates in person. And details of bipartite graphs appear in textbooks and software packages. Jakub gave his audience a lens into the data-analytic reasoning that led to their application as a solution for making online dating a culturally familiar experience.

The image loosened up the part of the presentation that was mostly about concepts and calculations.[26] Although odd for dating, the pumps-and-pipes version of Jakub's data solution was not far from the technical basis. Flow problems are part of physics and engineering, applications where they involve details that Jakub did not discuss as part of this meetup. The image then illustrates his reflective accomplishment of bringing those ideas to dating in a digital setting and then to the meetup presentation. In contrast to the wild idea of comparing the online dating platform to Harvard University, which responded to an unexpected question, the jump to water pumps was Jakub's idea from the beginning. He had even included graphical illustrations on his slides. Yet, both instances were reflections on explaining the difficulties of his data-analytic work to unfamiliar outsiders. They reveal the discussion of data science work as a distinct challenge that presenters tackled without any dedicated training.

Data scientists offered ideas that were not really part of their topic to make that topic accessible. Few matched Jakub's level of imagination, but others, too, proposed connections that opened their world to those around them. As a result, data science's formation did not hinge on a small set of vivid, if odd, ideas. It followed from a web of symbolic connections that articulated and eventually defined this new area of expert work. This process involved creative reflections either between the presenters and audience members or just in anticipation of them.

Matt, a data scientist at a digital communication startup, included a reference that shows how mundane but far-reaching these exercises could be. His work did not come with the rich imagery of romantic courtship. It was an administrative problem. However, he started his account with a familiar image, too. Matt described how he had visited different teams when he first joined his firm. As part of these introductions, he met the customer support department, and he shared a discovery from that encounter with his audience. It involved two people working "in Excel, trying to schedule everyone" on the team. This sight sounds familiar to anyone who has spent time in organizations in recent decades.[27] Matt described it with astonishment.

As a data scientist, Matt saw an opportunity, and he told his listeners about it. He built a quantitative model that would do the task for his two colleagues. As part of the story, Matt showed a photo of a sheet of paper with equations and some lines of his code on a slide, which he called "horrifying." But he assured his listeners that "out pops the schedule" that his colleagues could then "shove back to Excel." Matt had not explained how his model worked other than that it "defines the entire decision space as a polytope." The audience learned that it involved math and code and that the output of this code didn't require specialized expertise.

The image here is subtler than Jakub's pumps and pipes. Unlike water, which wasn't part of online matchmaking, Excel was really part of the scheduling work. But Matt's presentation still involved an imaginative turn. Excel played no role in his technical work optimizing email, telephone, and chat duties in the customer support team. The schedule that his analysis produced could open in any software that reads files with tabular information. A simple text editor would do. Matt included the Excel reference in his presentation to help those who didn't know the technical background of his model understand how it fits with his role as a data scientist.

Like Jakub, Matt treated the presentation of his work as a problem on its own. Both avoided technical details without hiding them entirely. The glimpses they shared offered a record of their data-analytic steps but shifted emphasis in a way that would allow others to follow the larger process and its logic. The speakers did not provide full documentation or comprehensive reports of that work at these meetup events. The ideas that went into describing the data scientist role were not part of the specialized technical expertise they used for their work. Instead, the speakers reflected on the situation and came up with ideas for explaining their work.

Data science presenters drew new connections in their technical work. Experts undergo extensive training until they understand their symbols, theories, and references, as well as the connections between them.[28] Scholarly communities often reject new connections.[29] But the meetups where Sa'diyya, Jakub, and others spoke were not part of an established academic discipline. Data scientists had room to consider symbolic connections across the boundaries of existing fields.[30] The uncertain situations they faced at meetups put them to the task. The reflective moments wherein data scientists connected technical details to familiar images started stitching together a new professional community.

Pumps and pipes and Excel sheets provided symbolic references that integrated data-analytic skills into a distinct stock of data science knowledge. They alone did not define a new data science role. They did not even reiterate the same technical steps. But they capture a key part of the process of defining data science. This process involved the reflective discussion and presentation of arcane expertise. Data science relies on specialized techniques, such as graphs and flow problems or the horrifying code Matt used. Although crucial for data science solutions, the details of each of these techniques are secondary to data science's definition. Presentations used images to articulate data-analytic experiences for which there were no words. Behind these images were at least several months of committed technical work and years of training and experience. Speakers used their talks to help listeners catch up in the few moments they had together.

CONCLUSION

Data science talks were not tight and complete. Speakers had a plan. They began with issues everyone could see. Then they showed the complications they could solve via technical tricks and solutions. Even forgiving audiences could become bewildered when speakers squeezed technical data-analytic processes into these public presentations. The remarks and questions were neither crystal clear nor incomprehensible, at least for those who could keep up. But even for them, the specific issues required some figuring out, creating uneasy moments at meetups. Speakers and listeners made progress together in a way that has abundant precedence in the wider social world once we look beyond the confines of technical expertise. Erving Goffman observed the pertinence of public performance dynamics in shifting attention, which were evident here in how the presenters discussed their work while also responding to the meetup situations. Sometimes these situations encountered moments of indecision, but speakers and listeners sent and responded to clues about options where things could go next. And these dynamics could infuse these gatherings with new energy, such as when the cues opened up new ideas for thinking about a data-analytic problem.

In the world of experts, these dynamics not only organized the gatherings but also generated a broader effect. The lively images they involved may seem out of place for technical issues, but imagination can be quite serious, profound, and productive. The small political groups that Tocqueville observed serve again as a reference point. Similar to his presentation of those gatherings as the foundation of democracy in the United States, the modern theorist Benedict Anderson proposed "imagined political communities" to connect the small gatherings to the larger society around them. Anderson drew attention to symbolic interconnections between people as an underlying mechanism.[31] Data science wasn't a country. However, where others mostly saw the state in its formal appearance, Anderson recognized people and what ties them together. If symbolic ties work for nations, they should easily aid an emergent profession.

At meetups, many, including the presenters, still had some trouble seeing such a community among data scientists. But as part of this nascent self-recognition, knowledge and technical ideas about work started functioning like anthems and coats of arms in the nation-building processes. An even more fitting, albeit again more arcane, image for this early stage may be that of "thought communities," which are groups of people with shared ideas.[32] The classic example was a group of scientists,[33] but shared thoughts do not have to be just technical. Political movements, churches, and, again, professions and nations are all thought communities. Jakub's and Matt's imaginative presentations tried to make their ideas accessible to the groups, thus rendering data science as a thought community.

These separate images don't show data science as a uniform group. But imagined communities don't come as coherent pictures in the first place. They emerge from smaller pieces, webs of connected ideas, such as flags and anthems, which form overlapping meanings in places such as newspaper columns. Data scientists drew on theories and technologies, including bipartite networks and the Python programming language, and discussed them at meetup events. Emergent groups assemble symbols into a network of ideas and gain momentum through interactions with the larger structure.[34] At meetup events, these interactions took different forms. They involved listening, taking notes, asking questions, and sometimes intense discussions of models, algorithms, or data structures. The statements of meetup presenters sent "behavioral cues" to their peers in the audience.[35] These cues produced ideas in situations of uncertainty that did not reproduce the familiar positions, as the case of aristocrats during the French Revolution showed. At data meetups, the uncertainty led speakers and listeners to interact in ways that reiterated, complicated, and, eventually, "yoked" older ideas into modern data science. Through this process, a community can form even though "most members will never know most of their fellow-members."[36] That is, if data hackers see themselves as a distinct professional role of which they want to be a part.

5

RELATIONS

D
ata science gained visibility on a vast scale, but its meaning emerged from immediate interactions and experiences. Meetups let participants explore technical ideas in presentations and direct discussions. While existing roles used the same ideas and techniques, temporarily questioning how much of data science's rise these events could explain, the history of quantitative thought has itself seen enough ruptures to render beliefs in direct effects of established expertise on data science's formation untenable. At this point, the meetup presenters have firmly claimed the analytical spotlight. The question now shifts from their agency at these events toward how they used it to recognize a distinct data scientist role.

Sociologists have shown how supposedly technical activities are really part of large collective forces and local social mechanisms, including for problems resembling the data science discussions.[1] Although major structural arrangements like status and gender matter here as elsewhere,[2] the main theories of expert work have zoomed in on concrete relationships, albeit for different reasons. Abbott's formal view stressed the interplay between different professions around competing claims over problem areas in a system of relations larger than personal connections. The informal view of expert work pays attention to more direct and constructive relationships between experts and the lay groups whose problems they address. These opposing views on expert work organize the interpretation of how hackers have defined data science during the meetup gatherings, which theories of interactions and symbolic links revealed as crucial lenses into data science's emergence.

Both hostile and amicable relations were easy to make out in data science's early appearances. Established scientists quickly called out data scientists as intruders in an echo of the familiar hostilities between formal groups. Data scientists cited one another as inspirations for understanding their role, giving credit to theories of informal relations. But neither of these observations explains how discussions among hackers doing data analysis led to the new idea of data science as something separate from existing roles. With meetups remaining outside of established settings, technical ideas, despite their ubiquity, could not only take funny forms but also slip into the background, creating a unique opportunity for developing the nontechnical sides of data science presentations: How did data science presenters contextualize the technical foundation at meetup events? How did they talk about technical issues? What did they leave out? What else did they say, and how?

The relational lens broadens the theoretical scope beyond problems of expert work to include insights into the strength of ties, their worth, or their dark sides.[3] The most recent push in this line of research has considered the interplay of relations and meaning,[4] while some general theories about relationships have pointed to their disciplining effect.[5] The network theorist Harrison White proposed the most comprehensive framework for explaining how relations induce behavior around brief interactions, closer collaboration, and mostly fleeting mutual awareness.[6]

White developed these ideas across a range of social settings, including professional ones, but relied on retrospective analyses of examples where relationships had fully formed. For relationships to shape the data scientist role, data hackers had to recognize themselves in relation to other roles rather than as part of them.

These theories then lead to different expectations for observations of relationships at the meetup presentations. Data scientists speaking about others with aversion would indicate their maturity in support of formal theories of professions. References to ties that advanced specific data science ideas and applications would lend support to informal theories of expert work. But they may also divert from these expectations in support of a more general explanation of collective emergence. Rather than having one or the other quality, relationships could just follow different dynamics around different types of interlocutors, as White's theory of relational discipline predicts. While those types of relations may complement one another to support a more robust professional role, they come with the shared challenges for data scientists to recognize themselves as part of a relation rather than part of an existing group. The meetup setting offers a rare window into how relationships come about in the eyes and interpretations of those entangled in them.

Evidence of relations was easy to find in meetup presentations but came with analytical challenges. Nontechnical remarks shifted the otherwise technical discussions by introducing the social context of data science work. Consistent with all three theoretical views, presenters discussed relations with different inflections and around different purposes. Audiences learned about interactions with colleagues and clients who got in the way of the implementation. The sheer appearance of them is not surprising. But the data scientists carefully untangled how those outsiders shaped their work, what the reason might be, and what the solution was. They didn't talk about this or that person only they knew; they talked about the kinds of interactions everyone could imagine.[7] More strikingly, data science presenters saw themselves in a complex entanglement with science, typically the solution for data scientists, and audiences learned how so. The core insight goes beyond all three existing theories: data science presenters solved these nontechnical issues without the "tool kits" available for their technical work,[8] relying on their own interpretation of themselves in their social contexts instead. This insight extends the pragmatist account of data science's emergence from previous chapters.

Insofar as data science creates distinct recognition for data-analytic work in the digital era, and insofar as that happened at meetups, these are the moments that reveal how data scientists recognized their professional role.[9] This chapter moves from concrete to more abstract relationships, starting with stories of colleagues, then of clients and, finally, of scientists. Unlike the usual workplace gossip, and in a departure from standard theories of expert work, the collective processing of those professional encounters at meetups led to reflections on the data scientist role. These insights extend the observations of reflexivity around the technical tasks from the previous chapter to interpretations that turned individual experiences into a distinct data scientist role.

COLLEAGUES: FROM CONFLICTS TO NEW ORGANIZATIONAL ARRANGEMENTS

Meetup presentations were about the work data scientists did. And work talk, even for technical roles, sooner or later turns to coworkers. How can it not? Colleagues socialize at work—some becoming friends outside or partners for life—and annoy one another when they compete for promotions or a superior's attention. These issues have received abundant attention, and human resources officers are ready to help out. The label may cast employees as exchangeable parts of a bureaucratic machine, which was how early organizational analysts saw them and other roles over a century ago.[10] But a different view has taken hold since then, one that conceives of workers as members of teams and considers their organizational fit, at least for office jobs and particularly in tech.[11] We now know that modern workplaces need a culture that lets coworkers connect to make an organization function.

This was also the world of work of data scientists. Presenters often mentioned others in their teams to recognize collective accomplishments. But like the presence of technical issues at meetups, the friendly acknowledgments of collective efforts where customs dictate such recognition say little about the emergence of a new profession. Sociologists have instead turned to confrontational interactions as an analytically sharper lens into emergent social processes.[12] Applying this strategy for data science meetups, a particularly vivid instance stands out as a first illustration.

This one began when an audience member, I call him Harry,[13] got up and addressed the speakers who were part of a panel discussion with the observation that "I think the word that you used is the stress that is going on within companies now because of all this data, and I'm finding, kind of on the front lines a little bit, that the, it's not just stress, it's, it is almost like a territorial thing going on . . . a real conflict."

The stress is visible not only in Harry's words but also in how he asked his question. It consisted of a series of fragments of observations. The "front lines" reference adds to the imaginative exaggerations some presenters used without a clear meaning other than making the comment sound more casual. All this speaks to the personal intensity of these collective situations and underlines that, in Harry's experience, relations may turn sour around data. His frustration offers direct support for the view of expert work as a series of conflicts over tasks. But as a practitioner and not a scholar, Harry wanted to know what to do about it.

The panelists confirmed they knew what he meant and, thus, the presence of tensions in data science's emergence, but they didn't help much. Their answers called for technical changes to mitigate conflicts without specifying concrete steps. They encouraged IT to defend their turf without business reasons. This engagement was maybe comforting—it showed Harry he wasn't alone—but also too vague to tell him how to handle the situation. Whatever the reasons for their hesitation, whether reservations about discussing conflicts on stage, or a lack of good ideas, the tip-toeing itself highlights a sensitive issue. And similar comments appeared on other occasions. What to make of these tensions between data scientists and others in their organizations and the apparent absence of standard solutions?

In contrast to the longstanding theoretical view on expert work, overt frustration was rarely the dominant theme. When a speaker, Quinn, at a different event, brought up similar observations,[14] for example, he explained that "data scientists are like the gatekeepers of information [and] just get buried in . . . stupid little things that people [their coworkers] should be able to answer on their own." The tensions did not seem to cause significant stress, but the situation required some ironing out. The "stupid little things" motivated a "monstrous overhaul of our whole data repository," Quinn continued to explain. While his account didn't reveal whether the change resolved all tensions with the other groups, it sketched out a concrete solution to the problem that Harry had raised. Harry may not have attended this presentation to learn about it, but those who were there got their own sense of "territorial things" and an idea about dealing with them. There is no need for a conflict, Quinn's take suggested. The audience learned about a technical setup that gives different sides specific tasks they can do or ask from one another.

A monstrous overhaul sounds like its own trouble, however. The intention was good, and Quinn explained that it "made data scientists responsible for the warehouse, the way it is designed," and the "experts on the taxonomy of the systems and how things are implemented and all that, where it is stored." What great news for data scientists. Audience members could bring back these ideas to their workplaces. But this proposal also had the slightly naive cheerfulness of a role on the rise claiming its place while overlooking incumbents. After all, data warehouses have been around long before data scientists entered the scene. Engineers who have overseen them in the past will perceive ideas like these as provocations. The ease with which Quinn discussed his solution ignored the kind of conflict mentioned in the widely popular *Harvard Business Review* introductions of data science.[15] More than providing a definite fix, his account turns the sensation of stress from complaints about others into images of data scientists negotiating relationships with neighboring organizational functions.

However optimistic Quinn's proposal was, the theme Harry's question made so vivid appeared in different facets at meetups, including in accounts of resistance. Another presenter, Rebecca, reiterated discussions around data access in a slightly different situation than Quinn's and with a different tone.[16] She had just joined her company and tried to secure access to internal datasets for her data science team. In her account, that process required starting to "talk to the people in the company who are in charge of the business systems" only to meet critical questions: "Why do you want to deal with the messy logs if we have these nice, clean data warehouses," Rebecca's colleagues had asked, we in the audience learned. The indicator of conflict in her comments was in the recognition of "pushback." The questions that she faced were defensive, not informational, drawing out more clearly the hostilities that are part of professional work in the standard theory.

The semipublic meetup setting also revealed a distinct insight into dynamics of professional emergence, however. Instead of brushing her colleagues' concerns aside or rallying against them, Rebecca shared her interpretation of those interactions. She explained that "the traditional data warehouse project involves sort of lots of work to enforce order on a rather chaotic system." This approach was in contrast to her team's data science approach, which she described as having "been more tactical, where we are more comfortable in dealing in the chaos . . . to solve the problem we need to solve [and not] lose key signals." Imposing order on chaos, her colleagues' aim, is a worthwhile exercise. So is finding key signals in chaos. The two approaches differ, but they also solve different problems.

What started as a story of more stress turned into an analytical assessment of Rebecca's warehouse colleagues. Rebecca didn't need a superior to ensure smooth operations like the LinkedIn data scientist in the *Harvard Business Review* article that introduced the role to a broader audience. She presented the situation that complicated her technical work from a perspective that stepped away from the frustrations of the encounter. Rebecca did not yield to the engineers, however. She articulated the data scientist role in how they do their work in their organizational context. In the meetup setting, a room full of attendees who had come to learn about data science got to see a reflective interpretation of its social entanglements.

The stress that Harry, the attendee, asked the panelists about and that sociological theory predicted resonated widely. Speakers offered technical solutions, which made sense to data scientists, but also showed reflexivity, which none of the standard theories predicted. And the two could work together: Toby, a presenter who chose to talk about past rather than ongoing projects,[17] shared insights combining both responses. Toby's problem had to with a database as well but not with issues of access that others could block. Instead, he wanted to create a new dataset of records of an online platform's operation, specifically, users' digital traces from clicks and queries, such as when they log into a service. This plan was less straightforward than it may sound today, when it is hard to imagine anything remaining unrecorded and where the main focus is on its avoidance. But to get to that point, someone has to set up a storage system in the first place. In this case, that person was Toby. And as an almost perfect echo of others and in line with standard theory, he described "sort of a constant battle with people" around his experience of proposing such a system.

The battle was not about the ethical concerns that critical voices rightly raise today. But neither was it about his coworkers worrying about a loss of influence, as the previous speaker had discussed. They "were afraid that [people] are just going to log stuff." In this context, "log stuff" refers to the storage of digital traces. Like other forms of storage, this can become a problem if it overwhelms available capacities. This concern sounds implausible today when additional storage in the cloud is virtually limitless and cheap. But fifteen years ago, such a decision could cause a platform to crash.

Like Rebecca, Toby arrived at a reflexive interpretation of the situation, offering more support for an alternative theoretical explanation of data science's emergence. He affirmed his skeptics' concerns in front of the audience, admitting he could not predict how much storage space the new system would need. The episode unfolded further in the past, however, and in the meetup presentation, he could share the full process of their attempts to gain intuition for how the system would work and avoid breakdowns. Toby even had a story that showed that the risk had paid off, describing how a colleague discovered an embarrassing problem in the platform's operation in the newly stored logs.

While the outcome is nice for Toby, this analysis gained significance from his telling of the story. It included a technical division of labor, like the first example, that recognized the different perspectives, like the previous one, to contextualize the struggle of its implementation. These stories show how data scientists analyzed the collective situation around their technical tasks. Just like these speakers reacted to the meetup situation, paying attention to what their audiences may and may not know, they saw themselves in relation to others, not just their own ideas.

All these separate presentations have shown traces of the hostilities that the standard theory identified in the system of professions. But when Harry's question mentioned data science's front lines, he didn't get a direct answer. Many others shared his experience, and members of the larger community and participants of other events had notes to share with one another. They discussed the stress each of them experienced around data-related activities in their workplaces: data access, data management, and data storage. These problems marked the interactions between technical and nontechnical coworkers, like in Harry's experience, but also between different technical groups.[18] Databases themselves were neither new nor the source of the problems. The problems came up around the uncertainties of working with datasets that the data scientists brought along but that others found threatening.

Sociological theories of expert work tend to focus on status concerns, but concrete technical problems were at the center of these meetup presentations. The uncertainty they described challenges information processing routines, which is the defining activity of formal organizations.[19] Data scientists' technical skills made them feel more at home in these situations.[20] Their presentations not only described why that challenge was worthwhile. They also demonstrated that making those arguments or sharing that information with others was part of what they did as data scientists. Instead of simply introducing themselves as superior experts, their accounts described the data scientist role as part of interdependent activities.

Meetup speakers presented data scientists as organizational actors as much as technical specialists. DJ Patil's early story about data science as the sexiest job of the twentieth century featured LinkedIn's CEO as the solution in a situation where no one else knew what to do. In contrast, the meetup presentations offered examples of how data scientists placed themselves in organizational problems. The organizations that the data scientists talked about are social settings. For a long time, organizations have prided themselves on having left behind old chains of command for more dynamic communication. Organizational culture has taken hold as a corporate buzzword since at least the 1980s,[21] and more recent innovations in communication technology have revived the idea and made it more concrete.[22] These processes are all part of the adjustment to the influx of social media solutions. But they are locally negotiated, not uniform, and therefore require local action. A basic insight for sociologists, some data scientists noticed these social dynamics as nonsociologists and in situations where they could apply what they had theorized.[23]

The methodological trick of analyzing contentious relations paid off for data science. Presenters shared stories of a variety of tensions with coworkers. The attendees had not been part of those conflicts. But conflicts were so common that listeners could easily imagine what was going on. The social process of data science's construction is larger than odd anecdotes in presentations. It gained momentum through the meetup presentations. Speakers and attendees used these occasions to collectively process the new impressions around the introduction of large-scale data analysis.

This insight casts Harry's meetup experience in a new light. About twenty minutes after he had asked about the conflicts he saw, and after the panelists had tried to offer solutions for a while, someone from the audience raised their hand. The person explained that she was "hearing two things." One was "a war between the IT/data people and business," referring to the question at the beginning of this section. The other was "that data scientists are hard to find," which had come up at some point during the discussion. This balanced summary echoes the empathetic descriptions of other presenters. Then the person offered a concrete solution, pointing out that she "didn't come to be a data scientist to not be a business person. I consider myself a business person." She invited Harry and the others to not "think of this as a war" and instead "think of incorporating data people into the business decisions."

This answer addresses the initial question directly, echoes what others have said elsewhere, and highlights a striking new take on the theoretical interpretation of conflicts between expert groups. This meetup participant envisioned the data scientist role as having the agency to navigate tensions and separate what were worries in people's minds and what were problems on the ground. Like many of the speakers, she defined the data scientist role in terms of its context, not only its technical skills and expertise. The proposal demonstrates the reflective work that goes into arriving at such an insight and its collective unfolding. This step of abstraction had nothing to do with quantitative training, but it was crucial in the definition of this expert role.

CLIENTS: FROM PRETTY PICTURES TO NEW PERSPECTIVES

The meetups brought together participants from different industries and fields of application, showing everyone how big and lively the data science community was becoming. Curiously, or perhaps not, presenters ventured from discussions of their technical issues and traded stories on colleagues. And those were not the only ones giving them headaches. Just like some speakers included remarks about non–data scientists inside their organizations, others shared experiences of dealing with non–data scientists even further apart, namely, their clients. Like doctors and lawyers, the classic professions serving clients and patients,[24] data scientists couldn't use their technical specialization as protection from those encounters and the headaches they bring along.[25] Consistent with recent theories for those established settings, the switch from colleagues to clients reveals evidence of

informal entanglements as crucial mechanisms in the construction of data science's novel expertise.

The point of departure for data science stories about clients
differs compared to the stories of relations with colleagues.
Unlike organizations that hired a data scientist, clients hadn't
committed to using data-analytic procedures. Once they agreed
to consult a data scientist, guarding their systems in the way that
some internal colleagues did would have undermined the whole
project. The same tensions may have still come up eventually.
But the initial problem for data scientists was to explain their
purpose. As they shared less common ground with clients, the
reports of those interactions should capture a more committed
side of data science's construction. The additional challenge may
plausibly revolve around flashy sales pitches; the relational extension of standard expertise, as recent theories would suggest; or
more of the reflexivity that data scientists have started to show
when addressing their peers and discussing their colleagues.

The problems start with data science's grounding in arcane
expertise that takes years to learn and makes the role hard to
explain. That expertise comes with textbooks and degrees that
certify its rigor. However, the defining challenge of data scientists lies less in reproducing existing knowledge and more in
applying that expertise to new problems, including the adjustments that Rebecca called "tactical" in the last section. These
steps usually follow a similar sequence, starting with the preparation and processing of datasets, then their analysis, and
eventually the interpretation of results and their linking to
decisions, such as who should date whom, Jakub's problem in
the previous chapter. Different data science applications face
similar issues as a result of these common steps. However,
while they help data scientists understand their work, they

provide no basis for a definite promise of what outsiders could expect from that work.

These challenges become evident around the implementation of data science solutions. The first tactical step, which was already central in encounters with colleagues, is a first inspection of messy datasets. One presenter, Alex,[26] shared with his meetup audience an "it's killing it slide," as he called it. Talking about clients, Alex explained that "the key thing to know about who is using our data, I describe them as they are oceanographers, not fly fishers," using common images rather than technical specifications. Those images were meant to capture technical changes from when "Twitter recognized that there was this world of oceanographers that needed data access that was different from the consumer access." To remain with his imagery, catching a single fish in a delicate procedure is not the main problem. Instead, the new project is about producing a map of the space in which the fish swim. The details remain murky, but no stress is in sight, only the sense of some confusion with the possibilities of modern datasets.

These comments about how Alex's services offered clients benefits from ongoing technological changes came as close to a sales pitch as I have seen meetup presentations go. But even he made clear that he didn't think of the attendees as the primary audience for his colorful story. He was only telling them, his peers, what he had prepared to tell outsiders. This setup casts the reference to fish in the sea as another reflective twist in data science presentations. Concerns with products, services, and specific consumers are common marketing issues. Many datasets and the techniques to analyze them exist independent of specific contemporary applications, leaving data scientists with a

more rudimentary problem. Alex worked out an idea for helping clients imagine what datasets mean for them when a data
scientist gets involved. There's no one new solution but a new
way of looking at the world.

Data scientists rarely hid the technical side of their work as
much as these odd images do. Even then, however, they used
the same analytic reflections with which they described their
technical steps for discussing the relations around themselves.
Joshua, a data scientist who ran a small consultancy, mentioned
his tactic for starting client conversations.[27] It involved a simple
dataset with which he illustrated different analytic procedures
for potential clients. Tellingly, this story came up as an off-script
remark, and when he named the dataset, he had a smirk on his
face. He smiled because he knew that everyone in the community knew it well. The geeky joke was that the speaker still used
it to create enlightening impressions for outsiders, which became
a lesson or at least an invitation for data scientists in the room
to articulate their role to outsiders. It was again only a carica-
ture of the true data science work, like the oceanographer story,
but one that remained closer to its technical foundation while
also recognizing that outsiders couldn't follow the full story.

With these comments at meetups, data scientists acknowledged and addressed a gulf between their and their clients'
understandings of data-analytic applications. These were no
sales calls, and data science wasn't standardized enough for tight
stories. Data science rarely allows specifying outcomes in advance
and the necessary steps to produce them, especially as new technologies and techniques become available and data scientists
apply them to new problems. Speakers used illustrative metaphors
or examples to bridge it. They took the perspective of those without a technical understanding of large datasets or statistical analyses. As a result, these comments at meetups positioned data

science in its social context, this time not inside of organizations but in their environment.

Data scientists did not only share the rhetorical tricks they had invented with their audiences. These tricks were one way in which presenters proposed navigating the uncertainty that was part of data science work in client interactions, but they were too particular for a standard narrative. While the versions so far have shown some reflexive creativity, they did not show much of the expertise construction that existing theories lead us to expect. Data science's emergence would find little support in those idiosyncratic solutions. But evidence of more systematic engagement emerged as others unpacked their relational experiences further to show what they meant for the data scientist role.

Noah, for example, who started a company that aimed to improve education with friends, told his audience that "the first thing that we learned is that, looking at the education system, it's not one-size-fits-all, it's everybody thinks that they're unique. We learned this lesson; we started giving schools, you know, standard, valid, reliable, best-practice feedback surveys. And they'd say to us, 'All right, fantastic, now our committee is gonna get together and edit the survey to make it for our district, 'cause there is no way that our district and the guys next door are going to wanna do the same thing.' And it's, you know, a valid perspective."

Initially, this report could fit right in with the earlier accounts of conflicts between colleagues, except that here the data scientists seemingly sacrificed turf, rather than having defended it. The teachers wanted the opposite of what Noah and his group had planned, and the teachers' ideas undermined the requirements of a rigorous survey. But Noah's inclusion of the situation in his meetup presentation showed him at least in

rhetorical control. While he sought the schools' business, the
teachers weren't at the meetup, and he could have presented a
more assertive version. His calling their perspective "valid" and
"a lesson" points at a relational dynamic wherein lay views
shaped data science thinking. Without references to battles or
territorial conflicts, Noah took another point of view than the
standard theory would have predicted, and he shared with his
audience that decision.

The concessions that Noah described tied into a deeply
technical issue. His data science group wanted to ensure com-
parability for its data collection efforts for different schools, following a standard scientific concern. But the teachers told
them that the ways in which students learned were too specific
because of differences across schools. Noah's group not only
appreciated the teachers' perspective; they also let teachers
adjust their surveys between schools and even groups of students. With this revision of their initial plan, Noah showed a
more committed version of recognizing the divide between
data science and clients than Alex's oceanographer reference or
Joshua's generic data analysis example. Integrated into the
meetup presentation, this was the same creative exercise, however, and another example for listeners to follow.

The change of direction was reflexive, not a savvy story to
please clients. Noah could have hidden the unfolding of events
for the audience and cast the solution as his innovative idea from
the start. But he retold the story of how they saw what the teachers explained to them about how education works. This version
inserts the turns that data-analytic work can take in response to
changing situations during its implementation into its collective
understanding. And Noah's experience was far from unique in
applied data collection projects.[28] Even academic scientists began
implementing more flexible designs around that time and have

kept negotiating the rigidity of survey formats.[29] Noah's client reference showed the meetup audience the complex interplay of technical ideas and the social context of their application. Data scientists resolved relational challenges on top of their technical challenges, and they told one another about these accomplishments.

Client relations entered meetup presentations, like those with coworkers, as the social contexts of this technical work. But they posed their own challenges. With less common ground compared to colleagues, presenters, rather than relying on accounts of what happened, if reflective ones, engaged in increasingly careful interpretive work to reconcile those encounters with their data science concerns. The following remarks by Claudia,[30] a data scientist at an online advertising agency, show how far this could go. Claudia began her presentation with the curious warning that "you really, really, really don't want me to optimize clicks. If you ever considered, please don't. Because what happens is—okay, here is the secret: If you ever want to have a great click-through campaign, all you need to do is to show the ad on the flashlight app. I don't care what you're advertising. It's a whole bunch of people fumbling in the dark. They will click on it eventually. So, you don't want to let me and predictive modeling loose on a bad proxy for an outcome because all that's going to find is probably not what you intended."

Much of Claudia's story is straightforward. She boasts how easily she could get ad clicks to stress that they weren't her concern and to mock click-through campaigns. This was no small joke. Advertisers shouldn't show ads to users who are likely to click on them, Claudia argued, questioning the core idea of online advertising. They should show them to users who are likely to *buy* the service or product after they see the ad. While this proposal makes sense, a lot is going on in how Claudia set it up, and her tone departs from Noah's enthusiastic story about fruitful lay-expert interactions for what looks like a return to the type of more hostile encounters better known from formal professions. These details require unpacking.

One problem with Claudia's story is the result of the rapid change in tech between then and now. Today, smartphones ship with an app that repurposes the photoflash into a flashlight. Such an app was not yet a standard feature when Claudia shared this story. Smartphone users had to download a specialized application that, to come without charge, may have included banner ads. Claudia invited her listeners to imagine someone using such an application to look for a key or wallet in the dark. This fictional user might then tap an advertisement that appears on the screen while searching the ground. However, that click was no indication that the user had any intention, let alone the time or patience, to buy or even consider buying the product in the ad. It would be an accident, which was Claudia's point.

The historical curiosity hides another reflective accomplishment, captured by the lack of any direct connection between the story and data science. This whole scenario was a launch pad for Claudia's concern with what specialists call "counterfactuals." Counterfactuals are crucial for scientists to arrive at insights. Scientists ask themselves if the outcome of a process remains the same after a single factor changes. This is the standard experimental reasoning where analysts expose the plants, rodents, or cell cultures to different conditions and track their responses. The same works on humans, for example, in clinical trials.[31] The result is an aggregate observation, an average value, which advances scientific insights but gives no information on a specific case, such as a recipient of Claudia's advertisements. As she put it, for "any single person's behavior . . . there is no way, ever, unless you have a time machine, to get data on the impact that an ad has." With the flashlight story thus illustrating analytical reasoning in this way, Claudia had snuck a technical idea into a template for conversations with outsiders who have no context for it but still take part in its implementation. There may be potential clients among the listeners, but Claudia is clearly not talking to them. She's addressing fellow data scientists, sharing her thoughts on interactions with clients. She returned to describing technical ideas for which she would "probably get killed and kicked off the plan in no time," even though "this is what you should be asking me to do, and I can do it." She found other ways to improve on the flashlight app option. In a generous interpretation, the work with lay problems again advanced expert knowledge as Claudia remained committed to getting the solution right. However, the point Claudia stressed most was how to put the wolf that is advanced statistical expertise into the sheep's clothing with which outsiders would feel comfortable.

For the meetup audience, Claudia created an elaborate story around her work as a data scientist. It shifted the focus away from the technical sides of the role to a relational side. Claudia showed some impatience as a muted form of frustration. However, her story challenged commercial but also scientific thinking by mobilizing an entire scene to make her point accessible. It caricatured Claudia's technical idea, and it added moving parts to a proposal that was already complex. Claudia gambled that some sarcasm would help deliver a point that questioned a major industry convention. Listeners who paid attention had a lot to learn. A technical idea entered the data science conversation as a reflection on a client relation and positioned the data scientist role without pigeonholing it.

Stories of clients and colleagues introduced different relational contexts into data science discussions. The shared experience and formalized status as insiders among coworkers brought out tensions. The different parties were fighting over the same territory, to use the words of Harry, the meetup attendee who raised the issue of conflict and front lines in an echo of some longstanding theoretical views. Data scientists faced different issues with clients in still having to gain access to problems they could work on and charge their fees for. They were further apart, potentially inducing new technical ideas, as another theoretical view would hold.

While observations around each type of relation resonated with one of the established theoretical views, both saw data scientists mobilize surprising reflexivity in stepping away from their own perspective, supporting a new theoretical direction. Those empathic moves first came together as part of the meetup interactions between presenters and their audiences with varying degrees of technical expertise. But that collective performance does not undermine the creativity among presenters. Data science took shape in the layering of the different perspectives that those speakers offered when processing experiences with outsiders. Those reflections were what the attendees got to learn about data science.

The different accounts of different types of relations also revolved around the different steps in data science work. As White predicted,[32] this difference reflects the social surroundings of those relations. The talk of colleagues focused on data access questions. The talk of client interactions is centered more on data analysis. Access issues come up once data scientists are inside organizations where others around them fear for their responsibilities. Clients don't have to worry about access issues if the analysis does not seem promising. They need to know what a data scientist can get out of their datasets. These shifting reference points capture how social structure organizes meaning making.[33] Individual presenters identified creative challenges within those relations in response to which they position and articulate the data scientist role.

These presenters did not complain that their clients' requests had made them do sloppy work. Their technical analyses worked well. But data science work doesn't end with data-analytic tasks.[34] The problems reflected that data science is complicated, especially with its entanglement with issues that data scientists can see but not control. Discussions of client interactions have helped data scientists recognize uncertainty as a defining part of their work for themselves and their listeners. The meetup situations may have made data scientists careful and sympathetic toward skeptics. Perhaps they secretly blamed others more for the trouble they encountered than they said publicly. But the pattern that emerges from these moments in their presentations suggests that at least part of their reflections induced evolving views of their situations, and whatever went on in their minds, that's what the audiences saw.

SCIENCE: FROM THE THEORY TO THE REALITY OF DATA ANALYSIS

Data scientists deal with colleagues and clients in the course of implementing their technical expertise. The further the distance across these sets of relations, the more creative the stories got.[35] But all still comes down to science, where data scientists trace their roots and which is a much more serious affair. In science, the scientific method, theory, and formalized procedures guide analysts through the uncertainties of their work. The comments on computer science, matrix algebra, and bipartite networks from the previous chapter showed some of those instances. Just now, Claudia motivated her challenge of online advertising conventions with scientific thinking around counterfactuals. While this deep connection should tie science into the presenters' concerns, it also complicates creative reflections on the relation of science to the supposedly novel role of the data scientist.

Claudia's situation illustrates this complexity. The solution was complicated, and the real problem was not the clients. The counterfactual logic not having solved her problem was "not a matter of big data or more data. It's a matter of this [situation] just doesn't exist," Claudia explained. A person could not both see an ad and not see an ad, which was the necessary counterfactual for telling whether the ad affected the person's purchasing decision. Comments like this one involving technical guidance that falls short of solving a problem made science's utility for data analysis its own storyline in data science discussions.

Even scientists struggle with science. Prevailing standards work for many studies, but scientists also encounter problems that do not fit with existing solutions and find new ones, occasionally defining entire scientific paradigms.[36] While such changes appear to insiders like "revolutions," to return to Thomas Kuhn's important idea, data scientists experience these situations outside the institutional structures of academic research. They stay in touch with scientific debates,[37] but their responses to problems with applying scientific standards make their experiences part of a pattern in work with abstract expertise that has only recently gained attention. It involves them developing scientific expertise from the outside, fitting the theoretical view of relational expertise or, potentially, to position themselves as a new competitor for established scientists, as the formal view would predict. Instead of these two familiar options, however, the most salient mechanism may again involve reflexivity in the relational arrangements, which the accounts of colleagues and clients have started to reveal.

Difficulties with science started small. For example, one presenter, Lucas, described how purely technical accounts of data processing steps look "nice and easy," while his experience was the opposite.[38] He stressed "the amount of time spent on making sure that your data flow is correct and reliable and solid." Lucas wanted the audience to understand that standard images of technical work in textbooks did not represent the work in practice. He had learned that lesson the hard way and hoped to spare others the same frustrations.

Lucas told his listeners that the insight came from a blog post whose author he described as a "programming philosopher." Programming and philosophy are odd allies, and there was no explanation of what the title meant. A blogger would have been the more intuitive designation for someone who writes such posts, but intuition was not what Lucas wanted to settle on. The author of his source had a PhD in applied mathematics and postdoctoral work using computer science under his belt. He had been a consultant for many years by the time he wrote the blog. These positions made for an impressive résumé without equipping him with a familiar profile. Instead, Lucas assigned meaning around what he got out of the blog, a new way of thinking, which is what philosophy offers. Why not call the person a programming philosopher, indeed? Although the issue had started with a critique of science's formalism, Lucas could still mobilize the cultural appearance of academic work for presenting his lessons to his audience.

These remarks reveal science's two sides from chapter 3 in the meetup reflections of data scientists. Even though science is

about discoveries, insiders and outsiders often pay closer attention to the people behind the insights and ideas. Disciplines have
their classics, and each new generation has rock-star researchers
who win awards and funding. The names of outstanding scholars become shorthand for the scientific ideas they introduced or
the methodologies they pioneered. Studies have shown that
these social dynamics disconnect the engagement with science
from scientific knowledge.[39] The programming philosopher
image is another instance of that process, just outside of academia and in the moment of its unfolding. Instead of exploring
data science's new contours in productive relations, like speakers did in the earlier remarks on relations to clients and colleagues, here they first reveal cracks in science and then not a
filler but new purposes for the debris.

Without the context of the sociology of science, Lucas's comment about abstract ideas and concrete analyses remained loose
and isolated, and he quickly returned to recognizing science's
authority. But this was a public presentation wherein Lucas's
experience with science became a chance for those in the audience to reflect on their own. It made a side of technical work
that tends to get buried in history and arcane discourse part of
the broader discussion.

Bewilderment among data scientists was not limited to initial data preparation steps. Another speaker, Anand, who worked
for an online fashion business, explained to his audience how he
had tried to anticipate fashion trends. Anand listed many ideas
and procedures, but he was still far from happy with what he had
achieved. And so he made sure the audience would understand
that "by no means is this problem, sort of, a cracked science
problem here," assuring them that "it is very hard." Like others,
Anand used casual language to lighten his talk—scientists only
"crack" problems in popular discourse; in practice, they answer

an ongoing stream of research questions. His warning and its rhetorical packaging then reiterate the tension between data-analytic work and analytical procedures in science. But this tension did not occur because colleagues got in the way or clients didn't get something. It was between what he had learned about data analysis from science and the data-analytic application he had implemented.

The problem was more in the view of science that Anand had mobilized than with science per se, but there is enough of a link between the two sides to see where he was coming from. While insiders mostly see their research slowly unfold, not as a sudden event that the cracking reference implied, before they get to that point they also engage scientific debates that have built up over centuries. By the time researchers learn the craft, they, too, encounter crisp laws, models, and bold statements with little left of the complex processes of their production. Students, like Anand was not too long before this appearance, study the outcomes in lectures, where they first see science through the eyes of lay outsiders and the labors of their predecessors as a collection of, in Anand's words, "cracked" problems. Only as they gain experience do they understand that their day-to-day work is much more messy and incremental.[40] Reporting on an experience outside of that standard trajectory, Anand presents an account of his struggle with learning the difference between impression and practice as one becomes an insider.[41]

This performance gave the audience impressions of the application of a data-analytic approach in a new setting to form their own ideas. Anand's choice of sharing that he felt lost doing his job positioned data science outside of the bastion of clarity he and many others thought science was. Now, he wasn't an academic researcher, nor were his problems clear scientific ones. No scientist has offered a definite model or law of people's fashion preferences. And although scientific insights into those choices exist, they remain too tentative and diffuse for Anand to have noticed them easily.[42] Whatever the solution, the challenge of getting an empirical analysis right to make significant progress, as all the speakers have stressed so far, is the defining feature of data-analytic work. This episode presented data science from a view that remained close to academic science and without explicitly acknowledging the distinct practice. Data scientists had science in mind for guidance and pushed further where that guidance ended, often where scientists have set their own limits. At meetups, they turned to one another in science's stead.

Data science presenters also did more careful interpretive work and contextualized personal experiences for their audiences. They exposed science's boundaries, which separate insiders from outsiders and insiders from one another. One dimension of this divide became visible when Peter, who worked for an image sharing platform, introduced several equations as "the really deep idea" and "the general recipe for statistical inference." Peter acknowledged that those deep ideas were difficult to understand. Instead of trying to teach them, he showed an alternative solution to the problem they were designed to address. Peter's approach involved no difficult equations. "You needed three essential things," he told his audience: "The ability to follow a straightforward logical argument, random number generation, and iteration." And even more comforting, "You were born with the first of these three things. And the last two are provided by any programming language with a decent library."

Like the other presenters, Peter did not pitch this solution as an alternative to science. He even cited a canonical scholar, Ronald Fisher, who had developed the ideas and explained that it had taken the invention of modern computers to give these ideas purchase. This is a casual version of the point that scholars of relational processes in expertise construction have diagnosed from the outside perspective of social scientific theory. Yet, coming from a technical expert, it involved critical reflection to invite listeners at the meetup to separate conventions and traditions in science from data-analytic practice and progress.

Peter's point reiterates insights at the meetup that are becoming a familiar feature of the data science story. Science does not follow a consistent definition of itself, and scientists are not as analytic in their thinking about themselves as they are about their research questions. Scientists want general insights, but often those insights follow from specific analyses. The scholarly community may accept an accomplishment, such as the invention of new statistical technique, but still reject the basis, as seen in the various situations in chapter 3 where quantitative solutions met resistance.[43] Peter's effort to engage with established scientific ideas and conventions of citing those influences is no guarantee for the acceptance of his ideas—scientists don't accept all things they say among each other, either. But data scientists started pursuing a different project. They looked for a place for themselves, not an attachment to familiar groups and their discourse. They found footing in reflections on the larger process of knowledge production around data analysis problems.

Other presentations recognized the project of finding a new place for technical work more explicitly. Yann,[44] who worked for a social media platform, had been an academic researcher and previously led the data science institute at a major university. He spoke at a meetup event about the attention AI was just starting to receive.[45] On stage, Yann recalled how during his days as an academic he and his collaborators had "started a research conspiracy." They had identified problems that would help them develop the new data-analytic approach and demonstrate its utility. Yann meant the conspiracy reference jokingly—after all, they worked in a university setting and obtained outside funding. The situation was not that Yann and his group had worked in secret; it was that their peers didn't pay attention. While the conspiracy description earned him the intended chuckles from the audience, it also set up a more significant point.

Yann explained a "very interesting phenomenon." He had noticed that "industry picked up on deep learning faster than academia" and, even more strikingly, how between "young people, you know, and not just, old, very old people," referring to academic researchers, "there is a bit of inertia there, or resistance." This story's setup leverages more lay stereotypes that see science aiming for new discoveries and breakthroughs when as insiders typically favor careful progress to ensure rigor.[46] Yann was also right that age plays a role in scientific movements,[47] but not all young scholars stand up to their predecessors, risking their careers in a system that senior colleagues control. The more rapid adoption of new techniques outside was not surprising for many insiders, but, as part of the meetup presentation, the idea resolved a real tension. It explained to listeners why one may find data science outside of science despite its close affinities.

Through discussions like these, data science meetups from the last decade continued versions of a collective struggle that has marked over two hundred years of quantitative thought. They are consistent with the dominant theory of conflicts between groups that result in some new knowledge getting denied a place in science. The reasons have less to do with the ideas and more with science's internal workings. And in line with the theories highlighting informal processes, the tensions did not involve direct confrontations. Data scientists experienced firsthand that science's appearance, like that of all social objects, belies its underlying processes. The presentational styles whereby speakers shared lessons from their personal experiences show the grip that impressions of science had on thinking about technical work. But rather than showing established theories simply complementing one another, these instances from data science discussions continue to reveal a novel idea about expert work. The responses to data analytic problems in light of guidance from science involved reflexive creativity that drew attention to issues without recognition in established disciplines.

This new theoretical dimension is fragile. A new professional role cannot count on enough protagonists with enough experience, like Yann and Peter had, to see the complete picture of how conflicts unfold in science. But even more junior meetup speakers noticed boundaries and even described their contexts without having witnessed their beginnings. The following dialogue emerged in a presentation by James, a particularly active member of the early data science community who had earned a PhD before accepting a job at a social networking platform. James came to the event to talk about a technique called stochastic gradient descent, or SGD for short. Before going into any details, he explained that "most people now accept [this as] the state of the art" and that it is "unbelievably simple intellectually." That sounded like the focus could be on the data-analytic intricacies, for once.

Despite the acceptance of those models and their simplicity, James found himself in the following exchange with an audience member. It started with a minor clarification question, but that question quickly unraveled:

Q: Is there a good recommended way to calculate standard errors?
A: [pause] Ah, for the estimates of these things?
Q: Yeah, we're statisticians, right? We want standard errors . . .
A: Well, the SGD is generally used in cases in which what we really want is predictions, not true estimates of parameters.

Then James elaborated: "There probably is literature on this, but I am not familiar with it, ahm, in large part because basically every paper . . . I have ever read on this topic has been written by a machine-learning person, and machine-learning people just don't care about standard errors [chuckle in the audience]. . . . If someone knows one, I'd love to hear about it, but I am not even sure they exist, let alone that they are [so far] usable. [pause] Sorry!"

This episode ended with a strong claim, but the first crucial moment was the pause at the beginning. James paused because the question surprised him. He understood what it asked. Standard errors are a basic concept in statistics, and he was more of a statistician than most. The question still threw James off because the technique he was discussing had come from a different discipline, machine learning, which is closer to computer science. From James's perspective, the justification for the question that "we're statisticians" made no sense at that moment. His irritation is then telling. It shows the ambiguity and depth of the divide that has appeared in different forms but most clearly in chapter 3's discussion of "two cultures" as a lived experience. Here, these two cultures clashed at a meetup in front of everyone to see.

James quickly steadied himself and gave an answer both cheeky and earnest about the general debate and his personal understanding of it. The technical part explained the focus on predictions over parameters. Like others who invoked technical concepts, James assumed listeners knew that standard errors are only relevant for interpreting parameters and that prediction analyses involve a different set of metrics. Then, he changed his tone and affirmed the question's concern by putting the blame on his own selective reading of the academic literature. He still teased a bit at the same time and to the wider audience's amusement when he said machine learning scholars don't care about something others care a lot about—suggesting with a smirk that they argue that they have more important concerns. James took the question seriously but retained the meetup's lightness in his answer and did not get defensive. His reflexive performance defused what could have become a small crisis.

The most profound part of the answer remained implicit. Like many of the presenters, James invited his audience to consider the relation between science's appearance and internal dynamics. His reflection organized different academic disciplines that deal with quantitative problems. Outsiders mostly see the results of scientific work. In general data science discussions, they may learn about this or that technique and how to implement and evaluate it. The earlier speakers' experiences and the different episodes in data science's history have shown that insiders argue over relevant problems and the intricacies of the analysis. For purists, it is not about whether an implementation solves a problem but about the principles that guide the solution. James's reaction to the question and Yann's earlier reference to a conspiracy offered their audiences glimpses of this struggle. Everyone in the room saw and felt that data science connected to existing ideas but fell into a larger divide. Rather than sorting out which side was right, James moved on to address a data-analytic problem.

The social processes of scientific knowledge production often only reveal themselves in retrospect and to specialists, such as those that informed chapter 3. Here, the meetups revealed them, too, and in real time. James may not have brought the core insight up as part of his presentation. But the openness of meetups brought participants from different intellectual traditions together. They had a shared interest in quantitative problems.

James was up to the task, and together they negotiated this new setting without the established academic traditions of how to think about quantitative problems.

The frictions, frustrations, and confusions did not mean that speakers wanted to abandon science. If anything, the title of "data scientist" signaled their allegiance to the institution of science, whether scientists liked it or not. However, the difficult experiences let presenters offer accounts of science in relation to data science that drew attention to social processes in science. The new image pointed out where science had not yet solved problems that seemed like science could solve them. Wondering why not, they looked at science from a distance that revealed its inner workings.

The social setting of science left its mark on what data scientists had to say. Stories of colleagues and clients involved concrete, practical problems that positioned data scientists next to those existing groups, proposing and defining new relationships. The accounts mentioned stress and used sarcasm. In contrast, stories of science remained less tangible. They concerned data-analytic practice and redefined the relationship between data science work and established disciplines. Instead of stress and empathy, the rhetorical markers of colleagues and clients, reflections on science showed concerns with confusion and orientation. As data scientists processed these responses together at meetups, the intersection of the three sets of relations positioned their role in the modern division of expert work. That did not mean opposition to any one of them, as some theoretical views predicted. It also didn't mean joint learning, as other theoretical ideas predicted. It meant the recognition of a distinct array of tensions and overlaps between existing social entities. The new arrangement came together around reflexive discussions of quantitative data analyses.

With enough confidence, this recognition involved the rejection of other affiliations, such as a split from both "annoying
research scientists" and "unsophisticated business analysts," as
one presenter put it.[48] These splits were not necessarily hostile,
as the speaker who apologized to those "who write checks" and
"traditional academics" showed. The move from the components
of data science work in the previous chapter to the relations
around it unpacks more of the wrestling of different existing
social entities into a new one. This "joking," as Andrew Abbott
called it,[49] required reflective work and mutual reassurance
among data scientists at these events.

CONCLUSION

Exercises in self-positioning are the cogs and wheels in data science presentations that moved the larger process forward.
Crowds of people were sitting and following someone talking
on a stage and showing slides about technical problems. There
was not much to see that would explain data science's emergence.
But the earlier chapters showed the significance of what went
on. Jakub's pumps and pipes image from the last chapter was a
version of complicated math and code issues like this chapter's
data warehouses and standard errors. These technical ideas were
only hard to get for outsiders. For insiders, they structured the
discussion. But even for them few details were clear, especially
as the collective setups of meetups made smooth discussions
impossible and required presenters and participants to think on
the spot.

This backdrop created a new conversational space. Since
insiders did not teach each other new expertise from scratch,
they found time to talk about other issues. These issues included

a crucial dimension of the construction of a new professional role: their social context. The classic view of professional emergence stresses the conflicts as a new expert group claims a set of problems as its own.[50] We saw some evidence of that at meetups. The most explicit reference appeared in stories of interactions with colleagues over control of datasets. Data scientists also shared their struggles with clients. Their stories of these relations had a more upbeat tone and generated new ideas, as more recent theories would predict. Between the two, and considering all three sets of relations, the pertinence of relational explanations of social emergence had the strongest support.

However, in contrast to standard theory, the most striking reactions of data scientists did not overlap with reports of conflicts nor with relational expertise construction. They came up across the stories but most clearly in reflections on science in light of data-analytic problems, which stood out because of the expression of confusion. Data scientists relied on science for much of their work, but sometimes, they encountered analytical problems science didn't solve. Presenters explained to the community that those limitations said more about science than about data-analytic work. They guided each other and stuck with the problems they addressed. All three sets of relationships produced stories consistent with a network theory of collective emergence. However, rather than focusing on the structural arrangement, this analysis of meetup presentations revealed the reflexivity that turns interactions with colleagues, clients, and science into a new arrangement that now has data scientists in its midst.

The chapter's focus on meetup talk captured how data scientists discussed where they found themselves. The stories positioned them in the social structure of data analytic work. How did they know who they were in those relationships?

6

IDENTITY

The puzzle of data science's emergence comes down to one last problem: How did data scientists turn their relational experiences of difference and deviance into a shared sense of self? Established professions rely on deep-seated images of their place in society, which are reproduced by orchestrated socialization during their training.[1] Younger cohorts in those lines of work may turn to their senior colleagues to envision who they want to be,[2] but early data scientists didn't have anyone to emulate. They used techniques from science but knew they were not scholars. They were close to hackers, but their focus on data-analytic problems made them too specialized and still stand out. To find themselves, they had to see these irregularities in one another, tie them to a shared experience, and translate those characteristics into a professional role.

Data scientists may not have had obvious role models to follow, but identity formation doesn't start or end within the confines of the workplace.[3] Everyday experiences around our gender, religion, ethnicity, and class are much more dominant aspects of who we are.[4] While their ubiquity can blur lines between identity and, say, interests or culture, it evades expert groups as an identity-defining context. Some theories would

locate the roots of a distinct data scientist identity in the relations that were the subject of the previous chapter. In this view,
identity follows less from the characteristics salient in everyday
life and more from our social embeddedness,[5] where shared identities of groups emerge from common relational profiles.[6] These
relationships can involve familiar social bonds to kin, friends, or
close colleagues but also instances of separation.[7] In the case of
data scientists, the relational alignment has involved the discussions of disputes with colleagues over data access, new perspectives that responded to skeptical clients, and the deeper reflections on the differences between scientific theory and data-analytic
practice. While relational theories reveal the roots of a new data
scientist identity in these empirical observations, they don't
explain how these arrangements become a sense of self that those
who had it could articulate to peers, outsiders, and newcomers.

This chapter adopts an intermediary perspective to discern
specific moments of identification that focus on how early data
scientists understood themselves. This analytic strategy still aims
to shed light on professional identity as an explanatory factor of
data science's emergence. But instead of specifying what their
first identity was, it unpacks their construction of a shared self-
understanding, considering external characteristics as much as
emotional connections.[8] This approach to studying data scientists' professional identity offers analytic traction for interpreting what early protagonists thought and said about the role in
which they found themselves.[9]

This analytic strategy pays off. Meetups featured technical
presentations, but just like presenters veered off to discuss social
relations at work, they tended to touch on topics that were even
less directly related. The host of one of the most prominent
meetup groups sometimes brought a few group-themed T-shirts
to give away. To decide who would get one, he wrote a few lines
of code on the laptop connected to the projector. The code

downloaded the list of participants from the platform's registration system and picked a name at random. He performed the data scientist role for everyone to see. It was just the prelude to the main presentation, and the host was not a partner, manager, department head, or had another position that was familiar from existing professions. But a mechanism similar to one that scholars of professions have observed for established groups can still unfold. Here, new members get to see improvising with code and the irony of using one's technical tools for community building as features of the data scientist role, where one might expect more careful planning and formalism.

However, the lack of scaffolding of an established profession left more work for the presenters. Whereas the meetup host's coding stunt on stage involved technical steps, others kept those connections hidden while discussing tasks more pertinent to the work. These accounts reveal the reflexive exercise of working out one's self-understanding as a practical activity involving concrete choices and decisions. This chapter first covers comments that are still intuitive—questions about personal trajectories, which reveal what data scientists did not identify with and how they negotiated their deviance. The analysis then continues with data scientists' sense of their current situations, of the community, and of their collective history and possible future. Answers to these questions follow from the same process as answers to more practical questions in earlier chapters. Data scientists, alone and together, reflect on their initial beliefs and subsequent experiences, always with an eye on their context.

HOW DID I GET HERE?

One of the professions' signature achievements is the clear paths leading new recruits in their folds. Lawyers have gone to law schools, medical doctors to medical schools, and scientists to graduate schools, and everyone wishing to follow them knows that. Leading hospitals, law firms, or academic departments may even require degrees from elite training institutions. Tech, the main setting of data science's emergence, on the other hand, proudly questions formal requirements. Founders have famously dropped out of college, and their firms advertise hiring procedures that do not insist on the standard résumé entries.[10] While this openness created opportunities for early data scientists, it undermined mutual recognition, leaving them to see others as their kind and figure out common grounds.

Data scientists had typically spent extensive time at some point learning technical skills and abstract concepts. In one of data science's founding stories, the LinkedIn data scientist had just finished a PhD in physics when he joined. In another, Jeff Hammerbacher, the protagonist, mentioned having earned an undergraduate degree in mathematics before he found his way to Facebook, still just a startup at the time. While both had technical degrees, their educational levels and specializations differed. And neither had anything to do with the social dynamics of users connecting to one another, on which they worked in their new jobs.

Data scientists were not the only ones without standard paths.[11] But even formalized promotions leave young professionals struggling with the adjustments to new roles.[12] The first data scientists found themselves in situations where no one, either inside or outside their workplaces, had defined the job they were supposed to do, often following training that required enormous specialization in entirely different fields. Those situations were not only hard to grasp for clients and colleagues, as the previous chapter showed. Data scientists wondered what was going on as well.

And so, as data science gained traction, the big question became: How does one become a data scientist? But while blogs, books, and podcasts started diffusing personal bios and career advice,[13] meetup speakers rarely made their own path into the data scientist role central. Similar to the avoidance of other popular or casual topics, they focused much more on what they *did* as data scientists. Small signs, like a presenter's training, still flashed up in the remarks. Quinn, from the last chapter, for example, had mentioned in passing that his "background is economics." However, the comment only came up as a means of introducing one of the first problems he worked on. Quinn had been "very excited about a two-sided marketplace," a technical concept from economics, and the platform for which he worked was "very interesting from that perspective," the audience learned. And in the end, the main story was about building a data-analytic system from scratch, which had nothing to do with his specialized training.

Quinn's mentioning of his background in passing continues to show the focus on the work itself over surrounding issues. But it reveals little of the uncertainty that has marked data science talks so far.[14] Where that was more prevalent, accounts got personal.

Twists in professional trajectories still entered data science conversations. Jeff Hammerbacher mentioned in his defining introduction of data science that he "studied mathematics in college and had been working for nearly a year on Wall Street" and that he "had some experience coding and a dismal GPA."[15] He expressed surprise about Facebook's having still hired him for rhetorical effect—he had a degree and experience, and his new boss and several of Facebook's early employees had attended the same school. However, the rest of Jeff's description of his work shows that his background had not prepared him for the new tasks. Yet he still accomplished them. He used what he knew to get started and the discrepancies he experienced to define the new role of the data scientist.

Startups, like Facebook at the time when Jeff joined, involve abundant uncertainties, especially for those who were the first in their roles.[16] Those situations are exciting to learn about in retrospect, but they easily confound systematic insight into the larger phenomenon, the emergence of a new line of work. They are also too rare to sustain a profession. Students at the end of their studies have loans to worry about or forgone wages to make up for. They need jobs, not adventures, at least for a start, and to grow, data science needs them.

And they became data scientists. One speaker in such a situation, Sanabel, had joined a social media firm not long before. This was her reasoning:

> I initially intended to be a journalist, and sort of felt like the writing was on the wall and that there was this insidious thing demolishing the wall, the separation between church and state, between advertising and editorial, and ended up studying mathematics and statistics, and ended up at a company doing analysis of content marketing, so, sort of what I was afraid of at the very beginning. But I think my sort of instincts led me in the right direction; I just sort of mixed up who I was working for.

The story's tone clearly reflects memories of what feels like life-defining decisions and the struggles they involve. While Sanabel's specific choices weren't completely obvious, her training in math and statistics seemingly anticipated the outcome. She started college before dedicated data science degrees spread widely, so hers was the next best preparation available, and the background makes her a fitting guest on a meetup stage. And yet, Sanabel included the uncertainty that has marked other sides of this work so much into the story of her trajectory.

Her journey began with an interest in journalism, a job involving vastly different expertise compared to what she studied. She gave a political reason for going against her interests. The entanglement of journalistic and commercial concerns in reporting didn't seem trustworthy, a problem that has occupied journalists for years.[17] But Sanabel offered no motivation in favor of the technical majors she chose instead, even though they were far from obvious. Worries around STEM retention show that most are happy to leave math and stats behind once they can.[18] Maybe Sanabel had talent and enjoyed them, and the earning prospects in those fields could have had something to do with the decision.[19] She didn't say, and there was most likely no one clear reason. First-year college students base their choice of major on no single factor.[20] In contrast to the goal-oriented strategies many see in students,[21] Sanabel altered her path twice. And she could recognize the irony of her turns.

Sanabel's story offers a new angle on the definition of data science at meetups. A listener may see her as having sacrificed idealism for personal gain. The data science job could look like a strategic decision following a political and monetary evaluation. But interests still mattered. Sanabel had picked a job closer to her initial interests amid a broad set of options that would have required the same technical skills. The tech boom shaped the careers of many college graduates of her generation. In another mix-up, it saw social scientists joining tech firms in customer support roles.[22] They, too, most likely considered their pay

checks. But the roles they took had no connection to the interests they presumably pursued in their majors.[23] Sanabel's story
documents how a topically interested and technically trained
person found their way into a nontechnical field as a data scientist before a visible path would point it out.

Sanabel was pragmatic. She recognized the larger socioeconomic situation of the labor market and looked for footholds.
There is a hidden logic to this approach. Career choices have no
one correct answer, and, as for many early data scientists, the job
she found was not yet available when she started her training.
They still involve big commitments. Sanabel's decision to study
mathematics and statistics is not the immediate alternative for
all those who worry about the commercial impact on journalism. But the full spectrum of options is rarely visible in the
moments when people consider what's next for them. The new
prominence of statistics changed what was possible for an entire
cohort of young people with technical skills or curiosities. And
confusion over choice was only the most immediate side of the
problem. Those who worked out the idea that defined Sanabel's
job had to look beyond those personal experiences and see the
space where they unfolded.

WHERE IS HERE?

The first steps into the world of work are intense for anyone. For
early data scientists, they coincided with moves into a novel role,
and the protagonists in the initial reflections described earlier
in this chapter found themselves with a lot to process. How much
the accounts reflected the stage in life and how much the uncertainty around data science's emergent status was not yet clear.

Only a more developed backdrop can bring out the distinct challenges of defining a new professional role.

Some early data scientists spoke from more settled perspectives,[24] with one standing out to show the contrast to previous stories: Cathy O'Neil, a meetup host and presenter and author of a book about the spread of algorithms and data science techniques. O'Neil had moved from academia to finance and then data science. She mined those changing impressions for those critical insights into a development many others only watched in awe—her book had the clever and telling title *Weapons of Math Destruction*. The path wasn't smooth, but its turns let O'Neil position her new experiences as a data scientist. The deeper reflections, which went far beyond the technical skills of a data scientist, elevated the recounting of professional events to the interpretation of a job's meaning.

The level of depth that filled a book wasn't standard, but several others showed similar reflective commitment. One meetup presenter, William, who had a similar background, focused his comments on more immediate conclusions. William started telling his audience that he had "worked as a quant," listing different firms in finance as his stops, before he "became a data scientist," first in finance and then in a tech startup with a finance focus. These were not the careers for which Cathy or William had trained. They still made sense in hindsight, with their reliance on resources attached to tasks involving numbers and demanding math expertise.[25]

Even though William did not process his impressions in a book-length critique, he dug deep to invest his comments with incisive experience. His presentation of it points to another side of data science's formation. William had introduced himself as "a recovering academic" and his move into data science as "rehab."

The comparison of leaving behind academic research for high-paying tech and finance jobs to overcoming addiction echoes a common reference among professionals, if an insensitive one. William extended familiar rhetoric from the imagery of mere recovery to a whole journey involving rehab. And the story draws attention to a distinct side of job changes. In addition to requiring skills and experiences, they put those pursuing them into new situations. New jobs come with new desks, new office neighbors, new teams, new locations of bathrooms and break rooms, and rules for wrapping up when it's time to go home. They have a special feeling to them.

The novelties that come with new jobs sooner or later turn into routine activities. Often, they differ little between one workplace and the next.[26] But the change from academic research into industry involved a change in the whole work environment. Graduate school takes years of one's early adult life, more hours than many formal jobs, and the anxiety of believing someone else is working on the same idea more quickly and clearly. The motivation for getting through that period is an academic research career with high status and a secure position as the reward. The loss of such a goal tears big holes into one's future plans. Sanabel presented her winding path from the choice of a college major into data science as a problem of twisted logic. For William, who was already on a longer journey, it was an emotional journey.

William's framing remained shallow for most who didn't share his experience, but others, and there were many in data science, reiterated them in ways that showed more of what they were going through. Benjamin was one more of those meetup presenters with advanced academic training. He didn't go as far as talking about rehab. He still painted a telling picture. The audience learned that his transition from academic research into data science started at a major physics laboratory until at one point, he "decided that you know what, this stuff I was reading about in *WIRED* magazine and on *Hacker News* and on *Tech-Crunch* was a little bit more exciting and interesting to me," referring to print and online tech publications. Those stories spoke to Benjamin, since he "had programmed every day . . . worked with big data essentially, [and] done a lot of machine learning" as a researcher. In his recollection, he had "those great skills" but "hit a bit of a brick wall."

Benjamin's wall was a material version of William's recovery analogy. It's different from the wall in Sanabel's earlier story, which had writing on it that warned Sanabel of a futile direction. Benjamin's didn't bear words to read. It was a barrier. He "was sort of in this science bubble," all his "friends were from academia," and all he "had ever thought about was being a physicist." The wall was surrounding this world. It "wasn't really clear what the next steps were," and it "took two to three years of stumbling around to figure it out."

Benjamin got through those years, as the meetup audience could see. He made it over the wall. And he took the experience seriously. Benjamin and William came to these meetups to present their startups offering training for academics who wanted to prepare for a transition into data science jobs. They had built gates into the wall, halfway houses for others to have less painful experiences. A few listeners maybe went home and applied to these training programs or reached out to hire graduates. But many had already gone through their own transitions. For the rest, these stories continue to develop data science as a shared social experience that is larger than the rooms and groups that met for these conversations. It requires not only understanding but also recognizing and claiming. Even this far away from specific quantitative problems, science looms large. The stories start to reveal an inside view of the divide separating science from the outside.

Data science's construction as a profession involved defining a new destination in the world of work. Sanabel's and Jeff's comments described moves from their training to data science roles. They described experiences of personal uncertainty at a time when there was no longer context for the uncertainty because data science had started to have meaning. Outsiders could easily overlook the defining features of those paths. Cathy, Benjamin, and William had already committed to a professional field. They underwent training to become academic scientists before they became data scientists. They had spent significant time in those fields, going through successes and failures and bonding or parting over both with their peers. They gave those experiences up as the basis of their daily work. These decisions were personal, but, like the others, they had a collective side. As a result, the emotional and reflective intensity of the presentation showed the vastness of the different contexts in which data hackers work. There are enough scientists across universities and other academic workplaces that many outsiders have different images to see. Those who move from one side to another have to cover the discrepancies of those institutional divides.

The divides between science and society and other social worlds are harder to picture than walls made of bricks, but they are just as real in their consequences. Whatever the image, shifts in professional paths present themselves differently depending on the direction from which one encounters them. Jordan, another speaker who was an academic researcher before he became a data scientist, neither invoked twisted logic nor emotional struggle. "Shocker" was all he had to say about his background, which included "scientific software engineering, math, stats." Jordan worked for a platform that aimed to help students learn. But he didn't use his math training to help students understand mathematics like math teachers would. He used it for data science, which he applied to aid students studying all sorts of subjects. The fields he listed as his background were no "shocker" because they were known to constitute data science by the time of his presentation.

Compared to the data scientists who experienced their transitions very much as a shock in their lives, Jordan had an ace up his sleeve. Like them, he listed the academic disciplines that were part of his research training but then added that he had been "doing analysis, inference, simulation, of," and this is crucial, "complex human systems." He further explained, "So this would be social networks, terror networks, ah, industrial systems, things like that." This self-presentation is again technical, but it includes telling details after some unpacking. Jordan's audience learned that he analyzed quantitative datasets, made inferences that referred to statistical estimation of the effect of some factors on an outcome, and ran simulations of human systems. The details have nothing to do with his work at a learning platform, but the basic operation of analyzing quantitative datasets fits, and he had experience covering vastly different problems.

How do they make his change into data science obvious, at least to him? Most would think of social networks, terror networks, and industrial systems separately and in different terms. Social networks today refer to social network platforms, such as Facebook or Twitter/X, and to a neighborhood or village community in the past. We talk about terrorist networks as terrorist groups or organizations. Industrial systems are either just industries or, depending on what Jordan had in mind, maybe business clusters. Each of these are entirely separate issues. But they were all complex human systems for Jordan, sets of relations, and instances of the larger idea of human systems. A learning platform was just another instance of humans doing something in the world.

This sense of continuity between different things in the world was rooted in a unique set of experiences. Like previous speakers, Jordan had obtained a doctoral degree in a technical field. But his advisor was a trained social scientist. She had specialized in using computational approaches for studying social networks long before they became synonymous with online platforms and their analysis widespread practice. Jordan's academic work involved approaching social dynamics and processes, which were as far afield then as the problems others faced once they became data scientists. Jordan had become used to moving between different sides of science even before he became a data scientist and, thus, before his peers.

Without strong embeddedness in an established research branch, Jordan noticed no twisted logic, withdrawal symptoms, or walls when he ventured outside of academic work. Others used the language of data science to make sense of their transitions. Jordan used it to describe to others work that was obvious to him already. These different uses of the new label amid the different trajectories show the significance of stories for understanding and articulating our place in the social world, including the world of work. Between the different accounts, data science emerged as a new reference that gave meaning where no existing stories were available. The data scientist role wasn't a purely logical or technical problem; it was a problem of recognition and interpretation of experiences, at least on the surface.

WHAT DOES THAT MAKE ME?

Stories of first jobs, new jobs, and different jobs can be engaging, but they are personal experiences and cannot define a professional role. But the stories also came up at meetups as self-introductions. They were the speakers' version of résumé summaries during a job interview or work encounter. Social conventions like these serve data scientists like professionals in established lines of work, but they don't help with what comes after placing oneself in a vacant spot next to other professional groups. Data scientists recognized oddities in their paths as a common thread, making shared weirdness a cornerstone of their new professional role and data science as a label for deviants.

By the time of these meetup introductions, data science definitions were easy to find. Drew Conway had posted his Venn diagram of math, stats, and coding skills, and Jeff Hammerbacher had published his chapter on his data science work at Facebook. A tweet that many quoted had introduced the data scientist role in humorous reference to dictionary-type definitions while retaining the ambiguous combination of statistics and computer science expertise. Hilary Mason and Chris Wiggins,[27] regular presenters at meetups, had published a blog post together. Their post introduced data science as OSEMN, which was an acronym for Obtain, Scrub, Explore, Model, and iNterpret. These were key data science steps, in their views, and OSEMN sounded like "awesome" when Hilary said it during her presentation. Others in the community cited those definitions during their introductions, sometimes with a twist. But the abundance of definitions did not overcome the disconnect between what one could read and what one did.

Meetup presenters connected their stories to the larger conversations that were going on at the time. Drew Conway embraced his background as a political scientist to cast social scientists as promising data scientists. When Jeff Hammerbacher came to speak,[28] he shared a story from when he asked what they thought of the data science title. Ironically, in light of its success, someone in his team "responded back and said, 'You know, ahm, maybe that's not such a good idea. There is this whole title structure called research scientist, so why don't we, why don't we keep research the title line?'" But Jeff had his reasons. He worried about "the premature specialization that could happen," with different members of his team focusing on accessing and setting up databases, estimating statistical models, and preparing reports. Jeff thought, "Everyone should be doing all of those things." He had a point, and many outside his team in the wider community agreed with this reasoning. They also faced their own resistance and still had to interpret their experience in light of it.

Those early pitches were taking place by the time the meetups were happening regularly and widely. Jeff ended his reiteration of them during a meetup presentation, noting that "you can look at various people's different [ideas] of what it means to do data science, but I think they all end up looking something like that." However, instead of just insisting on the value of the integrated expertise, he made the skepticism he had met years before part of his presentation. Similar to the comments from the previous chapter about colleagues, clients, and sciences, Jeff positioned data science in its social context, now on the basis of similarities in the nascent discussions rather than difference. The tension in his story still reiterates the fault lines that chapter 3 identified throughout data science's intellectual history in the midst of data science's contemporary construction. Jeff abstracted his version of them from personal experiences and gave them general meaning.

Those who defined data science for others shared their struggles getting there with their audiences. Jeff told listeners how he had sought reassurance from his network, DJ Patil recalled conversations with Jeff in his *Harvard Business Review* article, and Hilary mentioned early discussions with friends in the community. Like Jeff, she shared the bewilderment that made her seek out those conversations with the meetup attendees. She "insisted my title was scientist" when she "was coming from academia" to join an online communication technology platform, her listeners learned. "I didn't want something that would ruin my CV." The worry got her some laughter from the group. They knew by then that Hilary's CV was safe. But she knew academics often turn the intellectual divides into criteria for excluding those who have violated academic purity. "Better safe than sorry" was Hilary's initial motto.

The story of Hilary's anxiety was funny in hindsight, now with her being the meetup's speaker and star in the community. She still meant it as a lesson. Hilary reminded the audience that "'data scientist' didn't exist three years ago, three and a half years ago, as a field of practice." Of course, that could not have been the concern when she wanted to call herself a scientist. She can only see the meaning that data science's growing recognition has bestowed on her choice in hindsight. Hilary did not try to analyze a social process. But the anxieties she recalled in the story and the room's reaction bring out dynamics underpinning data science's emergence, the quick disappearance of the driving social mechanisms behind misleading impressions.

Stories of data scientists enduring personal and team members' feelings further infuse the new role with meaning. The uncertainties from the tasks and interactions with clients, colleagues, and existing expertise extend into the role's still-forming self-understanding. But they also remain circumstantial. Data science largely exists in opposition to formalized practices. Data science characteristics, experiences, and approaches only coalesced slowly into a professional identity. Rebecca, whose "pushback" from the database team featured in the previous chapter, went on to describe "sort of a philosophical difference, or shift, in some ways" when discussing the difference between data science and specialized data analysis tasks.[29] Her reference was the "tactical" approach to identifying and analyzing datasets. The philosophical difference did not only mean a different way of working with datasets. It meant for Rebecca the "belief in investing in people rather than tools." And for backup against the "pushback" she got from other teams and departments, she sought out "people who don't sort of just sit around hypothesizing or telling other people what to do." Her data scientists needed to be tacticians "who can actually write code themselves."

These personal reflections show how the technical approaches that undergirded data science work translated into a professional self-understanding. Meetup speakers connected their stories to more general ideas for how they were deviants because of their data-analytic work. Participants could take notes on how to handle situations they encountered and how to pursue their aspirations. These are crucial pieces of information for those present who want to join such a team. And they were part of a larger conversation about these issues at meetups. The comments were not a criticism of the type of activity to which they referred but questioned the need to focus on only one of them, at least for data scientists.

In contrast to much of the authoritative commentary on data science careers and definitions, these were still all personal reflections on professional experiences. The stories from the previous chapter had similar individual points of departure. The references to familiar encounters with colleagues, clients, and sciences elevated those to a more general level. They started carving out a professional role without much deliberate defining, a switch that the more internal focus of this chapter's stories has started to achieve through references to the emotional side of the personal trajectories. But feelings, even if more widely shared, remain too inaccessible to sustain an emerging profession.

WHAT ARE WE DOING?

The observations so far, which have focused on individual data scientists, still leave gaps in our understanding of the group's shared identity. The meetup speakers made their trajectories and work activities broadly accessible. At the center were still specific examples, even when they started to formulate a general data science story. This focus gave their accounts a solid foundation—they knew what they were talking about—but how could listeners and observers locate themselves in those stories?

Meetup speakers were not community organizers. They were pioneers among their peers and in their workplaces. They had thought carefully about the uprooting of their professional trajectories.[30] But they only really got to see others asking questions similar to their own during these meetups and events like them. Outside meetups, hiring decisions were, for our analysis here, an important part of data scientists' jobs: They had to identify profiles they thought would fit with their data science teams. The saying in the community was that one needed a data scientist to hire a data scientist. They were looking for versions of themselves. But the difficulty they noticed that outsiders had with understanding data science work came back to them when they had to understand the profiles of job candidates, who were all outsiders at the beginning. They wanted skills in statistics, but not just in hypothesis testing. They wanted data-related skills, but not only applied to implementing clean warehouses. What this meant was that who those data scientists identified as members of their community was not immediately clear.

Data scientists discussed the problem of hiring like they discussed other challenges of their jobs. For example, Jordan, the former researcher of complex human systems–turned–learning platform data scientist, explained his team was "looking for ontological skills." Anticipating the puzzled faces among listeners, he asked, "What does that mean?" And he told the audience that it meant that they were "looking for people that can reason about and formalize the world in a relatively general way." The explanation remains abstract, but at least nonspeakers of ancient Greek have something to hold on to.

What did Jordan mean by asking for the ability to reason about and formalize the world? All statistics and math are formal. Rules govern how we generate, manipulate, and interpret numbers. Some problems demand specialized solutions, but as such they underestimate and miss the ambiguity that defines social life. Formalism was the main condition for science's acceptance of statistics as a scientific exercise. And this was a trained scientist speaking. But formalizing is different from implementing formalized procedures. Jordan described the activity of translating the social world and lived experiences into abstract measures. He was looking for applicants who could recognize and navigate the ambiguity, not miss it and push it aside. In his case, these were problems around helping students understand ideas and concepts, which was clearly an unruly task.

Jordan had his own explanation. "For us, it's really data empathy," he specified. Again recognizing that not everyone might see what empathy has to do with all the technical tasks, he continued, "it's the ability to reason about the qualitative context in which data is born, are born," including that "I can put myself in the world" even though "I may not know a lot about that subject domain." Jordan didn't mean empathy in the familiar sense of understanding someone else's feelings. His adaptation to data analysis had a concrete goal, which was not compassion but "structuring models" and working with non–data scientists. His way of formulating those demands offered a reference for listeners to remember, as a key focus of data science, the people and their situations underlying the formal analyses.

Data science is not only a question of personal decisions and memories, whether around tasks or during professional trajectories. But it does not fit the standard descriptions of work involving numbers, either. Instead of following formal procedures, Jordan's view drew attention to the possibility of data scientists relying on observations in the world, which they then accommodate in formal analyses. They are not specialists in the abstract concepts and techniques that the scientists in chapter 3 defended as their jurisdiction. They are specialists in applying those techniques to concrete problems. Each application is a new professional problem. But they share similar challenges that those who engage with them can discuss and resolve together.

If data science was a formalized activity, one could tell if someone is a data scientist by how much of the relevant theories, techniques, and procedures they know. But speakers agreed that data science was not formalized and that it required formalizing as a tactical and pragmatic activity. How does this abstract consensus translate into mutual recognition?

Recall Quinn, the speaker who talked about the system that put the data scientists in charge in the previous chapter. Quinn later talked about how his team would identify data scientists. They did "what most people do, you know, we would bring people in and give them a bunch of logic problems, and, you know, whiteboard stuff." He and his team wanted to "assess whether they are smart." This solution would clearly identify who could code and understand statistical concepts or, in short, who knew the formalities. But it did not identify the "doers" that other speakers said data scientists typically were. While Quinn "didn't hire anyone wrong," he realized that "we just got terrible reason on people." He became frustrated with the approach he had seen others use.

As in the case of his struggle with colleagues, Quinn could share a solution. He described what amounted to one-day internships for identifying promising data science hires. Job candidates would get a question to address throughout the day and work with the team. While part of this included "hang[ing] out with them over lunch," the goal was that "at the end of the day, they present their findings to us." This sounds a bit loose, but it was a plan.[31] Quinn stressed that the ideas the candidates developed were "where we can go deep on, you know, what they have uncovered and we can pretty quickly pick up on, you know, what their strengths and weaknesses are, right, because, in a compressed time frame, somebody is naturally gonna gear toward the thing that they do best."

Like Quinn, data scientists had a hard time specifying what made them data scientists. They all explained that data science was about dealing with the messiness of analyzing problems and that indicators of technical competencies didn't reflect those skills. They talked about formalizing abilities, ontological skills, and tactical savviness. These are all abstract ideas as well, but listeners would have a hard time seeing their meaning in the context of quantitative data analysis. The speakers explained what they had in mind in reference to their personal experiences doing that work. Quinn's solution gave listeners an image they could hold on to: the idea that data science was a question of practice as much as the technical expertise informing it.

This image of quantitative data analysis stands in opposition to much of the bulwark that purists have built over the past two-hundred-some years. And maybe it appears here as an overly generous interpretation of substanceless attempts at self-justification. This group of deviants could just be too lazy to properly work out their ideas, but at least one tried. Benjamin, who had "hit a wall" when he first left academic research, proposed that data science "sort of breaks down into three broad categories" with respect to "the type of work that data teams do." These were "product analytics," "predictive modeling," and "data products." Benjamin explained each. The first required data scientists to "help their company or their team to optimize certain metrics" and "turn [insights] into actual products." The second involved "optimizing a certain number, like, for instance, fraud rate, and making it go down." The third required "working with data [and] creating algorithms" when "the end customer is actually the user of the website."

Benjamin showed that a more organized view of data science than others had offered on these stages was possible. Instead of insisting on the uncertainty, he saw the order in data science work. He had good reason. Benjamin told his audience that "the number-one thing we hear from the PhDs in our program when they're considering companies [is] 'I get what the company is doing at a high level, I get that the data is interesting, but what am I going to be doing, what am I specifically going to be going if I take this job?'" These are serious concerns, and they must have been difficult for Benjamin to hear. But like his conclusion, the backstory whereby he reached it set him apart from the other speakers. While they reflected on their own experience, Benjamin followed reports of the former researchers who were in the middle of their transitions. They were just entering rehab, as William put it, and wanted to know from him what was next. His categories offered answers.

However, in a striking turn of events, someone in the audience spoke up during the Q&A and said: "I just wanted to push you a little bit. . . . It seems to me [that] part of the value your graduates could add would be looking at the big picture and saying, look, here is where I could add value; here's what I could be doing."

Benjamin agreed. This proposal and Benjamin's immediate agreement dragged the new clarity back into the familiar disarray. The question extended the thinking of other speakers who had revealed the need for pragmatism in this line of work. And Benjamin immediately backtracked, adding, "The point is not so much to pigeonhole because most people with these backgrounds are really diverse, you know, can really do a diverse number of things." In between, he had even explained that the formal interviews for computer engineers rarely worked for data scientists, agreeing with the presentation about the day-long trials replacing formal exercises. Data science doesn't fit formal identifiers after all, even when trying.

This chapter's perspectives on data scientist careers, profiles, and activities cover different personal experiences and use different words to describe them. But they have also started to reveal a coherent narrative, with the various perspectives complementing one another to cover different ways of conceiving this work. This most recent episode's drama recalls the fragility of understanding an emerging professional role with uncertainty as a defining feature. But the presenters who brought data science to life at these events had one more card to play.

WHAT SHOULD WE BE DOING?

Data scientists built much of their presentations around what they had seen and done at work, recognizing the technical basis of the role. Elaborate statistical analyses demand a focus on specifics. The commitment extended to nontechnical comments during the presentations. And it came with a payoff. Speakers knew what they had seen and tried, putting them on familiar grounds when facing an audience they didn't know. But listeners needed to be able to follow the situations that speakers described for the stories to be understandable. When they couldn't, they asked questions. And presenters who wandered off too far, introducing generic categories or overly colorful images, were met with skepticism. They still had to bridge the gap between specific experiences and general salience.

While scientists value rigor and precision over all else, they allow themselves surprising liberty in one aspect: the notable colleagues and shared ancestors to whom scientists, like other communities, turn to remember who they are. Societies store their collective memories in the names of streets, schools, hospitals, holidays, and in music, film, and other cultural products.[32] Scientists remember their ancestors in awards, fellowships, and references in their scholarship. Each analysis aims to make a new contribution but retains connections to old ones, if only ceremonially.[33] Researchers leave aside the technical underpinning of established ideas and use them instead to position themselves in the stock of specialized knowledge.

Presenters brought this memory-making tradition to meetups. During one event that featured a panel discussion, rather than a presentation, the panelists wrestled with the old problem of whether data scientists should have specialized expertise or general skills. As one speaker insisted that there should be different types of data scientists, another jumped in. He warned that "I really feel like in some ways the orthogonality of these concepts is, is not an assumption we should start with," speaking up against the attempt to specify the data scientist role cleanly. His reason was that "when I look at who are good data scientists I know, they all have four characteristics. All highly tenacious, highly creative, very curious, and have deep technical skills." This view echoes how data scientists have described their work in the previous chapter. But instead of referring to personal experiences, the panelist invokes observations of "good data scientists." More specifically:

> So, you know, when we look at, for example, Claudia Perlich, she's a New York local who has been perhaps more successful in competitive data science than anyone in the world [and] in totally different areas. . . . I think that somebody like Claudia is, you could put her into a room with any kind of business problem and data, and the reason she has been successful as a data scientist is that she is good at being highly pragmatic and highly driven on the actual outcome to be achieved.

Like other comments that departed from personal experiences and concrete exercises, this one relied on technical concepts, creativity, curiosity, and skills. Listeners would have needed to experience them to follow without stories of a specific project, live coding on the projector, or slides showing database designs. This speaker used his own version of this strategy. He described his idea about data science in reference to a person he knew. The introduction of Claudia Perlich as a New York local was a friendly nod to the meetup's location. The praise of her as a successful data scientist relied on some insider achievements. Data science had adopted tournament-style competitions from the machine learning community, contests in which participants analyzed the same dataset and compared how well their models predicted an outcome. The best prediction won. Claudia, listeners learned, had built the best models, even, and this was crucial, for widely different problems. Tellingly, how she was able to do so remained unclear.

The speaker presented Claudia, a person, and a set of characteristics as a definition of what a data scientist was. The repeated success spoke to the speaker's tenacity claim. The different problems stood for curiosity and creativity. And the success in solving specialized problems for technical skills. Claudia, as a person, was supposedly imaginable to everyone in the audience. Whoever didn't know her could look up the accomplishments this speaker mentioned. She later would even come and speak on one of those meetup stages. In contrast to a formal definition, the reference to Claudia as a person with agency combined characteristics otherwise left in "orthogonal" categories.

The reference closed a major gap. Experts typically obtain degrees that certify their proficiency in an area of knowledge-based work. Standard certificates did not exist for data scientists at the time of these meetup events. Data scientists had degrees, too, but they were in various areas. The personal stories of trajectories into data science roles from earlier in this chapter don't translate into a shared understanding of data science. But shared images, like that of an exemplar data scientist, do.

The rhetorical trick extended personal views and experiences into ideas of a professional role. The panelist who had first proposed orthogonal types of data scientists then also said, "One thing that Claudia," returning to his co-panelist's earlier reference, "said: 'I never let other people pull my data for me.'" Claudia's rule supported his position that "it is critical that the person who's doing the algorithmic work have the ability to pull the data out of the system because it's an iterative process." But this version moves away from his own earlier view involving orthogonal-looking skills. The partial disagreement reflects the emergent status of the data science narrative. However, like in earlier disagreements, the consensus moves toward tactical approaches and pragmatism. Here, the reference to Claudia extended the specific versions of this idea into a rule with an authority behind it, a key feature of formal professions, albeit one undergoing informal construction during this event.

These references to Claudia still don't fully define data science. The new agreement between the panelists fell apart again when one of them talked about programming languages. He named one he found unnecessary, though allowing that "it is okay for a data scientist like Claudia" to have that expertise.[34] His co-panelist disagreed but added, "I guess it's a continuum," to not fully ruin the atmosphere. And another name entered the conversation, Jeff Hammerbacher, in an attempt to back one idea that didn't undermine the other.[35] Each of them had their points, remained open, and offered references that built bridges, if inadvertently.

These diverging views made this panel discussion a small-scale reproduction of the larger data science conversation. They extended the uncertainty around data science tasks and careers to a general understanding of the data scientist role. Without any single speaker trying, the audience saw their interaction reveal multiple views. What speakers had rationalized as tactical work, twisted career logics, and fear about what job they would do or how came down to a conversation among members of the community who spoke from some distance without losing touch. The uncertainty leaves data science vulnerable to anyone who has an idea for entirely different directions and finds listeners.

But at these meetups of the data science community, even diverting views complemented one another to build toward a more comprehensive understanding.

Meetup speakers did not only rely on notable peers to make points about data science. Like scientists, they remembered the ideas of those who came before them and benefited from their forebears.[36] Each new generation finds the same reference points for guidance. Speakers cited the same classic authors and works that statisticians and computer scientists may recognize, such as John von Neumann or even Thomas Bayes, if sometimes in different ways. But they also offered new candidates to consider as guiding a definition of data science.

The tradition and format of scientific discourse have an established place for memorialization in the introductions and footnotes of academic writing. Meetup presentations didn't. One presenter, in unusually formal wear, still turned to such a format for presenting an oddly large vision of where data science work was heading. Whereas most discussed the intricacies of data science work, his pitch was the automation of data science.[37] Like others, this speaker contextualized his pitch, but he dug much deeper than they, getting further away from concrete data science exercises when promising an "actual demonstration that looks at a problem that is more than two thousand years old." And rather than occupying an expert community, this problem required the "greatest mind of its generation, a guy named Hero, who was a professor at Alexandria, to solve." He even managed that feat "without big data tools; in fact, he used just basic algebra."

This introduction tried to do what other stories avoided. It highlighted a problem that wasn't a problem any longer, an authority, and it mentioned big data as a modern accomplishment. Instead of exposing the messiness of this work, the presenter informed the audience that they were in the privileged position of bearing witness when "for the first time in public, we're going to show you that the tool can automatically derive a formula that it took Hero several years to build and literally his creative genius, to figure out how to do." What a special moment.

The speaker delivered on his promise. Numbers that reproduced the formula Hero had defined two thousand years ago started to appear on the screen. But the irony of someone using a modern computer, the culmination of innumerable hours of work of those who had invented and assembled it and built the software to make it run, to do what someone had achieved by hand so long ago exposes the accomplishment as a cheap publicity stunt. The choice of Hero's problem leverages the significance of two thousand years of mathematical ideas but not any of today's problems. A cynical interpretation of the pitch would reverse the logic and make the tool look two thousand years late. Whether this worked for the audience or not, the story sidetracks the larger data science conversation, directing it away from the tactical work and toward a singular accomplishment. It recalls the role of presenters in shaping that story and underscores the massive but still fragile processes behind the agreement across so many other presentations.

Not all stories of ideas predating data science diverged so much from the emerging data science narrative. Another speaker, Getu, offered a more familiar version. He started talking about weather forecasting as one of the oldest forms of data science. Following a few remarks on the problem's myth-based roots, Getu introduced "a particular fellow by the name of Admiral Robert FitzRoy," a British naval officer who captained the ship on Charles Darwin's famous journey. But that accomplishment was not Getu's interest. He moved on to describe FitzRoy as "somebody who decided that it was as particularly important despite inaccuracy to present predictions for weather." For context, Getu explained that "in the 1850s, Admiral FitzRoy was particularly concerned about how storms essentially decimated ships and the men manning them. And he decided that . . . the time was ripe to start displaying and, ah, pronouncing predictions for storms. . . . In 1861, ah, he presented the first meteorological report in the *Times*. Ahm, it involved a series of basic meteorological readings in a variety of cities in the UK." It was "fascinating" to Getu "that [FitzRoy] decided to take this leap." But in contrast to the Hero story, this one was not about the protagonist's specific achievement. The audience learned about the ridicule of the reports FitzRoy had put in the *Times* and opposition from parliament. More like the panel's reference to Claudia, Getu talked about FitzRoy because of his intuition in collecting and analyzing numerical information. In this specific case, he stressed, the motivation was saving people's lives.

Getu extended the discussions of the data scientist role from personal experiences and acquaintances to a yet more general foundation. His presentation of FitzRoy justified the focus on datasets over definite ideas or skills and techniques for analyzing them. The references to peers like Claudia and Jeff first broadened personal data science experiences without resorting to formal categories. References to historical figures like Fitz-Roy came with memory that has solidified over centuries to make ideas about data science even more widely accessible. But they needed the kind of interpretive work Getu had done and avoid the standard great-man narrative that the story of Hero reproduced.

FitzRoy was easy to claim for data science because he was not a standard reference in academic statistics. But that outsider status was not a necessary condition for new ideas in meetup remarks. Chris Wiggins, a repeat meetup speaker who had defined data science early on with Hilary Mason, offered a similar data science spin on standard references without problems. He noted that "Leo Breiman and John Tukey, you know, these were people who were highly fluent mathematical statisticians, and then went out and did dirty, dirty consulting, right." Leo Breiman and John Tukey were both modern scientists who had lived until the early 2000s. They missed the rise of the data scientist role, but Chris introduced them as "the people who framed the intellectual foundation on which data science now sits." The introduction may not have been necessary for many data scientists, but it gave those in the audience who were new and still focused on the techniques a historical context.

Chris was sensitive to the possible discrepancy between clean quantitative analysis and the messiness of their practical application. He reminded his listeners that "Breiman had a proper tenured position" and "wrote a beautiful book on mathematical probability at UCLA" but then "just like walked the earth in Santa Monica, taking these crazy consulting gigs." These gigs weren't the point. Chris explained that those activities "gave us CART, and like, which begat, you know, he gave us random forest," referring to machine learning techniques. The moral of the story was that "these beautiful, very applied ideas in data science came from interacting with real, messy problems." And so, the accounts of data science work, experiences, and views get a broadly accepted foundation.

Many of the pages from this and earlier chapters ring through these statements. Leo Breiman published the article discussing the "two cultures" of statistical modeling, which appeared at the end of chapter 3, together with the pushback from some members of the statistics community. The other stories of data sciences applications may not have had the same impact. But they followed the same principles, continuously connecting disparate experiences. Where does this shared understanding leave data scientists in their day-to-day work?

WHO ARE WE?

Stories about notable peers and famous ancestors are more accessible and easier to collectively remember than those of specific work experiences or job trajectories. They place the passing meetup events into their larger context, offering orientation. But they sacrificed connections to concrete problems, leaving the placement somewhat loose and leaving more to do for those who tried to catch up.

As a final trick, data scientists used meetups to place themselves between the evolving problems of quantitative data analyses. Chris, who had just told his listeners about Breiman and Tukey, quickly returned to the "messy problems" of practicing data scientists. Staying in the academic context, he separated data scientists from specialized researchers in terms of "this thing where you interact with somebody from a different discipline." Still referring to uniformly specialized problems typical of academic research, these interactions, Chris told the audience, trade "better predictive accuracy on learning cats' faces from pictures" for "an understanding of how some system works." Instead of looking at eminent scholars for technical ideas, he looked at them for how they worked, and he translated those approaches into the present.

The idea of interdisciplinary interactions generalizes the stories from the previous chapter without leaving the historical moment, like some of the solutions in this chapter did. The speakers who discussed their coworker and client interactions recognized the central role those relations played in their technical work. But they did not assign a general meaning to them. Chris connected the willingness to break out of areas of specialization to the data scientist role. His argument was not that every messy problem leads to general insight. Not every pure problem leads to general insight, either. But he identified benefits in engaging with different groups from introducing a broader set of issues.

Chris was formulating this broader argument in front of the meetup audience. While he had worked in an environment with no tradition of quantitative analysis, he integrated the idea of interdisciplinary interactions into his presentation in reference to a previous speaker at the same event, Hannah Wallach,[38] a trained computer scientist who had moved to an interdisciplinary industry lab and talked about such interactions just before. Hannah discussed their benefits in some detail, explaining that "very few computer scientists or engineers would consider developing models or tools for analyzing astronomy data without involving astronomers." She then asked: "So, why then is so many methods for analyzing social data developed without social scientists?"

Hannah's question responded to the prominence of data scientists with purely technical training in areas that had been the domain of social scientists. LinkedIn's and Facebook's first data scientists, as well as many of those who have appeared in these pages, are examples of that trend. Hannah's rhetorical question highlighted potential problems. And her tentative answer sketched the problem's full significance. She speculated that "in part, it is because we have really strong intuitions about the social world." They don't think to ask social scientists, she reasoned, even if there is a clear need, as her analogy to astronomy had suggested. Hannah advocated for collaborations as part of a larger call to make machine learning applications in societal contexts transparent, safe, and useful.

Hannah's was a more reasoned argument for the interactions that Chris described as a defining feature of data scientists. But it was not the full answer. Hannah had acknowledged earlier in her talk that "it is very much the case that interdisciplinary [work] is hard" and, pausing for an empathetic nod, "it is also kind of time-consuming." These observations flesh out the data scientist role, connecting points made by earlier meetup speakers. A day-long trial like Quinn proposed takes more time than a formal job interview, and tactical and creative approaches to messy datasets are harder to implement than straightforward solutions. Hannah resolves the tension between competing visions for science from chapter 3 in the new definition of data science. And the whole scene of her developing these points on stage captures how data scientists reflected on their work and themselves as an expert group.

The context of Hannah's presentation reveals the magnitude of that process. She brought slides that used the layout of Drew Conway's Venn diagram for discussing the interdisciplinary collaborations, including him in the conversation, as Chris had involved her in his and as the speakers at another event had involved Claudia and Jeff. She also mentioned a colleague from her work named Duncan Watts, who had made the point about the deceptively obvious explanation of social problems. Even more strikingly, Chris had qualified that, unlike Hannah, he hadn't "had the pleasure of collaborating with real, honest social scientists" when he included her point in his presentation, only to go on and publish a book with a historian a few years later titled *How Data Happened*. To bring these connections full circle, the book cited Hannah's point on the opening pages, quoting from another talk she had given.[39]

A fuller image of data science's collective construction is emerging. Data scientists recognized their distinct role in references to their colleagues and clients and to sciences. They answer the questions that followed from that insight, determining who they were and could be, in reference to one another. They talked about one another, about Claudia, Jeff, Hannah, Duncan, and many others, plus those they imagined to be part of their group even though they weren't around any longer. Those references were not inward-looking. They all came together from different backgrounds. Those backgrounds shaped what they saw individually. The references to one another worked with those observations more than just repeating them. The openness of meetups offered the chance to challenge and revise the observations and interpretations.

They did not create this web of concrete and imagined interconnections and relations strategically but made specific references and engaged with others purposefully. And the effects became evident. One speaker who had first introduced Claudia also shared his impression that "data science has the potential to bring together a community of like-minded people who believe that good decisions are made using data." Another speaker at a different event remembered the old days when he was part of "these little, you know, ninja teams on the side" as a motivation to his audience to try "a little exercise I like to give people to do: When you guys are getting ready for bed tonight, just stop, and like put down your toothbrush, your comb, look in the mirror, smile at yourself, and say: 'I do analytics, I am sexy.' Okay? And for the first time in any of our careers, a lot of people would not argue with this, right, so enjoy it." This was not a call for revolution. He knew that "eventually, the hype will die down." The point was that this was still a new era for technical people who were "gonna have a very nice, stable career path."

CONCLUSION

Data scientists have tied different ideas and images around what they have done and seen into a professional identity. Like their takes on technical questions and work relations, they have assembled their self-understanding from personal experiences and insights: their training and professional trajectories, the profiles in their teams, and their views of others in the community. Even broader ideas retained specific references, if to quantitative analysts who had long passed away. The choices of speakers of what they highlighted in those accounts revealed identity construction as a distinct activity in the emergence of the data scientist role. Rather than specifying the data scientist identity, these observations have further shown how data scientists mobilize reflexive creativity to reconcile established views of quantitative expertise with modern data analysis applications.

The question of identity construction came with its own theoretical concerns, but the findings from this analysis inform the larger debate on expert work. The comments included different references to formal features of expert work, such as academic disciplines, organizational units, résumé entries, and canonical ideas. These are the features that the theory of expert work as a system of institutionalized groups highlights. But there were, once again, just as many indicators supporting the side of the theoretical debate that emphasizes informal processes. These included the proposals to peers for getting past formal indicators and the interactions in which panelists challenged one another's views of data science. Rather than supporting one view more than another, the observations of the data science case supported a novel theoretical focus.

For data hackers to recognize themselves as data scientists, they went beyond their technical expertise and engaged in analytical reflections of their social contexts. Whereas these reflections concerned the interactions at meetups and in work situations during the last two chapters, here they concerned the data scientists themselves. However, rather than proposing themselves as solutions for others, they unpacked how their sense of themselves had come together. The presenters did not provide answers, in other words. They laid out their own path as guidance for others to use for their own situations. This pattern calls for turning to pragmatist philosophers and focusing on reflexivity as a creative practice in expert work.

This direction reconciles the conundrum of how technical data science expertise could spread without institutional scaffolding and beyond close relationships between experts, their clients, and their technical devices. Early data hackers developed and shared analytical thinking about their technical problems and personal situations so that others could adopt and arrive at similar conclusions. The conclusions were that their experiences deviated from established roles and trajectories and best fit with the new narrative of the data scientist.

CONCLUSION

Data scientists are fixtures in industries, scholarly fields, and societies around the world today. The role is an appealing career option for some and for many more represents the human face of the last decade's changes, both good and bad, in the digital landscape. This book analyzed its origins. Focusing on observations from New York City, one of data science's birthplaces, I have argued that the data scientist role emerged from discussions held among scattered hackers about technical activities in their social contexts in ways that led to new conclusions. Their interpretations were crucial for moving on from established expert roles toward the data science idea. However, only the shared commitment to quantitative data analysis with its vast sociotechnical infrastructure and an eye on specific problems ensured agreements. Their collective reflections, even on seemingly casual experiences, led to an increasingly coherent understanding of the data scientist. In theory-speak, the protagonists coupled *relational discipline* with *reflexive creativity*.[1]

The book's six chapters have documented the empirical foundation for my explanation of data science's emergence. This conclusion remains brief. It connects this book's insights to (1) the existing accounts of data scientists and (2) the larger sociological understanding of expert work and (3) ends with practical takeaways.

WHAT IS DATA SCIENCE?

The book's observations and argument added to the existing writing about data scientists as an emerging profession. The first addition came from my empirical angle. The speakers at the New York City meetups in the early 2010s were the predecessors of the data scientists that have informed other accounts.[2] While this analysis missed parallel discussions on the West Coast, the situation in New York captured data science discussions outside of the support of Silicon Valley's tech culture and institutions.[3] As a result, this analysis discovered the role of data hackers amid novel technical challenges when data science was not yet a shared idea and had no local legacy. This setup brought to the fore the concerns and community of early data scientists.

A second addition to existing accounts came from considering data science's emergence in both its practical implementation and its academic roots. While both sides have received attention before,[4] my joint analysis revealed a deeper divide in quantitative expertise made salient by data science than previous accounts have noted. This backdrop is important. The ongoing prominence fostered popular discussions of the promises and dangers of data science. But the issue that started them, the problem of meaningfully analyzing formal datasets, has occupied statisticians, applied mathematicians, and many others for hundreds of years. This history turned the popular movement from the last decade into a powerful lens for capturing otherwise arcane social processes. Once in place, it showed that before data hackers could impose their ideas on users of digital technologies and bask in lay excitement, they had to negotiate science and other forms of intellectual work, one of the social world's defining divides.[5]

Finally, the book's focus on casual interactions, the jovial after-work get-togethers, has also placed data science's emergence closer to everyday collective activities. While other research has noted the significance of meetups in the world of data scientists,[6] it has also framed these sites as new professional venues. In contrast, my analysis highlighted the continuity that meetups create between the technical focus of data science discussions and many other collective concerns ranging from politics to artistic or leisurely pursuits. The social dynamics around interactions, creativity, and reflexivity that data scientists displayed may, therefore, inform our perspective on a broader set of social movements that form around a shared stock of knowledge.

Several of my core observations were still consistent with existing arguments. Ambiguity was ubiquitous, although uncertainty was a much more prevalent experience among these early data scientists, adding key nuance. This analysis also offered no insights to ease worries about data science's consequences—the struggle of early data hackers to understand their role has no bearing on the damage some of their applications have done to democracy and everyday life. But whereas existing contributions have focused on implications for the institutionalization of the profession, I have scrutinized the interplay of structure and practice as the early data scientists navigated the uncertainty and found clarity in the idea of a distinct role. Instead of casting them as passive agents of economic and technological changes, my account has positioned data scientists as actors who can take charge of their work and its consequences and pointed out instances in which they have called one another out.

The data scientist role continued to thrive after I left the field.[7] It has spread far beyond the United States,[8] and dedicated professional associations have replaced the passing remarks during meetings of established scientific societies, as have training programs and schools and calls for a code of ethics.[9] These are all key features that scholars of expert work have listed since the 1950s and 1960s as defining characteristics of professions.

However, much suggests that the particular institutionalization of data scientists has led the field to resemble specialized occupations that fit neatly into workplaces rather than the classic professions, which are characterized by significant autonomy over their tasks and expertise. In universities and training programs, data science remains under the control of statisticians, with other disciplines on hand for some specialized extensions into engineering and the social sciences. The code of ethics has not become more than a laudable idea, and there is no indication that membership in any professional association is relevant for practicing data scientists.

These developments point away from the distinctiveness that the early groups sought during their after-work gatherings. While this trajectory is far from unique to data scientists—even lawyers rarely embody the classic image of the autonomous professional[10]—it recalls the fragility of work amid larger social and economic forces, including the recent rise of generative AI applications. But the skepticism toward definite requirements of professional status in the newer sociology of professions raises questions about their significance for evaluating data science. A formal organization representing the community would have benefits. However, the more decisive question for this early stage is whether the activities of data scientists have shaped this area of technical expertise. In no plausible scenario could an analysis revisit the same developments with, say, statisticians involved rather than data scientists. However, the pushback of statisticians and other neighboring groups has added alternative ideas to those original voices. They gave a strong indication that the marks that data scientists have left come at least in part from their recognition as a distinct role.

The final verdict must include qualifications, but the pattern reveals the early data science movement as a robust professional initiative. The analysis indicated diverse views among data scientists, and the dominant image today does not cover all of data science. Just like early data hackers stepped out of their existing roles and jobs to redefine themselves, their successors have reflected on data science's challenges during the following decade. But several examples show that the data science community lives on. In one specific episode, a data scientist who helped many join the community got bullied online—tellingly, by someone who was supposedly leading a data science association. Many prominent data scientists stood up in their peer's defense. In another instance, a data scientist who worked for the state of Florida spoke out against orders to issue false COVID statistics. The community rallied behind her and applauded her commitment to professional ethics. Finally, a nonprofit organization offering pro bono data science services has been around long enough to have celebrated its ten-year anniversary.[11] While established groups could have been involved in these events, they all occurred at precisely the intersections of practical problems and technical expertise that purists rejected and data scientists embraced.

These are only scattered indicators, but they illustrate how the increasingly established group can still recognize issues that matter and find new directions. My analysis of data scientists at gatherings in New York City has shown how the back-and-forth within the community let them recognize uncertainties over new directions and resolve those glitches. Even the weight of massive intellectual legacies, technological machinery, and popular debates did not stop them. Similarly, future events will shape but not dictate data science's development.

PROFESSIONS AND EXPERTISE AS COLLECTIVE ACTION

My argument about data science's emergence advances the literature on expert work. Like many existing analyses of data scientists, mine has found evidence of the two dominant views in sociology. Data scientists have significantly benefited from the formalisms of academia, including statistical theory and computer science, and of the corporate world, including reporting structures and task responsibilities. Even the experiences of early data scientists showed conflicts between competing groups, which is the core concern of Andrew Abbott's famous theory of professions defending their jurisdictions. However, the analysis also revealed abundant informal processes in the construction of data science expertise, including relations between the protagonists, between them and the larger community of coders and the technologies they used, as well as in the interactions between data scientists and their lay clients. All these observations are consistent with the larger theoretical framework that Gil Eyal assembled to replace Abbott's more formal view.

Rather than suggesting that both were correct for their respective cases, a possibility I considered in the introduction, the analysis of the data science case uncovered major shortcomings. The interplay of the activities of data scientists and their larger backdrop pointed to a more dynamic alternative. This new theory of reflexive creativity and relational discipline places the two opposing views along a continuum for understanding areas of expert work. Instead of looking for evidence of formalism or informal processes, this view considers the relative explanatory purchase of each one for a specific case. The results will still support Abbott's theory if the degree of institutionalization gives experts a basis to defend against intruders. They will support Eyal's theory if a case covers weakly institutionalized niches where experts and others assemble new knowledge or techniques. But it also integrates a vast space between those two scenarios and beyond into its analytical scope. My theoretical view is sensitive to the fleeting activities of incipient groups amid the much more salient technological, intellectual, cultural, or economic processes. All the collective attempts that never left a mark in the system of professions or the bundles of relational expertise become part of the sociological account.

The practice-focused view can explain problems that don't fit into the standard expertise settings. The pragmatist thinking that informed my reflexive creativity argument had previously explained surprising observations in formal organizations and everyday life.[12] The emergent data science case and the meetups have demonstrated its utility for understanding more fluid settings. And as my theoretical framework made the social context an independent dimension from the individual activities, the insights from the data science analysis can inform studies of a range of problems, including political movements, economic developments, and cultural movements, both in the artistic sense and in the sense of local customs. Specific findings will differ across these areas, but the theoretical framework helps discern how people recognize themselves and one another in their social contexts, whether this is governmental institutions; theaters and performance spaces; or cities, towns, and their histories. Those larger forces, states, capitalism, and religious ideologies, almost always retain the upper hand. But this theoretical framework integrates the failures and occasional successes of emergent activities into a set of collective movements following discernible patterns.

Like Abbott, Eyal, Larson, and others, I have considered expert work as a collective endeavor within more extensive social processes. The reflexive and relational mechanisms I identified added to the insights of the specialized studies from recent decades. Moreover, my analysis situated them within data science as a social object. The comprehensive view transcended standard analytical frames but caught a major force in the modern social world.

In the tradeoff between empirical significance and scholarly grip, this choice favored the former without losing sight of the latter. It added data science's emergence to the stock of sociological knowledge. More payoff may follow as social life becomes easier to capture and analytical techniques become available for discerning it. These opportunities were not yet on the horizon of many defining contributions to professions, limiting the utility of their design choices as templates for us. My account's iterations between theoretical ideas and empirical analyses of a major social process aimed to adapt the promise of the past era to the affordances of the present. The classics cannot tell us what to do, but they can help steer new technical machinery toward sociological insights.

For sociology to keep up with the future of the world of work and collective life, this more inclusive and dynamic theoretical view is crucial. Research has shown that formal occupational labels capture less of the labor market than we once thought.[13] This change does not mean that all careers will become more fluid or that formal structures are undesirable.[14] However, it underlines the benefits of a new understanding of how groups emerge as pathways to empirically grounded formalisms. And these changes go far beyond the labor market setting or the world of work. Social progress and digital infrastructures have changed how we organize ourselves and others and how we discuss and pursue shared interests, beliefs, and practices.[15] Whoever embarks on new directions will experience confusion, just as data scientists once did. The view of their responses as reflexive creativity within relational contexts guides how we understand what comes of these incipient activities.

TAKEAWAYS

Finally, this account of data science's emergence provides some more immediate takeaways for readers with different stakes in data science: data scientists themselves; those venturing, like early data scientists, somewhere new; bystanders who prefer staying put but are glad to see others on the move; and researchers who want to follow other emergent movements to understand what they accomplish and how they accomplish it but also what they might endanger.

This book provides younger data scientists with a portrait of their profession during its infancy; it reminds veterans of what it once was. It doesn't tell them how to do their job or organize their profession today. However, it can serve as a reference point for deciding what they want to make of their role. Just as the name "data scientist" indicated to outsiders more novelty than insiders believed there was, its continuity belies the changes that any line of work undergoes. Today's data scientists can interpret their role in new ways, including around motivations that have receded between then and now. As for the early data scientists, any initiative taken today starts with immediate problems but then also has to include allies and others in the conversation. This time around, they may consider taking more charge of formally establishing their role than their predecessors have.

Readers who are considering a career in data science can take this account as a guide into the conundrum around the profession. There are still ample opportunities in data science, and the more who pursue them, having learned from the failures of data science's early days, the better for everyone. However, since there is an increasingly clear image of data science, the experience will differ from the original experiences. This analysis of data science's early days has shown that new directions don't come from strategy. They come from commitment to tasks and the perceptiveness of one's surroundings to guide the commitments. Another way to follow data scientists then means finding new commitments and others to pursue them with, if only loosely, as well as beneficiaries. The early protagonists didn't seek out their positions; they had learned skills and expertise for other reasons and then adjusted their trajectories. By definition, this approach would then lead to something other than data science. But it works for a range of problems, including nontechnical ones.

While new directions are not for everyone, whoever likes to see them happen can still get in on the action. The data scientists were able to get together because others offered spaces to meet. The problem of gathering places is an important concern in urban planning for organizing collective life. Many causes require specialized setups; data scientists, for instance, needed projectors to share their code, models, and results. Universities, startups, and coworking spaces stepped up. They had their own interests while also observing the norm in the hacker community of keeping business out of technical gatherings. Data science's emergence offered a reminder that social movements need spaces to meet, even those with deep roots in digital technologies, and especially when they are pursuing aims other than broadly public ones. These spaces require ongoing effort and negotiation for many to involve themselves.

Lastly, as new groups gather to address smaller or larger problems, other researchers may want to follow those efforts to help us understand how society changes and finds continuity. The fluidity of those moments is potentially crucial but also hard to capture. Although my analysis of data science's emergence has benefited from hindsight, its underlying observations covered the time when everything happened. The hackers who discussed the pros and cons of data science as an answer to the problems they experienced did not know how big their cause would become; nor did I when watching them. The result was a fragmented picture that missed some important places that shaped data science. The tactics of the abductive method helped keep track of initial expectations and surprising impressions. This documentation of its application can serve as an inventory of tricks to try when following newly unfolding social processes where they happen and hopefully avoid mistakes causing one to miss the relevant action.

This was no definite analysis of data science's emergence. A more careful design would likely have led to a different set of sites for field observations, more comprehensive interviews, and more formal modeling. I have tried to account for these limitations in the argument I have made with the observations I had and the snippets I showed. However, these limitations were also an inevitable part of a discovery-oriented research process.

In that sense, this study has captured the tension between rigor and novelty, which is the defining tension of science. It thereby recorded and discerned not only displays and reports of uncertainty among data scientists, as others have, but also the experience of their resolution as it happened. Since no discovery-oriented research activity can avoid uncertainty, the struggles of early data hackers offer a reflection point for related situations. And their moves in discussions of practical problems to questions of themselves, their social contexts, and their intellectual histories serve as a reflection point for all others in intellectual communities to consider how larger processes reveal themselves in personal experiences.

EPILOGUE

This study came to an abrupt end when I had to defend my dissertation to start a new job. While that's not the scientific way to wrap up research, and I hadn't yet really solved the problem of data science's emergence, the process I analyzed was showing signs of closure. The social world helped out as the profession was getting in the way.

Tellingly, few of the signs appeared where I looked most closely. The job description analysis was promising but didn't offer the final word on data science; the talks at meetups showed more confidence in data science but still remained provisional. Surprisingly, a sign of data science's progress flared up during a research break. I was on a videocall with my college roommate, a physicist by training, when he mentioned having started dabbling in data science. Such a side hustle wouldn't sound like much of a surprise for someone with his training today, but back then, it showed me how far those tentative ideas I had watched come together had spread.

The next hint followed only a few months later but again far away from New York City's meetup scene. I was home in Europe meeting with another friend from college, a fellow social scientist with whom I had prepared course exercises for a statistics professor. I knew that my friend had gotten a master's degree in statistics and then started working for a bank. Now he told me about his new job as a data scientist. And this was not all: When I told him about my meetup experiences in New York City, he excitedly explained that he was watching those very same meetup talks on YouTube. These instances showed that what I had seen up close had grown into a common experience reaching far beyond Silicon Valley or New York City.

The signs were not limited to personal stories. As part of my effort to track data science's contours, I had continued to follow up with whoever had to do with data science and wanted to talk to me. One chat was with a founder who had started a recruitment business for data scientists and other data-related roles. He made the casual comment that his operation required "zero dollars for marketing" because "everyone knows data science anyway." The self-evident status of data science secured the livelihood of a non–data scientist. This and other hints started to show that data science was making progress as a new line of work. And while the stories captured its connections to technical fields such as physics and statistics, the practical application of those skills dominated.

My ongoing conversations also took me deep inside the academic establishment during interviews with an acting and a former chair of a statistics department. Both were serious academics, not the hoodie-wearing hackers from the places where I did most of my research. Their willingness to talk to a sociology graduate student showed their concern with data science, but this interest expressed itself differently. The acting department chair recognized the merit of some of what data scientists did but made sure I understood that statisticians had been doing the same all along. He pointed out what problems statisticians addressed that data scientists supposedly ignored. In a striking contrast, the former department chair was excited about data science. While he also saw a much longer history than the new label suggested, he viewed the new interest as a revival of concerns that excessive theory and mathematical formalism had undermined in statistics.

These conversations came late in my research, but they added crucial details. The opposing views of these two statisticians revealed a version of the conflict that sociological theory had led me to expect from the beginning. I had seen signs of it among data scientists, but this was the most striking evidence. The specific reactions also brought the conflict to issues inside and outside of scientific research and practical work. After all, data scientists did not threaten to take over any of those statisticians' applied work. They were tenured academics. This insight confirmed my initial hunches about data science's prospects but also made the project much more complicated. While the question of how academic departments adopted data science would have required an entirely new research strategy, within the scope I had defined, it required new reflections on the materials I had collected.

This wasn't even the biggest problem that came up in the project's final months. The full mess I had gotten myself into dawned on me one Friday in October 2015. Much of that day was like many days during my time in the field. I attended a data science–themed event on my campus in the morning and had a meetup scheduled in midtown for the evening. One detail that stood out was the clustering of multiple events on one day. But this wasn't entirely unusual. The odd occurrence was that the two main presenters were from the social sciences world in which I was just getting started. They had slightly idiosyncratic profiles, and both had mentioned connections to data science to me, but they were still granted tenure by their fellow sociologists. To make the day more bizarre, a third event on that day in the city featured my advisor, who had stayed out of the data science world to my knowledge since his endorsement of my project a few years before. After having spent those years tracking down data science, data science now came knocking on my door.

Data science had not only made a mark on the paths of some young folks getting started and on the academics closest to its underlying expertise. It was seeping into fields further away, including my own. And signs of that spread would only increase the more I followed up. The founder of the academic association that featured the first academic mentioning of data science in print in the 1990s was a friend of the sociologists who had built the area of research that had attracted me to the discipline in the first place. The statistician for whom I prepared exercise materials as an undergraduate student organized a data science–themed conference soon after I had left. As these different impressions of data science came together, indicating maturity, I not only located a novel kind of tension but also found myself increasingly caught up in those larger social forces.

While these were daunting analytical challenges, I didn't yet understand the full implications. I was still in the field, continued to gather observations, especially at meetups. But even during one of those routine visits, new signs of data science's closure appeared. I sat in the audience when someone sat down next to me and said "hi." I recognized my new neighbor from the Introduction to Data Science lecture a few years earlier. Back then, he stood out as an advanced undergraduate student. I knew he had completed a master's degree in statistics in the meantime. Now I learned what he had been doing subsequently, which included a stint in finance and then a data science role with a more meaningful purpose. And as if these were not again enough signs of closure, during the Q&A, someone asked a question, which made my neighbor turn around and then to me, in surprise. It was a mutual friend from the lecture, sitting a few rows behind us. This unplanned reunion showed what a big-small world data science had become.

Whatever stone I turned, I found some hint that data science had matured. The study that had begun without a clear outcome now addressed what sociological theory, and my naive hopes, predicted it would. The exact form was impossible to know beforehand. It still didn't have a main professional association that most data scientists were members of or state-sanctioned licensing, both key elements of the strictest definitions of autonomous professions. Still impressed by what the classics had concluded in their times, I didn't recognize the relevant features today right away. I retained email alerts about open data science positions for assurance that the role continued to exist and worried about analytical and theoretical challenges that followed from my position in data science's development. My neighbor's reaction to my telling him about my involvement in data science, namely, my studying its emergence, led him to think for a moment and then respond, "That's wild." Meant nicely, I still wondered if the whole endeavor might have become too wild.

There was not much time to worry. The work continued, and solutions and answers came together. I took a detour and developed some of the methodological ideas I had in response to seeing data scientists work, joining forces with someone from a different tradition of thinking as an external check on my ideas. I also took a job far away from New York and its intellectual scene, getting some distance from the unfolding I had watched so closely. These steps helped me see the patterns in data science's emergence. They also fell outside of what standard research methodology counsels or helps us think through. What counts in the end, however, is that I came away from all this with a better understanding of what happened among the data nerds and hackers as they assembled the idea of data science.

ACKNOWLEDGMENTS

This study received much help long before becoming a book project and more since then. It started as a dissertation idea, and I thank Peter Bearman, my thesis advisor and mentor, and Josh Whitford, who has offered guidance throughout and beyond. Both endorsed my hunch and let me run with it. Encouraging early engagement came from Mathijs de Vaan and Joscha Legewie; they even volunteered their profiles for me to test my emerging definition of a data scientist.

The community of data scientists deserves significant thanks. The most instrumental person for this project was Rachel Schutt, the instructor of the Introduction to Data Science course where it all began. Rachel agreed to have many conversations with me and connected me to others in the field. Cathy O'Neil and Jared Lander provided additional perspectives on the world I wanted to study. In sociology, Mitchell Duneier set me up with my first stack of books on the topic, Matt Salganik made me believe in the apprenticeship idea, and Duncan Watts introduced me to the origin myths.

Gil Eyal, Cathrine Turco, and David Stark saw the first set of results when they joined my thesis committee. Their critiques showed me I still had work to do. Their engagement with my pushback made me believe I could get it right. The defense became a real intellectual moment in which the idea of a book started.

A lot more needed to happen for my argument to come together. Henning Hillmann provided an environment where I could start over and the collegiality to do so effectively. Laura Nelson, David Ribes, and Janet Vertesi helped me navigate tricky junctions during the analysis. Stefan Timmermans injected fresh momentum by showing me how writing works. Gil commented on the new version and invited me to present in his group, where Diane Vaughan shared thoughts that helped me lock in the argument. Joan Robinson and Andrew Schrank were close allies during the most intense writing months. Exchanging drafts with Joan set free new energy. Conversations with Andrew gave me the confidence to finish this manuscript.

Socialization into academic work is messy. I thank Claudius Hildebrand for his camaraderie during this process early on. Jeremy Kuhnle had my back during the later phase, and Achim Edelmann most recently. Since our first days in graduate school, Kinga Makovi and Byungkyu Lee have been professional inspirations and personal friends, and they never said no to reading an undercooked idea. Fabien Accominotti, Ryan Hagen, Pilar Opazo, Benjamin Rohr, Alix Rule, Eun Kyong Shin, and Daniel Tadmon, all close peers, offered comments and examples of outstanding scholarship. In the community of specialists, Sophie Mützel and Robert Dorschel have given me the assurance to push this project forward.

Supportive institutional settings have helped as well. My first ideas for this study benefited from the feedback of fellow members of the CODES, SKAT, and XS workshops at Columbia, and the NYLON group at New York University. As the book idea took shape in Mannheim, my MZES Mittelbau friends, including Johanna Gereke, Anna Kaiser, David Kretschmer, Lars Leszczensky, Sebastian Pink, and Tobias Roth, warmly welcomed me and volunteered as audiences. My reading group friends Florian Andersen, Marcel Kappes, and Pavel Dimitrov Chachev kept me engaged, as did Sofia Aouani and Ida Gaede later in Paris. At the CSO, Manisha Anantharaman, Olivier Borraz, Patrick Castel, Simon Cordonnier, Sophie Dubuisson-Quellier, Martin Giraudeau, Léonie Hénaut, Jeanne Lazarus, Emmanuel Lazega, Kevin Mellet, Christine Musselin, Jérôme Pélisse, and Olivier Pilmis made me feel I had found a place to work. My Sciences Po colleagues Jean-Philippe Cointet, Vincent Lépinay, Jen Schradie, Sylvain Parasie, Guillaume Lachenal, and Dominique Cordon read early drafts.

At Columbia University Press, Eric Schwartz saw the book come together before I could and helped me get there. Alyssa M. Napier continued this immense support during the final steps of the process. Financial support came from a European Research Council grant (ERC StG #101117844).

This book required significant personal investment. I thank my family for their patience throughout these years. Katharina Burgdorf not only put up with me on this trip and weighed in when I wasn't sure where to go but also added stops and detours of her own to make it a richer, more beautiful experience. I cannot thank her enough.

METHODOLOGICAL APPENDIX

This book studies a classic problem in sociology: the emergence of a professional role. It describes several well-documented processes around technological change, symbolic interactionism, relational meaning making, and identity formation as they converged in data science's emergence. While the topic and some dynamics were familiar, data science and the analysis of an unsettled case posed new challenges. But help was in sight. Diane Vaughan's decades-long experience of using retrospective observations to reconstruct emergent situations provided a powerful methodological template. Iddo Tavory and Stefan Timmermans turned the iterations between the visible patterns and the collection of new data points according to existing theories that were part of that approach into an abduction-oriented program, which I adopted for my analysis. This section provides a formal overview of my application of such a procedure to complement the analytical presentation in chapter 1.

The core research design challenge came from the inside perspective necessary for capturing an incipient process, the moving in and out of the collective dynamics to discern their unfolding. I used three main strategies to ensure systematic observations. First, each iteration followed methodological principles, which solidified as a mix of qualitative and quantitative analyses. Second, as I assembled my empirical strategy, I remained alert to different views and directions. My extensive notes and memos allowed me to go back to those observations and follow up. Third, I accounted for the limitations in my analytical focus on semipublic events in New York City. Finally, the research that my peers conducted between my data collection and final analysis let me position this study in the context of their findings.

The following summary presents this strategy in discrete steps. While failing to unpack the evolving perspective from the first few chapters, this version presents the full scope and outlines a template, at least in part, for studying related problems.

EXPLORATION

This study most heavily rests on observations of the tech scene between September 2012 and February 2016. During this time, I followed academic discussions, talked to data scientists and those dealing with them, and used their techniques and technologies to process large-scale datasets, including two thousand early data scientist job descriptions and tens of thousands of job descriptions around them. The most conservative tallying identifies seventy-one specific encounters with the community of early data nerds and hackers. These include interviews and conversations and, especially, dozens of meetup events featuring data and tech presentations and discussions. Many of those events had multiple presentations, bringing the number of accounts of data work I followed to over one hundred, all in the context of groups of active members who chatted with one another before and after presentations, asked questions, and cracked jokes. This section details how I assembled my observations and analyzed them in an exploratory phase that mapped out the contours of data science's formation. While the project evolved to keep track of the emergent case, it had a clear start. I turned from a student of data science into a researcher of data science in October 2012, when I announced to my Introduction to Data Science instructor that I would like to talk to her to set up a sociological study of data science as a novel profession. My notes document conversations about the topic with my academic advisors, their endorsement of the idea, and suggestions for moving forward. The switch came as the regular encounters with practicing data scientists had increased my confidence that the new label was not only the product of superficial hype but came with a committed movement. I had not settled yet on meetups as a strategic setting, but my initial conversations pointed them out as sites where data scientists socialized. One interview connection proposed that we set aside time during a meetup gathering, while another suggested that I attend the meetup that they were organizing.

The initial impressions confirmed two basic ideas that seemed central to moving forward with the study. One was data science's technical foundation, no matter how similar or different from established statistics. I decided to pursue that technical side via my own analysis of data science and explored different techniques and technologies from data science. The second conclusion was that I would keep attending meetups. Their analytical promise wasn't immediately evident, but their endorsements in conversations and the seamless transition from the classroom to them highlighted those events as sites that data scientists took seriously. While this focus risked missing perspectives from quieter and more focused data scientists, it captured data science's public-facing activities and, thus, the main research question. After about a year of testing these different strategies, the most focused years of meetup observations were 2014 and 2015, when I attended forty-eight events, twenty-four each year.

Like its beginning, the study didn't follow a metric that indicated its conclusion, but, in hindsight, it still ended with signs of closure. My last set of field notes on a meetup was from February 2016. There was no definite indication of data science's maturity at that point, but it was time to move on, and the three and a half years since the start had generated enough material to analyze. Looking back, however, my notes from that event show that the process I had set out to observe had also evolved into a new phase. The uncertainty from the beginning was giving way to the scaffolding that would bear data science. The guest at this data science meetup was also the host of another data science meetup group, a practicing data scientist, and one of my first data science instructors a few years before. He greeted me when we crossed paths before his presentation, and then, as part of his opening remarks, he listed classical statisticians as the sources of his ideas, including Bill Cleveland as the person who supposedly coined the label "data science." This mixing of the meetup community and the critical reflection showed that data scientists had become a group that understood itself.

With the original observations concluded, I started reviewing my notes. They consisted of records of my interactions, whether conversations, interviews, documents, or public presentations, and included reflections I had made to prepare for meetings, notes of things that were said and how, and, for the events, observations of what happened, who was around, and so on. Since laptops were ubiquitous at these gatherings, I used mine to keep notes just like others used theirs to write down coding tricks. As part of my adoption of data science technologies,

I had started using a popular programming editor, Emacs, in which I then typed up my observations as text documents. For conversations over lunch or while standing around before an event got started, I would write down my recollections once I got back to my desk. This material came together as over four hundred pages of notes of events, several folders of contextual materials and observations, thousands of lines of code, and hours of video recordings, all covering the vibrant period that was data science's early days.

Following my exit from the field, I started coding my notes. The themes I identified as high-level codes that I assigned to notes included math, statistics, data, ML, tools, substance, reflexivity, and, somewhat oddly, logistic regression. Logistic regression was odd because it was much more specific compared to the others, but it was the proverbial key to data science. For math, I had eight subcodes, including Greek letters, matrix, probability, and linear algebra. For statistics, I had regression, now as a family of statistical techniques, LOESS curve, gradient, and information theory. For ML, I had labels that included supervised learning, decision trees, and random forests. For tools, I had R, memory, XML, python, and hadoop. For substance, I had domain, credit rating, clicks, finance, cancer, and Netflix, among others. For reflexivity, I had book, competition, ethics, blog posts, kaggle, and surprise, and some names of semi-prominent figures who appeared in presentations of fellow data scientists.

Some themes were less prominent than I had expected, while others gained more clarity. This initial analysis was still part of my dissertation. But before it produced insights, I noted major questions. The original proposal included a qualitative component as context for two extensive quantitative analyses of data science jobs and data science's academic roots. I had planned to conduct interviews and qualitative case studies. However, as the abductive method counsels, I adjusted my focus as the initial analysis of my field notes and the event recordings revealed more intricate themes in the meetup world and a more inclusive scope. The empirical strategy that I ended up taking captured the broader data science community.

This discovery led to a shift in focus to micro-level dynamics. The notes helped reorganize my larger set of materials. Many of the groups kept video recordings of their events. In March 2016, I started using my coded field notes to identify the most revealing presentations, using one level of analysis to gain access to a deeper level of analysis. In addition to recovering those recordings for events I attended, I used the opportunity to add twelve events between 2012 and 2015 from my usual groups that seemed particularly relevant and refined the analysis of the evolving research direction. Cameras could only capture the presentations, but as a result of my extensive personal attendance, I knew that they were more representative of the events than the audience and that this focus was important. This step showed that while many of those presentations added nuance, I had reached theoretical saturation, and I used them to supplement my overall materials.

These observations became the main foundation for my initial set of memos, which I organized around five main themes: data, products, skills, identity, and social world. This analysis used longer quotes from the field, which I scrutinized in this new context for systematic patterns. They evolved further into memos on technology, organizations, work, community, and discipline. Within the themes, I then identified an additional and, reflecting the new level of granularity, more refined set of codes.

This overview ended my first analytical phase. I consolidated my observations, organized them, extracted themes, revisited the observations, enriched them around the themes, and wrote up the patterns I started seeing. The overarching idea that came together in this iteration positioned data science between a corporate movement, hackers, and organized nonprofit programmers. I ended up viewing data science as a "thought community." While useful in getting away from some of the standard portrayals of data science as a profession or discipline, it was also vague and vanished in a plethora of detailed observations, as the feedback I received pointed out. So, the next round required "pruning," which clarified my observations and led to sharper theoretical insights.

PRECISION

To get from an initial inspection to a precise sociological analysis, I refined my theoretical lens. A large spreadsheet helped synthesize the insights from the earlier memos and organized them around theoretical themes. The two worked in tandem. I aimed to make a sharper argument by going beyond questions of what data science had become—a community with distinct contours rather than a classic discipline or profession—to consider how the data nerds and hackers had pulled off that accomplishment.

One standard point of departure would be rational action theory, which explains how actors pursue their interests. But this logic assumed that data hackers knew what there is to optimize. The stories in the nascent data science community did not reveal a coherent strategy, however, or even recognized steps they could learn about. I found a theoretical framework that could deal with such ambiguity in pragmatist philosophy, which explains how actors respond to problems they encounter. These ideas helped me discern the struggles I had seen among data scientists trying to figure out the practical problems. Questions remained about how those activities fit into the larger division of labor and the collective processes that undergirded the construction of the data science community. As a solution, I linked the ideas from pragmatism with theories of role structures and their network-analytic implementations. These theoretical approaches gave the complex process that my initial analysis of the data science scene revealed theoretical scaffolding.

Much of my focus was on further discerning the meetup presentations, including accounts of the tools and techniques that data scientists used in their work, their workplace experiences, and their sense of community. I looked for evidence through the lens of an intricate theoretical framework that I believed could explain data science's emergence. While I already organized the observations around what relationships data scientists discussed with clients or colleagues, I broke them up further along dimensions I believed needed consideration. I distinguished accounts by what interpretive logic they mobilized.

Parallel to discerning these narrow patterns, I tried to tie them into a bigger picture. In the analytical spreadsheet, I mapped out the full argument in a schematic fashion with columns for puzzles and questions, theories and empirical evidence, and summaries. By moving back and forth between theoretical ideas and these full representations of my field observations, I hoped to produce a more concise and still comprehensive argument of data science's formation than my descriptive account of its appearance.

This process paid off. The initial analysis had tracked the novel data science case through analogies to the familiar cases of corporate programmers and activist hackers. The new theoretical lens revealed more clearly the social dynamics undergirding data science's emergence. I reconsidered the framing of the case and started to see data science within the divide in science. This angle was not immediately obvious for two reasons. One was that the sociology of professions and the sociology of science are distinct specialized debates, motivating a choice of placing data science in one or the other. The second reason has to do with my empirical observations. As I've tried to show throughout the book, data scientists had more immediate concerns than placing themselves as a group in the world of academic disciplines. However, once I had made that conceptual move, new patterns emerged from the empirical material.

The closer inspection of how data scientists discussed their work and the implementation of their procedures in light of social scientific thinking also led me to the abductive method. In contrast to how it featured in the final argument, namely, as the methodological framework for the qualitative analysis, back then, I discovered it as part of the analysis of data science work. Despite its recognition in epistemology, abduction was just starting to become a social scientific methodology. The analysis of the data scientists led me to Charles S. Peirce and then to Tavory and Timmermans's version of the method for qualitative research that eventually came to serve as a frame for this analysis.

Despite much progress, however, the new precision also started to undermine the more complete understanding of data science's emergence. For example, I hadn't considered identity as an important analytical dimension. First, outside of explicit discussions of identity politics and similar issues, identity does not reveal itself easily. It was especially clouded in the early data science phase. It is clear in hindsight that a common identity was key to data hackers' coming together and gaining lay salience. But their overt concern was much more with what they did than who they were. Second, there is an uneasy relationship among sociologists with identity. It always lurks in the background, which makes it easy to mistake it for the active driver of a sociological phenomenon, a mistake I wanted to avoid.

The abductive research method still helped me detect it. As part of my analytical procedure, I continued to share my results with different workshop audiences. In one of these settings, in 2017, a specialist in adolescent ethnic identity formation commented that, from his perspective, I was basically studying the identity formation of data scientists. The fact that the participant had extensive experience studying identity but no specific understanding of my case and saw relevant indicators in my material convinced me that I should look closer in my material. A few months later, the next iteration included an explicit account of data scientists' identity formation.

These refinements of the initial exploration led to a new version of my argument in 2018. While much more precise, this version had overcorrected for the limitations of the first version. I had worked myself into excessively nuanced observations about the formation of data science. Although I had also posited data science more between science and applied work, this new empirical framing remained underdeveloped as a sociological problem. Instead of analyzing the presentations of online dating and quantitative finance applications as lenses into the meetup setting, this intermediary step focused on what those accounts revealed about something larger that was going on in their workplaces. It overlooked the meetups as a concrete part of the process of data science's emergence.

CONTEXTUALIZATION

For this third step, which started about three years into the analysis and six years following the study's beginning, I repeated the earlier ones but considered the full picture and specific observations. Rather than accounting for all the nuance, I focused on the pieces that were relevant for explaining data science's emergence from what I had already considered and from what I had missed.

Sociological theory once again guided the overhaul. Beyond high-level references to Dewey and Pierce, which informed my initial pragmatism focus, I turned to Herbert Mead to better account for tensions around the selves of the early data hackers as they became data scientists. And to ensure a modern interpretation, I considered Hans Joas's focus on creativity and recent empirical studies. This led to a framework in which I separated "practical creativity" from "reflexive creativity." This division finally captured the unique challenges and dynamics around the problems data scientists faced in what they did as part of their roles and compared who they were.

The pragmatist lens also accounted for what data scientist presenters did on the stages of meetup events. It thereby moved the analysis beyond the personal experiences they presented to capture the process that unfolded through the collective events. The lens still missed the larger changes as part of which data science appeared on the scene. Turning to historical research, I retraced earlier instances of data science and reread the existing writing on the evolution of statistical thinking. This writing had been part of my initial preparation for the study, but original observations pushed it into the background. To integrate those ideas into the analysis, I complemented my firsthand observations by collecting documents through searches in digital databases that mentioned data science, as well as following up with debates from the last two decades that were referenced in conversations about data science.

The patterns I noted from the historical writing and the analysis of more recent documents led me to Karl Polanyi's idea of the double movement. Polanyi is better known as a theorist of economic processes. And a problem in economic sociology was where I first worked with his theoretical ideas. But data scientists emerged amid a larger commercial interest in quantitative analyses, thanks to the technological innovations that had made datasets more abundant and accessible.

This framework guided a new analysis of the historical background of data science. The processes Polanyi analyzed in the economy unfolded more slowly than what happened in any single meetup event or even the sequence I got to follow during my few years in the field. Whereas my initial review of that research had tried to learn about the origins of contemporary ideas, the double movement concept drew attention to social dynamics unfolding between the established scientific fields and countermovements, including the data hackers who flocked around the data science idea.

This application of Polanyi's theory for understanding the economy did not immediately map onto data science's formation. Unlike the market and social forces Polanyi discerned, the scholars, scientists, and hackers in data science constitute a much more isolated and selective community, even outside today's academic setting. However, it did draw my attention to a pattern that I had missed before: the stillborn countermovements of problem-oriented quantitative experts meeting the pushback of purist scholars throughout at least the past two hundred years of statistical thinking.

In addition to viewing the data science presentations in their historical context, I also integrated the technical issues they discussed into the analysis. The idea of a data science–of–data science analysis was part of the earliest conversations about the project. But while I was aware of sociological analyses of technical systems, I worried about the multiple challenges around qualitatively analyzing a quantitative analysis that I implemented myself to produce formal insights into the data science case. With the field observations now carrying the main empirical weight and a historically grounded theoretical framework, the reflexive large-scale data analysis became newly effective. In addition to providing a specific example of the tasks that are part of data science, this integration also returned to very early concerns with how different models and algorithms intervene in private, social, and economic life. This new version reanalyzed the job post study I had conducted previously from an outside perspective. Instead of only discerning the patterns it revealed from the job descriptions, I discerned how it had come about, offering a window into how the application of these devices creates intermediary objects that connect otherwise disparate hackers.

As a final refocusing strategy, I revisited the main field site, the meetup landscape, starting from my initial encounter. Since several data science meetup groups were already in place when I joined, I had too quickly taken them for granted. But they only began meeting shortly before this study started, and others still formed during the time of my data collection. A better understanding of what these events were sociologically and of what happened during those meetings allowed me to connect the observations of data scientists to the larger social processes surrounding them. I knew the story of the meetup.com founder, where New York City played a central role, and I knew of colleagues who had arrived at meetups for different research concerns. In this analytic overhaul, I reviewed the writing on meetups more systematically. I used those insights to go beyond the meetups I knew and view them as part of a larger process.

This step raised some new methodological questions. While the project had a clear starting point in my announcement to my doctoral thesis advisor and to the data science instructor, my first-ever meetup attendance predated that recognition. Yet, it also covered the same topics data science meetups would cover later and a future leader of the community of data scientists. These observations stretched even the abductive method's focus on broadening the perspective on immediate observations, since they were from outside of my formal data collection activities. They still had direct connections to the problem I studied, and the lack of strategy was beneficial for capturing the twists and turns of data science's emergence. The empirical problem required ana-lytical adjustments. This additional analytical step grounded this study in the situation the first data scientists faced, namely, one in which there was no data science.

These revisions added no new empirical observations. How-ever, the integration of those existing observations into the anal-ysis transformed the sociological insight that followed from the initial version. This phase leveraged the abductive methodology as it accounted for the emerging patterns, such as the connec-tion between historical developments, sociotechnical arrange-ments, gatherings, and public performances. At this point, the argument came together around the completion of the minute analyses of the previous phases and these contextualizations.

COMPLETION

The final stretch involved the writing of the manuscript. By this point, the notes, memos, spreadsheets, presentations, and discussions had helped me formulate a robust argument. The presentation of that argument in a manuscript still offered an opportunity for another set of analytical reflections. Like before, I continued to balance details from the field and the larger social context of data science's emergence, as well as my novel interpretations and the existing understanding of such processes. While the pieces were available, I now integrated them into a linear presentation. I still obtained feedback, which led me to swap chapters for a more coherent account. However, mostly, the final presentation helped me clip off details and nuances that I once considered important but that eventually obscured the explanation of data science's emergence.

NOTES

INTRODUCTION

1. Vindu Goel, "Facebook Tinkers with Users' Emotions in News Feed Experiment, Stirring Outcry," *New York Times*, June 29, 2014; Matthew Rosenberg, Nicholas Confessore, and Carole Cadwalladr, "How Trump Consultants Exploited the Facebook Data of Millions," *New York Times*, March 17, 2018.
2. Cathy O'Neil, *Weapons of Math Destruction: How Big Data Increases Inequality and Threatens Democracy* (Crown, 2016); Virginia Eubanks, *Automating Inequality: How High-Tech Tools Profile, Police, and Punish the Poor* (St. Martin's, 2018).
3. See, e.g., Paulina Restrepo-Echavarría and Maria A. Arias, "U.S., European Economies and the Great Recession," Federal Reserve Bank of St. Louis, April 21, 2017; Ferran Brunet, "The Great Recession and the American and European Economic Governance Challenges," *Europe en Formation* 360, no. 2 (2011): 59–78.
4. Christopher M. Kelty, *Two Bits: The Cultural Significance of Free Software* (Duke University Press, 2008); E. Gabriella Coleman, "Coding Freedom: The Ethics and Aesthetics of Hacking," (Princeton University Press, 2013); Aaron Swartz, *The Boy Who Could Change the World: The Writings of Aaron Swartz* (New Press, 2016).
5. Shoshana Zuboff, *The Age of Surveillance Capitalism: The Fight for a Human Future at the New Frontier of Power* (Profile, 2019); Safiya Umoja Noble, *Algorithms of Oppression: How Search Engines Reinforce*

Racism (New York University Press, 2018); Steve Lohr, *Data-Ism: The Revolution Transforming Decision Making, Consumer Behavior, and Almost Everything Else* (HarperCollins, 2015); Steffen Mau, *Das metrische Wir: Über die Quantifizierung des Sozialen* (Suhrkamp, 2017); Eubanks, *Automating Inequality*; O'Neil, *Weapons of Math Destruction*.

6. David Donoho, "Fifty Years of Data Science," paper presented at the Tukey Centennial workshop, Princeton, NJ, 2015; David Ribes, "STS, Meet Data Science, Once Again," *Science, Technology, & Human Values* 44, no. 3 (2019): 514–39; Sandra González-Bailón, *Decoding the Social World: Data Science and the Unintended Consequences of Communication* (MIT Press, 2017).

7. "Data science," https://en.wikipedia.org/wiki/Data_science.

8. Carl Shan, Henry Wang, William Chen, and Max Song, *The Data Science Handbook: Advice and Insights from 25 Amazing Data Scientists* (self-published, 2015); Jeff Hammerbacher, "Information Platforms and the Rise of the Data Scientist," in *Beautiful Data: The Stories Behind Elegant Data Solutions*, ed. Toby Segaran and Jeff Hammerbacher (O'Reilly Media, 2009); M. Loukides, *What Is Data Science?* (O'Reilly Media, 2011); Rachel Schutt and Cathy O'Neil, *Doing Data Science* (O'Reilly Media, 2013).

9. Katy Börner et al., "Skill Discrepancies Between Research, Education, and Jobs Reveal the Critical Need to Supply Soft Skills for the Data Economy," *Proceedings of the National Academy of Sciences* 115, no. 50 (2018): 12630–37; Netta Avnoon, "Data Scientists' Identity Work: Omnivorous Symbolic Boundaries in Skills Acquisition," *Work, Employment, and Society* 35, no. 2 (2021): 332–49; Robert Dorschel and Philipp Brandt, "Professionalization Via Ambiguity: The Discursive Construction of Data Scientists in Higher Education and the Labor Market," *Zeitschrift für Soziologie* 50, no. 3–4 (2021): 193–210; Ribes, "STS, Meet Data Science, Once Again."

10. Peter L. Berger and Thomas Luckmann, *The Social Construction of Reality: A Treatise in the Sociology of Knowledge* (Doubleday, 1966); Eviatar Zerubavel, *Social Mindscapes: An Invitation to Cognitive Sociology* (Harvard University Press, 1997).

11. Noortje Marres, *Digital Sociology: The Reinvention of Social Research* (Wiley, 2017); Avnoon, "Data Scientists' Identity Work"; Dorschel and

Bradt, "Professionalization Via Ambiguity"; Zuboff, *The Age of Surveillance Capitalism.*

12. Zeynep Tufekci, *Twitter and Tear Gas: The Power and Fragility of Networked Protest* (Yale University Press, 2017); O'Neil, *Weapons of Math Destruction*; Eubanks, *Automating Inequality*; Noble, *Algorithms of Oppression.*

13. Sarah Williams, *Data Action: Using Data for Public Good* (MIT Press, 2020); Gonzáles-Bailón, *Decoding the Social World.*

14. Matthew J. Salganik, *Bit by Bit: Social Research in the Digital Age* (Princeton University Press, 2018); Philipp Brandt, "Sociology's Stake in Data Science," *Sociologica* 16, no. 2 (2022): 149–66.

15. Andrew Abbott, *The System of Professions: An Essay on the Division of Expert Labor* (University of Chicago Press, 1988); Gil Eyal, "For a Sociology of Expertise: The Social Origins of the Autism Epidemic," *American Journal of Sociology* 118, no. 4 (2013): 863.

16. Eyal, "For a Sociology of Expertise," integrated a larger stream of research, including Harry M. Collins and Robert Evans, *Rethinking Expertise* (University of Chicago Press, 2007); Steven Epstein, *Impure Science: AIDS, Activism, and the Politics of Knowledge* (University of California Press, 1996); Thomas F. Gieryn, "Boundary-Work and the Demarcation of Science from Non-science: Strains and Interests in Professional Ideologies of Scientists," *American Sociological Review* 48, no. 6 (1983): 781–95; Susan Leigh Star, *Ecologies of Knowledge: Work and Politics in Science and Technology* (State University of New York Press, 1995); Bruno Latour, *Science in Action: How to Follow Scientists and Engineers Through Society* (Harvard University Press, 1987).

17. See Sida Liu, "Boundaries and Professions: Toward a Processual Theory of Action," *Journal of Professions and Organization* 5, no. 1 (2018): 45–57, for a comprehensive discussion. This literature has a long tradition that includes Magali Sarfatti Larson, *The Rise of Professionalism: A Sociological Analysis* (University of California Press, 1977); Eliot Freidson, *Profession of Medicine: A Study of the Sociology of Applied Knowledge* (University of Chicago Press, 1988); Eliot Freidson, *Professional Powers: A Study of the Institutionalization of Formal Knowledge* (University of Chicago Press, 1986); Eliot Freidson, *Professionalism Reborn: Theory, Prophecy, and Policy* (University of Chicago

Press, 1994); Eliot Freidson, *Professionalism: The Third Logic* (University of Chicago Press, 2001), even going back to E. C. Hughes, "Professions," *Daedalus* 92, no. 4 (1963): 655–68. Kevin T. Leicht and Mary L Fennell, "The Changing Organizational Context of Professional Work," *Annual Review of Sociology* 23, no. 1 (1997): 215–31; and Elizabeth H. Gorman and Rebecca L. Sandefur, "'Golden Age,' Quiescence, and Revival: How the Sociology of Professions Became the Study of Knowledge-Based Work," *Work and Occupations* 38, no. 3 (2011): 275–302, have offered comprehensive summaries of the debate's trajectory until the most recent turn.

18. William J. Goode, "Community Within a Community: The Professions," *American Sociological Review* 22, no. 2 (1957): 194–200; Harold L. Wilensky, "The Professionalization of Everyone," *American Journal of Sociology* 70, no. 2 (1964): 137–58; Hughes, "Professions."

19. Larson, *The Rise of Professionalism*; and Abbott, *The System of Professions*, were particularly explicit in this criticism.

20. Dietrich Rueschemeyer, *Lawyers and Their Society: A Comparative Study of the Legal Profession in Germany and in the United States* (Harvard University Press, 1973); Joseph Ben-David, *The Scientist's Role in Society: A Comparative Study* (Prentice Hall, 1971); Freidson, *Professional Powers*.

21. Rue Bucher and Anselm Strauss, "Professions in Process," *American Journal of Sociology* 66, no. 4 (1961): 325–34; Freidson, *Profession of Medicine*.

22. Freidson, *Profession of Medicine*.

23. Larson, *The Rise of Professionalism*, xvi–xvii.

24. Beth A. Bechky, "Object Lessons: Workplace Artifacts as Representations of Occupational Jurisdiction," *American Journal of Sociology* 109, no. 3 (2003): 720–52; Beth A. Bechky, "Sharing Meaning Across Occupational Communities: The Transformation of Understanding on a Production Floor," *Organization Science* 14, no. 3 (2003): 312–30; Daniel A. Menchik, "Decisions About Knowledge in Medical Practice: The Effect of Temporal Features of a Task," *American Journal of Sociology* 120, no. 3 (2014): 701–49; Rebecca L. Sandefur, "Elements of Professional Expertise: Understanding Relational and Substantive Expertise Through Lawyers' Impact," *American Sociological Review* 80,

no. 5 (2015): 909–33; Damon J. Phillips, Catherine J. Turco, and Ezra W. Zuckerman, "Betrayal as Market Barrier: Identity-Based Limits to Diversification Among High-Status Corporate Law Firms," *American Journal of Sociology* 118, no. 4 (2013): 1023–54; Wendy Nelson Espeland and Michael Sauder, "Rankings and Reactivity: How Public Measures Recreate Social Worlds," *American Journal of Sociology* 113, no. 1 (2007): 1–40.

25. Michael G. Pratt, Kevin W. Rockmann, and Jeffrey B. Kaufmann, "Constructing Professional Identity: The Role of Work and Identity Learning Cycles in the Customization of Identity Among Medical Residents," *Academy of Management Journal* 49, no. 2 (2006): 235–62; Herminia Ibarra, "Provisional Selves: Experimenting with Image and Identity in Professional Adaptation," *Administrative Science Quarterly* 44, no. 4 (1999): 764–91.

26. Brianna Barker Caza, and Stephanie Creary, "The Construction of Professional Identity," in *Perspectives on Contemporary Professional Work*, ed. A. Wilkinson, D. Hislop, and C. Coupland (Elgar, 2016), 259–85.

27. Léonie Hénaut, Jennifer C. Lena, and Fabien Accominotti, "Poly-occupationalism: Expertise Stretch and Status Stretch in the Postindustrial Era," *American Sociological Review* 88, no. 5 (2023): 872–900.

28. Thomas H. Davenport and D. J. Patil. "Data Scientist: The Sexiest Job of the 21st Century," *Harvard Business Review* 90, no. 10 (2012): 70–76; Hammerbacher, "Information Platforms"; Hilary Mason and Chris Wiggins, "A Taxonomy of Data Science," *dataists.com*, April 22, 2010, https://web.archive.org/web/20160220042455/dataists.com/2010/09/a-taxonomy-of-data-science/.

29. Abbott, *The System of Professions*, chap. 9, discovered a legal profession that had been forgotten.

30. Coleman, "Coding Freedom."

31. Theodore M. Porter, *The Rise of Statistical Thinking, 1820–1900* (Princeton University Press, 1986); Theodore M. Porter, *Trust in Numbers: The Pursuit of Objectivity in Science and Public Life* (Princeton University Press, 1995); Alain Desrosières, *The Politics of Large Numbers: A History of Statistical Reasoning* (Harvard University Press, 1998).

32. Joseph Ben-David, *The Scientist's Role in Society: A Comparative Study* (Prentice Hall, 1971); Robert K. Merton, "Science, Technology and Society in Seventeenth Century England," *Osiris* 4 (1938): 360–632.

33. Steven Shapin, *The Scientific Life: A Moral History of a Late Modern Vocation* (University of Chicago Press, 2008).

34. Ben-David, *The Scientist's Role in Society*.

35. Michael Park, Erin Leahey, and Russell J. Funk, "Papers and Patents Are Becoming Less Disruptive Over Time," *Nature* 613, no. 7942 (2023): 138–44.

36. Henry M. Cowles, *The Scientific Method* (Harvard University Press, 2020).

37. Though not the "gentlemen" scientists in Steven Shapin, "'A Scholar and a Gentleman': The Problematic Identity of the Scientific Practitioner in Early Modern England," *History of Science* 29, no. 3 (1991): 279–327.

38. Desrosières, *The Politics of Large Numbers*, 63, citing Robin L. Plackett, "Studies in the History of Probability and Statistics. XXIX: The Discovery of the Method of Least Squares," *Biometrika* 59, no. 2 (1972): 239–51.

39. Francis Galton, "Kinship and Correlation," *North American Review* 150, no. 401 (1890): 421.

40. See Philipp Brandt and Stefan Timmermans, "Abductive Logic of Inquiry for Quantitative Research in the Digital Age," *Sociological Science* 8 (2021): 191–210; and Iddo Tavory and Stefan Timmermans, *Abductive Analysis: Theorizing Qualitative Research* (University of Chicago Press, 2014), for discussions of this problem in quantitative and qualitative research and reviews of different arguments.

41. Tavory and Timmermans, *Abductive Analysis*, 4.

42. Tavory and Timmermans, *Abductive Analysis*, 54.

43. Tavory and Timmermans propose three "movements," mnemonics, defamiliarization, and revisiting observations (2014). I focus on the second one here because it best describes the gist of their recommendations.

44. Chris Wiggins and Matthew L. Jones, *How Data Happened: A History from the Age of Reason to the Age of Algorithms* (Norton, 2023);

González-Bailón, *Decoding the Social World*; Donoho, "50 Years"; Kelty, *Two Bits*; Coleman, *Coding Freedom*.

45. Tavory and Timmermans, *Abductive Analysis*, 61.

46. Diane Vaughan, "NASA Revisited: Theory, Analogy, and Public Sociology," *American Journal of Sociology* 112, no. 2 (2006): 353–93.

47. Tavory and Timmermans, *Abductive Analysis*, 62.

48. This argument integrates sociology's two foundational concerns with structure and action. For discipline, on the structural side, I draw on Harrison C. White, *Identity and Control: How Social Formations Emerge*, 2nd. ed. (Princeton University Press, 2008). Agency comes from pragmatism; see John Dewey, *Human Nature and Conduct* (Modern Library, 1922); together with Joas's interpretation in terms of creativity. Hans Joas, *Die Kreativität des Handelns* (Suhrkamp, 1992). On reflexivity, see also Margaret S. Archer, *Making Our Way Through the World: Human Reflexivity and Social Mobility* (Cambridge University Press, 2007).

49. https://economicgraph.linkedin.com/research/LinkedIns-2017-US -Emerging-Jobs-Report; https://www.kaggle.com/surveys/2017.

1. ENCOUNTERS

1. Thomas H. Davenport and DJ Patil, "Data Scientist: The Sexiest Job of the 21st Century," *Harvard Business Review* 90, no. 10 (2012): 72.

2. Venn diagram: http://drewconway.com/zia/2013/3/26/the-data-science -venn-diagram; tweet: https://twitter.com/josh_wills/status/198093512 149958656?lang=en.

3. See, for example, Cathy O'Neil, *Weapons of Math Destruction: How Big Data Increases Inequality and Threatens Democracy* (Crown, 2016); Matthew J. Salganik, *Bit by Bit: Social Research in the Digital Age* (Princeton University Press, 2018).

4. This statement refers to the focal period of the late 2000s and early 2010s. The idea of data science appeared in print already in the 1990s, as chapter 3 will discuss in detail.

5. Jeff Hammerbacher, "Information Platforms and the Rise of the Data Scientist," in *Beautiful Data: The Stories Behind Elegant Data Solutions*, ed. Toby Segaran and Jeff Hammerbacher: (O'Reilly Media, 2009): 83–4.

6. Hammerbacher, "Information Platforms," 77.

7. Davenport and Patil, "Data Scientist," 71.

8. Both Hammerbacher's Facebook and Patil's LinkedIn have done well in the meantime, and even then Hammerbacher observed that "three teams working with three separate technology stacks have evolved similar platforms for processing large amounts of data." Hammerbacher, "Information Platforms," 92.

9. This framing suggests links to Michel Foucault's idea of strategy without strategists; see Michel Foucault and François Ewald, *Dispositive der Macht: Über Sexualität, Wissen und Wahrheit* (Merve Verlag, 1978), 132.

10. I am using the instructor's real name because she has published about the class together with her coinstructor: Rachel Schutt and Cathy O'Neil, *Doing Data Science* (O'Reilly Media, 2013).

11. Those were Francis Galton's words, which I first discussed in the introduction when I introduced the abductive method; Francis Galton, "Kinship and Correlation," *North American Review* 150, no. 401 (1890): 421.

12. This kind of conflict is a central idea in Andrew Abbott, *The System of Professions: An Essay on the Division of Expert Labor* (University of Chicago Press, 1988).

13. The literature mainly building on Abbott, *The System of Professions*, and which Elizabeth H. Gorman and Rebecca L. Sandefur, "'Golden Age,' Quiescence, and Revival: How the Sociology of Professions Became the Study of Knowledge-Based Work," *Work and Occupations* 38, no. 3 (2011): 275–302; and Sida Liu, "Boundaries and Professions: Toward a Processual Theory of Action," *Journal of Professions and Organization* 5, no. 1 (2018): 45–57, have summarized.

14. The literature Eyal integrated into a framework focused on the informal side of expertise, here, with a focus on the interplay of experts and their techniques. Gil Eyal, "For a Sociology of Expertise: The Social Origins of the Autism Epidemic," *American Journal of Sociology* 118, no. 4 (2013): 863–907; Harry M. Collins, "The Meaning of Data: Open and Closed Evidential Cultures in the Search for Gravitational Waves," *American Journal of Sociology* 104, no. 2 (1998): 293–338.

15. Iddo Tavory and Stefan Timmermans, "A Pragmatist Approach to Causality in Ethnography," *American Journal of Sociology* 119, no. 3 (2013): 682–714.

16. Iddo Tavory and Stefan Timmermans, *Abductive Analysis: Theorizing Qualitative Research* (Chicago: University of Chicago Press, 2014), 58–61.

17. That was at the time of my observations and with respect to the literature that could guide my incipient research endeavors. A few scholars have since turned to considering meetups as professional spaces: Netta Avnoon, "The Gates to the Profession Are Open: The Alternative Institutionalization of Data Science," *Theory and Society* 53, no. 2 (2024): 239–71; Daniel DellaPosta and Victor Nee, "Emergence of Diverse and Specialized Knowledge in a Metropolitan Tech Cluster," *Social Science Research* 86 (2020): 102377.

18. Libby Schweber, *Disciplining Statistics: Demography and Vital Statistics in France and England, 1830–1885* (Duke University Press, 2006).

19. E. Gabriella Coleman, *Coding Freedom: The Ethics and Aesthetics of Hacking* (Princeton University Press, 2013); Christopher M. Kelty, *Two Bits: The Cultural Significance of Free Software* (Duke University Press, 2008).

20. Timmermans and Tavory, *Abductive Analysis*, 54–58.

21. Monika Krause, "On Sociological Reflexivity," *Sociological Theory* 39, no. 1 (2021): 3–18.

22. Adrianne Jeffries, "The Long and Curious History of Meetup.com," *Observer*, January 2011, https://observer.com/2011/01/the-long-and-curious-history-of-meetupcom/; Max Nisen, "The Unusual Career Path of Meetup CEO Scott Heiferman," *Business Insider*, June 2013, https://www.businessinsider.fr/us/scott-heiferman-startup-career-history-2013-6.

23. Robert Putnam, "Bowling Alone," *Journal of Democracy* 6, no. 1 (1995): 65–78; Robert Putnam, *Bowling Alone: The Collapse and Revival of American Community* (Simon & Schuster, 2000).

24. Bruce D. Weinberg and Christine B. Williams, "The 2004 US Presidential Campaign: Impact of Hybrid Offline and Online 'Meetup' Communities," *Journal of Direct, Data and Digital Marketing Practice* 8 (2006): 46–57.

25. Ayan Kumar Bhowmick, Soumajit Pramanik, Sayan Pathak, and Bivas Mitra, "On the Splitting Dynamics of Meetup Social Groups," paper presented at the Proceedings of the International AAAI Conference on Web and Social Media, 2020; DellaPosta and Nee, "Emergence of Diverse and Specialized Knowledge."

26. Many have questioned Putnam's analysis and thus his conclusions, implying he hadn't uncovered a problem that needed fixing, which is not to say that there were no problems that did. See Alejandro Portes, "Social Capital: Its Origins and Applications in Modern Sociology," *Annual Review of Sociology* 24 (1998); Byungkyu Lee and Peter Bearman, "Important Matters in Political Context," *Sociological Science* 4 (2017): 1–30.

27. Jiawei Chen, Xiying Wang, Jordan Beck, Chuqing Wu, and John M. Carroll, "Beyond Leaders and Followers: Understanding Participation Dynamics in Event-Based Social Networks," *International Journal of Human–Computer Interaction* 35, no. 20 (2019): 1892–905.

28. Chen et al., "Beyond Leaders and Followers"; Stephen Ricken, Louise Barkhuus, and Quentin Jones, "Going Online to Meet Offline: Organizational Practices of Social Activities Through Meetup," paper presented at the Proceedings of the 8th International Conference on Communities and Technologies, 2017.

29. Chen et al., "Beyond Leaders and Followers," 1898–99.

30. Chen et al., "Beyond Leaders and Followers," 1897.

31. DellaPosta and Nee, "Emergence of Diverse and Specialized Knowledge."

32. Chicago (7,718), New York (23,270), and San Francisco (17,647).

33. Bhowmick et al., "On the Splitting Dynamics."

34. Soumajit Pramanik, Midhun Gundapuneni, Sayan Pathak, and Bivas Mitra, "Can I Foresee the Success of My Meetup Group?," paper presented at the 2016 IEEE/ACM International Conference on Advances in Social Networks Analysis and Mining (ASONAM), 2016.

35. Eliot Freidson, *Professional Powers: A Study of the Institutionalization of Formal Knowledge* (University of Chicago Press, 1986); Eliot Freidson, *Professionalism: The Third Logic* (University of Chicago Press, 2001).

36. William J. Goode, "Community Within a Community: The Professions," *American Sociological Review* 22, no. 2 (1957): 194–200.

37. Beth A. Bechky, "Sharing Meaning Across Occupational Communities: The Transformation of Understanding on a Production Floor," *Organization Science* 14, no. 3 (2003): 312–30; Gil Eyal, "For a Sociology of Expertise: The Social Origins of the Autism Epidemic," *American Journal of Sociology* 118, no. 4 (2013): 863–907; Mirko Noordegraaf, "Hybrid Professionalism and Beyond: (New) Forms of Public Professionalism in Changing Organizational and Societal Contexts," *Journal of Professions and Organization* 2, no. 2 (2015): 187–206; Magali Sarfatti Larson, *The Rise of Professionalism: A Sociological Analysis* (University of California Press, 1977); Eliot Freidson, *Profession of Medicine: A Study of the Sociology of Applied Knowledge* (University of Chicago Press, 1988); Abbott, *The System of Professions*.

38. Paul DiMaggio and Walter Powell, "The Iron Cage Revisited: Institutional Isomorphism and Collective Rationality in Organizational Fields," *American Sociological Review* 48, no. 2 (1983): 147–60; Peter L. Berger and Thomas Luckmann, *The Social Construction of Reality: A Treatise in the Sociology of Knowledge* (Doubleday, 1966).

39. James Samuel Coleman, *Foundations of Social Theory* (Belknap Press of Harvard University Press, 1990).

40. Mark S. Granovetter, *Getting a Job: A Study of Contacts and Careers*, 2nd ed. (University of Chicago Press, 1995); Ronald S. Burt, *Brokerage and Closure: An Introduction to Social Capital* (Oxford University Press, 2005); Matthew Desmond, "Disposable Ties and the Urban Poor," *American Journal of Sociology* 117, no. 5 (2012): 1295–335.

41. Everyday group events are embedded in layers of institutions and social structures. William H. Sewell, "A Theory of Structure: Duality, Agency, and Transformation," *American Journal of Sociology* 98, no. 1 (1992): 1–29.

42. E.g., Roger V. Gould, *Insurgent Identities: Class, Community, and Protest in Paris from 1848 to the Commune* (University of Chicago Press, 1995); Forrest Briscoe and Sean Safford, "The Nixon-in-China Effect: Activism, Imitation, and the Institutionalization of Contentious Practices," *Administrative Science Quarterly* 53, no. 3 (2008): 460–91; Emmanuel Lazega, "Networks and Institutionalization: A

Neo-Structural Approach," *Connections* 37, no. 1–2 (2018): 7–22; Emily Erikson and Mark Hamilton, "Companies and the Rise of Economic Thought: The Institutional Foundations of Early Economics in England, 1550–1720," *American Journal of Sociology* 124, no. 1 (2018): 111–49.

43. E.g., see Scott Frickel and Neil Gross, "A General Theory of Scientific/Intellectual Movements," *American Sociological Review* 70, no. 2 (2005): 204–32.

44. E.g., Emily Erikson and Peter Bearman, "Malfeasance and the Foundations for Global Trade: The Structure of English Trade in the East Indies, 1601–1833," *American Journal of Sociology* 112, no. 1 (2006): 195–230; Ivan Ermakoff, "The Structure of Contingency," *American Journal of Sociology* 121, no. 1 (2015): 64–125.

45. Alexis de Tocqueville, *Democracy in America* (1840), ed. Eduardo Nolla, trans. James T. Schleifer, 2 vols. (Liberty Fund, 2012), 979.

46. Tocqueville, *Democracy in America*, 979.

47. We can think of this comparison of the early United States from Tocqueville's perspective and data science as an instance of Vaughan's analogical theorizing or Krause's call for considering the "larger diversity in the world." Diane Vaughan, "NASA Revisited: Theory, Analogy, and Public Sociology," *American Journal of Sociology* 112, no. 2 (2006): 353–93; Diana Vaughan, "Theorizing Disaster: Analogy, Historical Ethnography, and the *Challenger* Accident," *Ethnography* 5, no. 3 (2004): 315–47; Monika Krause, "On Sociological Reflexivity," *Sociological Theory* 39, no. 1 (2021): 3–18.

48. This observation moves away from the Tocquevillian argument, which was about voluntary groups and democracy as customs. It connects those insights to the everyday appearance of democracy, more tied to the constitutional implementation, not the philosophy or theory.

49. Another productive analogy would be to collective movements in the sense of Marwell and Oliver's *Critical Mass in Collective Action*, especially the discussion of how group leaders secure involvement. However, such a perspective requires adjustments, as the meetup attendees are mostly organizing to overcome uncertainty and isolation rather than to pursue a common cause, which is the focus in Marwell and Oliver. Gerald Marwell and Pamela Oliver, *The Critical Mass in Collective Action* (Cambridge University Press, 1993), 89.

50. AnnaLee Saxenian, *Regional Advantage: Culture and Competition in Silicon Valley and Route 128* (Harvard University Press, 1996).

51. Based on Pramanik et al., close to the time of my observations, and population counts from Google for 2016, 17180/8469000=.002 for New York and 13381/871000=.015 for San Francisco; Pramanik et al., "Can I Foresee the Success."

52. DellaPosta and Nee, "Emergence of Diverse and Specialized Knowledge," 2.

53. The uniqueness is a limitation from a perspective that seeks general explanations. But no general explanation is likely to account for the mechanisms unfolding in San Francisco and in New York or in other places where data science formed. New York as a place is also large enough to make the mechanisms that unfolded there relevant for understanding data science broadly.

54. Tellingly, one of them became a data scientist and the other a professor of sociology.

55. My initial technical exercises induced enough momentum into this project to lead to a publication once more competent colleagues added their expertise: Mark Anthony Hoffman, Jean-Philippe Cointet, Philipp Brandt, Newton Key, and Peter Bearman, "The (Protestant) Bible, the (Printed) Sermon, and the Word(s): The Semantic Structure of the Conformist and Dissenting Bible, 1660–1780," *Poetics* 68 (2018): 89–103.

56. The work only appeared publicly in oral form in Alix Rule and Philipp Brandt, "Dynamic Art Objects: The Evolving Structural Composition of the Global Art Scene," SUNBELT International Social Networks Research Association Conference, Hamburg, Germany, 2013; For a more sophisticated version, see Alix Rule, Zhongyu Wang, Rupayan Basu, et al., "Using Simple NLP Tools to Trace the Globalization of the Art World," *Proceedings of the ACL 2014 Workshop on Language Technologies and Computational Social Science* (Baltimore, 2014), 66–70.

57. Hammerbacher, "Data Scientist," 84, 83.

58. Harold Garfinkel, "The Rational Properties of Scientific and Common Sense Activities," *Behavioral Science* 5, no. 1 (1960): 72.

59. Abbott, *The System of Professions*, 281.

2. THE WORK

1. Lauren A. Rivera, *Pedigree: How Elite Students Get Elite Jobs* (Princeton University Press, 2015); Kim A. Weeden, "Why Do Some Occupations Pay More Than Others? Social Closure and Earnings Inequality in the United States," *American Journal of Sociology* 108, no. 1 (2002): 55–101; Siwei Cheng and Barum Park, "Flows and Boundaries: A Network Approach to Studying Occupational Mobility in the Labor Market," *American Journal of Sociology* 126, no. 3 (2020): 577–631.

2. Thomas H. Davenport and DJ Patil, "Data Scientist: The Sexiest Job of the 21st Century," *Harvard Business Review* 90, no. 10 (2012): 70–76; James Manyika, Michael Chui, Brad Brown, Jaques Bughin, Richard Dobbs, Charles Roxburgh, and Angela Hung Byers, *Big Data: The Next Frontier for Innovation, Competition, and Productivity* (McKinsey Global Institute, 2011).

3. Bruno Latour and Steve Woolgar, *Laboratory Life: The Construction of Scientific Facts* (Princeton University Press, 1986).

4. Harry Collins, *Gravity's Ghost: Scientific Discovery in the Twenty-First Century* (University of Chicago Press, 2011); Beth A. Bechky, "Object Lessons: Workplace Artifacts as Representations of Occupational Jurisdiction," *American Journal of Sociology* 109, no. 3 (2003): 720–52; Daniel Beunza and David Stark, "Tools of the Trade: The Socio-Technology of Arbitrage in a Wall Street Trading Room," *Industrial and Corporate Change* 13, no. 2 (2004): 369–400; Donald MacKenzie, "Material Signals: A Historical Sociology of High-Frequency Trading," *American Journal of Sociology* 123, no. 6 (2018): 1635–83; Donald MacKenzie, "Statistical Theory and Social Interests a Case-Study," *Social Studies of Science* 8, no. 1 (1978): 35–83.

5. Josh Whitford and Francesco Zirpoli, "Pragmatism, Practice, and the Boundaries of Organization," *Organization Science* 25, no. 6 (2014): 1823–39; David Stark, *The Sense of Dissonance: Accounts of Worth in Economic Life* (Princeton University Press, 2009); Hila Lifshitz-Assaf, "Dismantling Knowledge Boundaries at NASA: The Critical Role of Professional Identity in Open Innovation," *Administrative Science Quarterly* 63, no. 4 (2018): 746–82.

6. John Dewey, *Logic: The Theory of Inquiry* (Henry Holt, 1938), 105.

7. Technical readers will find many sections rudimentary and maybe even discover mistakes or opportunities for better solutions. But they may still be able to develop a new perspective on their technical expertise from the way that this chapter discusses its application.

8. Emmanuelle Marchal, Kevin Mellet, and Géraldine Rieucau, "Job Board Toolkits: Internet Matchmaking and Changes in Job Advertisements." *Human Relations* 60, no. 7 (2007): 1091–113; David H. Autor, "Wiring the Labor Market." *Journal of Economic Perspectives* 15, no. 1 (2001): 25–40.

9. Website operators also typically dislike the idea of scrapers extracting their content and taking away capacities from actual users.

10. There is more technological infrastructure necessary for making Python work, but that's beyond the scope of this book.

11. I implemented an automated extraction solution for a different problem, where I ran my code in the cloud and saved tweets for over a year. Job posts were less continuous than tweets and didn't need such a solution.

12. Not all of these dots appear data scientist positions. I collected posts for other positions for analytic leverage, as I will explain. The data scientist positions were still concentrated on the coasts at this time.

13. This data structure is also much more efficient for storage. The few job ads I wanted to see would have easily fit in a spreadsheet, but LinkedIn's database needed to save resources. It could also easily accommodate varying types of information.

14. This number only refers to queries on LinkedIn, which was not the most popular website but was one with good coverage and data access. The aim was not an accurate statistic of the total labor market size, which industry reports had already provided.

15. Any coder will know the forum stackoverflow.com, which has an effective system for collecting and curating questions and organizing answers by their utility for users who left a vote.

16. E.g., Alix Rule, Jean-Philippe Cointet, and Peter S. Bearman, "Lexical Shifts, Substantive Changes, and Continuity in State of the Union Discourse, 1790–2014," *Proceedings of the National Academy of Sciences* 112, no. 35 (2015): 10837–44; Laura K. Nelson, "Computational Grounded Theory: A Methodological Framework," *Sociological*

Methods & Research 49, no. 1 (2020): 3–42; Alina Arseniev-Koehler, "Theoretical Foundations and Limits of Word Embeddings: What Types of Meaning Can They Capture?," *Sociological Methods & Research* 53, no. 4 (2022): 1753–93; Justin Grimmer, Margaret E. Roberts, and Brandon M. Stewart, *Text as Data: A New Framework for Machine Learning and the Social Sciences* (Princeton University Press, 2022).

17. Some pioneers had thought carefully about extracting social relations from written records, but they had strategically chosen reports and documents that captured the social world's rich ambiguities to discern them analytically: Roberto Franzosi, "From Words to Numbers: A Generalized and Linguistics-Based Coding Procedure for Collecting Textual Data," *Sociological Methodology* 19 (1989): 263–98; John W. Mohr, "Soldiers, Mothers, Tramps and Others: Discourse Roles in the 1907 New York City Charity Directory," *Poetics* 22, no. 4 (1994): 327–57; Peter S. Bearman and Katherine Stovel, "Becoming a Nazi: A Model for Narrative Networks," *Poetics* 27, no. 2–3 (2000): 69–90; David R. Gibson, "Taking Turns and Talking Ties: Networks and Conversational Interaction," *American Journal of Sociology* 110, no. 6 (2005): 1561–97.

18. Sinan Aral and Marshall Van Alstyne, "The Diversity-Bandwidth Trade-Off," *American Journal of Sociology* 117, no. 1 (2011): 90–171.

19. Echoing the emerging community of data scientists with their different backgrounds, the two scholars were an information scientist and an economist who had published in a sociology journal.

20. A century ago, for example, some saw that the frequency of words in a language follows a pattern, now known as Zipf's Law.

21. Around the time of their research, a sophisticated method for identifying topics in large corpora of texts appeared in the community, which spread in the years after they had published their article. I would go on and implement these more sophisticated techniques as well, but the cryptic style of job posts undermined this technique's promise. David M. Blei and John D. Lafferty, "Topic Models," in *Text Mining* (Chapman and Hall/CRC, 2009), 101–24; John W. Mohr and Petko Bogdanov, "Introduction—Topic Models: What They Are and Why They Matter," *Poetics* 41, no. 6 (2013): 545–69.

22. Aral and Van Alstyne, "The Diversity-Bandwidth Trade-Off," 122.

23. They used the unsupervised machine learning technique of *k*-means clustering to sort emails into groups. The job postings analysis didn't require this step because the job titles defined the topics.

24. The technical names of these measures are the "coefficient of variation of the mean frequencies of [a] keyword" and the "intratopic frequency of [a] keyword." Aral and Van Alstyne, "The Diversity-Bandwidth Trade-Off," 122.

25. Monika Krause, "On Sociological Reflexivity," *Sociological Theory* 39, no. 1 (2021): 3–18.

26. Arthur L. Stinchcombe, *Theoretical Methods in Social History* (Academic Press, 1978), chap. 2.

27. John P. Heinz and Edward O. Laumann, *Chicago Lawyers: The Social Structure of the Bar* (Russell Sage Foundation/American Bar Foundation, 1982); John P. Heinz, *Urban Lawyers: The New Social Structure of the Bar* (University of Chicago Press, 2005); Damon J. Phillips, Catherine J. Turco, and Ezra W. Zuckerman, "Betrayal as Market Barrier: Identity-Based Limits to Diversification Among High-Status Corporate Law Firms," *American Journal of Sociology* 118, no. 4 (2013): 1023–54; Wendy Nelson Espeland and Michael Sauder, "Rankings and Reactivity: How Public Measures Recreate Social Worlds," *American Journal of Sociology* 113, no. 1 (2007): 1–40; Michael Sauder and Wendy Nelson Espeland, "The Discipline of Rankings: Tight Coupling and Organizational Change," *American Sociological Review* 74, no. 1 (2009): 63–82; Rebecca L. Sandefur, "Elements of Professional Expertise: Understanding Relational and Substantive Expertise Through Lawyers' Impact," *American Sociological Review* 80, no. 5 (2015): 909–33.

28. E.g., Steven P. Vallas, "The Concept of Skill—a Critical Review," *Work and Occupations* 17, no. 4 (1990): 379–98; Robin Fincham, "Knowledge Work as Occupational Strategy: Comparing IT and Management Consulting," *New Technology, Work and Employment* 21, no. 1 (2006): 16–28; Daniel Muzio, Stephen Ackroyd, and J. Chanlat, "Introduction: Lawyers, Doctors and Business Consultants," in *Redirections in the Study of Expert Labour: Established Professions and New Expert Occupations*, ed. Daniel Muzio, Stephen Ackroyd, and J. Chanlat (Palgrave Macmillan, 2008).

29. Philip Kraft, *Programmers and Managers: The Routinization of Computer Programming in the United States* (Springer-Verlag, 1977); Elizabeth H. Gorman and Rebecca L. Sandefur, "'Golden Age,' Quiescence, and Revival: How the Sociology of Professions Became the Study of Knowledge-Based Work," *Work and Occupations* 38, no. 3 (2011): 275–302; Muzio, Ackroyd, and Chanlat, "Introduction: Lawyers, Doctors and Business Consultants."

30. Kraft, *Programmers and Managers*.

31. Attorneys may show slightly more fragmentation than expected, with classifier iterations only capturing 80 percent of the job descriptions in the test samples. This variability most likely results from law's institutional status, which makes it easy for job descriptions to leave out words that others use without making job seekers less likely to recognize them as attorney job posts. The results for risk analyst positions also indicate less coherent overlap, with iterations extracting skills that are representative of only about 70 percent of the remaining descriptions. This variation reflects the reliance on standardized methods in risk analysis as well as its institutional status as a finance function, two features that undermine the need for detailed descriptions.

32. Andrew Abbott, *The System of Professions: An Essay on the Division of Expert Labor* (University of Chicago Press, 1988); Gil Eyal, "For a Sociology of Expertise: The Social Origins of the Autism Epidemic," *American Journal of Sociology* 118, no. 4 (2013): 863–907; Eliot Freidson, *Professionalism: The Third Logic* (University of Chicago Press, 2001).

33. I tried to get some handle on that problem by disproportionately retrieving older posts.

34. Blei and Lafferty, "Topic Models"; James A. Evans, "Industry Induces Academic Science to Know Less About More," *American Journal of Sociology* 116, no. 2 (2010): 389–452; Jacob G. Foster, Andrey Rzhetsky, and James A. Evans, "Tradition and Innovation in Scientists' Research Strategies," *American Sociological Review* 80, no. 5 (2015): 875–908; Uri Shwed and Peter S. Bearman, "The Temporal Structure of Scientific Consensus Formation," *American Sociological Review* 75, no. 6 (2010): 817–40.

35. The main focus is on centralized and decentralized structures; Shwed and Bearman have recovered even more specific temporal patterns.

One branch of research has shown the intricacies of highly specialized knowledge, including in scientific disciplines. In contrast, technical expertise that fits with different types of problems, such as in legal expertise. Abbott, *The System of Professions*; Delia Baldassarri and Mario Diani, "The Integrative Power of Civic Networks," *American Journal of Sociology* 113, no. 3 (2007): 735–80; Albert-Laszlo Barabasi, Hawoong Jeong, Zoltan Néda, Erzsebet Ravasz, Andras Schubert, and Tamas Vicsek, "Evolution of the Social Network of Scientific Collaborations," *Physica A: Statistical Mechanics and Its Applications* 311, no. 3–4 (2002): 590–614; James Moody, "The Structure of a Social Science Collaboration Network: Disciplinary Cohesion from 1963 to 1999," *American Sociological Review* 69, no. 2 (2004): 213–38; Shwed and Bearman, "The Temporal Structure of Scientific Consensus Formation"; Arthur L. Stinchcombe, *When Formality Works: Authority and Abstraction in Law and Organizations* (University of Chicago Press, 2001).

36. Technically, I first create a bipartite network with job positions and skills as two types of nodes. I project this network on the level of job positions, such that two positions have a tie between them if they share one or more skills. Ronald L. Breiger, "The Duality of Persons and Groups," *Social Forces* 53, no. 2 (1974): 181–90; Sophie Mützel and Ronald Breiger, "Duality Beyond Persons and Groups," in *The Oxford Handbook of Social Networks* (Oxford University Press, 2020), 392. A sliding window filter accounts for temporal changes in relevant skill combinations by dropping older ones as time passes. Gueorgi Kossinets and Duncan J. Watts, "Origins of Homophily in an Evolving Social Network," *American Journal of Sociology* 115, no. 2 (2009): 405–50. I then estimate the Newman modularity of the network to infer underlying fragmentation into subsets of positions that ask for similar skills. M. E. J. Newman and M. Girvan, "Finding and Evaluating Community Structure in Networks," *Phys. Rev. E* 69, no. 2 (2004): 026113. This community detection strategy reveals fragmentation as the basis for considering specializations and their overlaps and thus the kind of expertise that combines them. Daniel Navon and Uri Shwed, "The Chromosome 22q11.2 Deletion: From the Unification of Biomedical Fields to a New Kind of Genetic Condition." *Social Science &*

Medicine 75, no. 9 (2012): 1633–41. I consider the pattern of tie (skill) densities in professional specializations and overlaps between specializations, revealed by the modularity estimation, as a formal model of professional expertise. Integrative expertise combines skills that apply to distinct specializations. In contrast, universal overlap indicates generally shared skills and expertise to which specific problems can be added as they arise. The results section discusses the interpretation of these models.

37. This implementation was inspired by White, Boorman and Breiger's strategy for networks of social relations. Harrison White, Scott Boorman, and Ronald Breiger, "Social Structure from Multiple Networks. I. Blockmodels of Roles and Positions," *American Journal of Sociology* 81, no. 4 (1976): 730–80.

38. The raw matrix indicates extreme fragmentation. Both images lead to the same conclusions as they fail to signal integration.

39. AnnaLee Saxenian, *Regional Advantage: Culture and Competition in Silicon Valley and Route 128* (Harvard University Press, 1996).

40. The previous analysis has shown that computer engineering is so specialized that there's no representation in shared words in job posts, and I will exclude this case. I excluded risk analyst positions from this discussion, since the classifier didn't work quite as well for them. The classifier still worked much better than it did for software engineers, and the results were consistent with the reported pattern. The images for risk analyst positions resemble those of financial advisors, except for an outlier specialization of risk analyst positions that slightly distorts their uniformly specialized image without suggesting integration.

41. This figure only shows the most recent period, since these were no emergent roles and the images were stable for earlier years.

42. I followed Stinchcombe's thinking on theory construction. Stinchcombe, *Theoretical Methods*, chap. 2.

3. SCIENCE AND DATA

1. The clearest version of this critique appeared in David Donoho, "50 Years of Data Science," read at the Tukey Centennial workshop, Princeton, NJ.

2. E.g., Peter S. Bearman, *Relations Into Rhetorics: Local Elite Structure in Norfolk, England, 1540–1640* (Rutgers University Press, 1993); Emily Erikson, *Between Monopoly and Free Trade: The English East India Company, 1600–1757* (Princeton University Press, 2014); Ivan Ermakoff, *Ruling Oneself Out: A Theory of Collective Abdications* (Duke University Press, 2008); Ivan Ermakoff, "The Structure of Contingency," *American Journal of Sociology* 121, no. 1 (2015): 64–125; Roger V. Gould, *Insurgent Identities: Class, Community, and Protest in Paris from 1848 to the Commune* (University of Chicago Press, 1995); Peter Hedström, Rickard Sandell, and Charlotta Stern, "Mesolevel Networks and the Diffusion of Social Movements: The Case of the Swedish Social Democratic Party," *American Journal of Sociology* 106, no. 1 (2000): 145–72; Henning Hillmann, *The Corsairs of Saint-Malo: Network Organization of a Merchant Elite Under the Ancien Régime* (Columbia University Press, 2021).

3. This discussion moves on from the simple question of whether statisticians felt they had received adequate recognition from data scientists.

4. Abbott used this duality as an analytical setup for all learned professions. It is also implicit in studies that consider the tensions and relations between experts and lay outsiders: Andrew Abbott, "Status and Status Strain in the Professions," *American Journal of Sociology* 86, no. 4 (1981): 819–35; Gil Eyal, "For a Sociology of Expertise: The Social Origins of the Autism Epidemic," *American Journal of Sociology* 118, no. 4 (2013): 863–907; Thomas F. Gieryn, "Boundary-Work and the Demarcation of Science from Non-Science: Strains and Interests in Professional Ideologies of Scientists," *American Sociological Review* 48, no. 6 (1983): 781–95; Brian Wynne, "Misunderstood Misunderstanding: Social Identities and Public Uptake of Science," *Public Understanding of Science* 1, no. 3 (1992): 281–304.

5. D. DellaPosta, Y. Shi, and M. Macy, "Why Do Liberals Drink Lattes?," *American Journal of Sociology* 120, no. 5 (2015): 1473–511.

6. E.g., Harry M. Collins, "The Meaning of Data: Open and Closed Evidential Cultures in the Search for Gravitational Waves," *American Journal of Sociology* 104, no. 2 (1998): 293–338.

7. Ambiguities in sciences have spurred much scientific inquiry that have shown the inventiveness of scientists signaling rigor with gentleman

status or abstract formulas used not for insight but rhetoric. Here, it complicates the naive idea that data science follows from or relates to sciences in a clear way, since one is new and the other is old. Deirdre N. McCloskey, *The Rhetoric of Economics* (University of Wisconsin Press, 1998); Steven Shapin, "'A Scholar and a Gentleman': The Problematic Identity of the Scientific Practitioner in Early Modern England," *History of Science* 29, no. 3 (1991): 279–327.

8. Donoho was the most vocal response; Donoho, "50 Years."

9. Joseph Ben-David, *The Scientist's Role in Society: A Comparative Study* (Prentice Hall, 1971), chap. 3.

10. Ben-David, *The Scientist's Role in Society*, chap. 2.

11. Philipp Brandt and Sean Safford, "La globalisation à la croisée des stratégies organisationnelles et des institutions nationales," In *La société des organisations*, ed. Olivier Borraz (Presses de Sciences Po, 2022).

12. This framing refers to explicit calls for "data science." Practices that many call data science today have a much longer history, which the rest of the chapter discusses.

13. Chikio Hayashi, "What Is Data Science? Fundamental Concepts and a Heuristic Example," in *Data Science, Classification, and Related Methods* (Springer, 1996), 40.

14. Erin Leahey, Christine M. Beckman, and Taryn L. Stanko, "Prominent but Less Productive: The Impact of Interdisciplinarity on Scientists' Research," *Administrative Science Quarterly* 62, no. 1 (2017): 105–39; Tobias Stark, J. Rambaran, and Daniel McFarland, "The Meeting of Minds: Forging Social and Intellectual Networks Within Universities," *Sociological Science* 7 (2020).

15. Andrew Abbott, *Chaos of Disciplines* (University of Chicago Press, 2001); Gieryn, "Boundary-Work and the Demarcation of Science from Non-Science"; Leahey, Beckman, and Stanko, "Prominent but Less Productive."

16. The scientific association at whose meeting Hayashi presented continued to use the data science label in, e.g., Martin Schader, Wolfgang A. Gaul, and Maurizio Vichi, "Between Data Science and Applied Data Analysis," Proceedings of the 26th Annual Conference of the Gesellschaft für Klassifikation E.V., University of Mannheim,

July 22–24, 2002, 2003. There was also a dedicated journal in the early 2000s and calls for an academic discipline in F. Jack Smith, "Data Science as an Academic Discipline," *Data Science Journal* 5 (2006): 163–64.

17. Burt implemented a technical analysis of this duality: Ronald S. Burt, "Social Contagion and Innovation: Cohesion Versus Structural Equivalence," *American Journal of Sociology* 92, no. 6 (1987): 1287–335.

18. E.g., Jason Owen-Smith and Walter W. Powell, "Careers and Contradictions: Faculty Responses to the Transformation of Knowledge and Its Uses in the Life Sciences," *Research in the Sociology of Work* 10 (2001).

19. William S. Cleveland, "Data Science: An Action Plan for Expanding the Technical Areas of the Field of Statistics," *International Statistical Review* 69, no. 1 (2001): 21.

20. Frickel and Gross, "A General Theory of Scientific/Intellectual Movements."

21. Jeff C. F. Wu, "Statistics = Data Science?," slide deck, 1997, 10.

22. Wu, "Statistics = Data Science?," 12.

23. The sociology of science that started with Robert Merton and includes today's science of science movement.

24. E.g., Robert K. Merton, "Priorities in Scientific Discovery: A Chapter in the Sociology of Science," *American Sociological Review* 22, no. 6 (1957): 635–59.

25. Freda B. Lynn, "Diffusing Through Disciplines: Insiders, Outsiders, and Socially Influenced Citation Behavior," *Social Forces* 93, no. 1 (2014): 355–82; Peter McMahan and Daniel A. McFarland, "Creative Destruction: The Structural Consequences of Scientific Curation," *American Sociological Review* 86, no. 2 (2021): 341–76; Etienne Ollion and Andrew Abbott, "French Connections: The Reception of French Sociologists in the USA (1970–2012)," *Archives Européennes de Sociologie* 57, no. 2 (2016): 331.

26. Chapters 5 and 6 will analyze this recognition further; one clear example is in Rachel Schutt and Cathy O'Neil, *Doing Data Science* (O'Reilly Media, 2013).

27. Thomas S. Kuhn, *The Structure of Scientific Revolutions*, 2nd ed. (University of Chicago Press, 1970).

28. Even recent discussions about the transparency of academic research focus more on general steps than the underlying decisions and reasoning.

29. The intuitive interpretation of a positive association between studying and scores is that more studying leads to better results. However, that's not necessarily the case. Better scores may motivate students to study more, or parents with more money may have time to sit their kids down to study and pay for tutors to instill the relevant knowledge, or confidence to not be nervous in a test, or to simply ask questions during one. Social science students learn in their second semester about these complications with interpreting associations under the tagline "correlation is not causation." Now, even if an association doesn't come with a meaning attached to it, first we needed to be able to observe an association, which was the focus a century and a half ago.

30. MacKenzie considered these different backgrounds for contextualizing Pearson's support of eugenics and Yule's opposition. Donald MacKenzie, "Statistical Theory and Social Interests: A Case-Study," *Social Studies of Science* 8, no. 1 (1978): 35–83; see also Donald A. MacKenzie, *Statistics in Britain, 1865–1930: The Social Construction of Scientific Knowledge* (Edinburgh University Press, 1981).

31. MacKenzie, "Statistical Theory and Social Interests," 38.

32. MacKenzie, "Statistical Theory and Social Interests," 45.

33. MacKenzie made them accessible by showing their association with the political orientations and class affiliations of Yule and Pearson. See MacKenzie, "Statistical Theory and Social Interests."

34. Particularly Stinchcombe's ideas support this line of thinking. Arthur L. Stinchcombe, *When Formality Works: Authority and Abstraction in Law and Organizations* (University of Chicago Press, 2001).

35. The observations in this section and the previous section reiterate the ideas of pragmatist philosophy from chapter 2.

36. See Alain Desrosières, *The Politics of Large Numbers: A History of Statistical Reasoning* (Harvard University Press, 1998), 63; Robin L. Plackett, "Studies in the History of Probability and Statistics. XXIX: The Discovery of the Method of Least Squares," *Biometrika* 59, no. 2 (1972): 239–51.

37. Stephen M. Stigler, *The History of Statistics* (Harvard University Press, 1990), 57.

38. Stigler, *The History of Statistics*, 57.

39. Stigler, *The History of Statistics*, 57.

40. Stigler, *The History of Statistics*, 55–61.

41. E.g., Rogers Brubaker, *Citizenship and Nationhood in France and Germany* (Harvard University Press, 2009); DellaPosta et al., "Why Do Liberals Drink Lattes?"; Isin Guler, Mauro F. Guillén, and John Muir Macpherson, "Global Competition, Institutions, and the Diffusion of Organizational Practices: The International Spread of ISO 9000 Quality Certificates," *Administrative Science Quarterly* 47, no. 2 (2002): 207–32.

42. To borrow the image that Polanyi developed for the economy. Karl Polanyi, *The Great Transformation: The Political and Economic Origins of Our Time* (Beacon, 2001).

43. Wendy Nelson Espeland and Michael Sauder, "Rankings and Reactivity: How Public Measures Recreate Social Worlds," *American Journal of Sociology* 113, no. 1 (2007): 1–40; Christine Musselin, "University Governance in Meso and Macro Perspectives," *Annual Review of Sociology* 47 (2021); Evan Schofer and John W. Meyer, "The Worldwide Expansion of Higher Education in the Twentieth Century," *American Sociological Review* 70, no. 6 (2005): 898–920.

44. E.g., Pierre Azoulay, Joshua S. Graff Zivin, and Gustavo Manso, "Incentives and Creativity: Evidence from the Academic Life Sciences," *The RAND Journal of Economics* 42, no. 3 (2011): 527–54; Marion Fourcade, *Economists and Societies: Discipline and Profession in the United States, Britain, and France, 1890s to 1990s* (Princeton University Press, 2009); Jacob G. Foster, Andrey Rzhetsky, and James A. Evans, "Tradition and Innovation in Scientists' Research Strategies," *American Sociological Review* 80, no. 5 (2015): 875–908; Michael Park, Erin Leahey, and Russell J. Funk, "Papers and Patents Are Becoming Less Disruptive Over Time," *Nature* 613, no. 7942 (2023): 138–44.

45. Gross and Frickel, "A General Theory of Scientific/Intellectual Movements."

46. Schweber, *Disciplining Statistics*, 98.

47. Schweber, *Disciplining Statistics*, 99.

48. Schweber, *Disciplining Statistics*.

49. Leifer offers a general account; Dorschel and Brandt showed the applicability of this idea to data science's rise. Eric M. Leifer, "Interaction Preludes to Role Setting: Exploratory Local Action," *American Sociological Review* 53, no. 6 (1988): 865–78; Robert Dorschel and Philipp Brandt, "Professionalization Via Ambiguity. The Discursive Construction of Data Scientists in Higher Education and the Labor Market," *Zeitschrift für Soziologie* 50, no. 3–4 (2021): 193–210.

50. Charles Camic and Yu Xie, "The Statistical Turn in American Social Science: Columbia University, 1890 to 1915," *American Sociological Review* 59, no. 5 (1994): 773–805.

51. Camic and Xie, "The Statistical Turn in American Social Science," 792; citing Franklin H. Giddings, *Exact Methods in Sociology* (1899); Franklin H. Giddings, "The Concepts and Methods of Sociology," *Science* 20, no. 515 (1904): 624–34.

52. Camic and Xie, "The Statistical Turn in American Social Science," 793; citing Giddings, *Exact Methods in Sociology*, 151–52.

53. Originally in Susan Leigh Star, and James R. Griesemer, "Institutional Ecology, Translations, and Boundary Objects: Amateurs and Professionals in Berkeley's Museum of Vertebrate Zoology, 1907–39," *Social Studies of Science* 19, no. 3 (1989): 387–420; but consider also Pascale Trompette and Dominique Vinck, "Revisiting the Notion of Boundary Object," *Revue d'Anthropologie des Connaissances* 3, no. 3–1 (2009).

54. Context matters for the place of statistics in science, like for other institutional projects. For state making, for example, Tilly argued that war mattered; Gorski suggested religion. Philip S. Gorski, *The Disciplinary Revolution* (University of Chicago Press, 2003); Charles Tilly, *Coercion, Capital, and European States, AD 990–1992* (Blackwell, 1992).

55. Camic and Xie, "The Statistical Turn in American Social Science."

56. Besides the department structure, one key was their openness to applied work, even involving industrial research activities. But not only in the United States did practical problems motivate scholarly progress. Ben-David, *The Scientist's Role in Society*; Theodore M. Porter, *Trust in Numbers: The Pursuit of Objectivity in Science and Public Life* (Princeton University Press, 1995).

57. Ben-David, *The Scientist's Role in Society*, 149.

58. Their own institutions hesitated to recognize statistics as a distinct discipline, leaving them to rely on their connections among one another, often outside of universities. Ben-David, *The Scientist's Role in Society*, 152.

59. This cooperation helped facilitate a "consciousness" for a separate discipline, which finally manifested itself in the founding of a dedicated institute in 1935. Allen T. Craig, "Our Silver Anniversary," *Annals of Mathematical Statistics* 31, no. 4 (1960): 835–37; Ben-David, *The Scientist's Role in Society*, 150.

60. Abbott, *Chaos of Disciplines*, proposed a fractal pattern to describe this progress, which Shwed and Bearman, "The Temporal Structure of Scientific Consensus Formation," have shown to be part of a range of patterns, including one of spiraling.

61. Michael Park, Erin Leahey, and Russell J. Funk, "Papers and Patents Are Becoming Less Disruptive Over Time," *Nature* 613, no. 7942 (2023): 138–44.

62. E.g., Philipp Brandt, "Sociology's Stake in Data Science," *Sociologica* 16, no. 2 (2022): 149–66; Sandra González-Bailón, *Decoding the Social World: Data Science and the Unintended Consequences of Communication* (MIT Press, 2017); D. Lazer, A. Pentland, L. Adamic, et al., "Social Science: Computational Social Science," *Science* 323, no. 5915 (2009): 721–23; David M. J. Lazer, Alex Pentland, Duncan J. Watts, et al., "Computational Social Science: Obstacles and Opportunities," *Science* 369, no. 6507 (2020): 1060–62.

63. Leo Breiman, "Statistical Modeling: The Two Cultures (with Comments and a Rejoinder by the Author)," *Statistical Science* 16, no. 3 (2001): 199–231.

64. Breiman, "Statistical Modeling," 199.

65. David R. Cox, "[Statistical Modeling: The Two Cultures]: Comment," *Statistical Science* 16, no. 3 (2001): 218.

66. Emanuel Parzen, "[Statistical Modeling: The Two Cultures]: Comment," *Statistical Science* 16, no. 3 (2001): 224.

67. "On Chomsky and the Two Cultures of Statistical Learning," https://norvig.com/chomsky.html.

68. The myth and ceremony argument originally unpacked organizational process, but the underlying idea applies to the organization of science

as well. J. W. Meyer and B. Rowan, "Institutionalized Organizations: Formal Structure as Myth and Ceremony," *American Journal of Sociology* 83, no. 2 (1977): 340–63.

69. Mark A. Pachucki and Ronald L. Breiger, "Cultural Holes: Beyond Relationality in Social Networks and Culture," *Annual Review of Sociology* 36 (2010): 205–24.

4. INTERACTIONS

1. For the original discussion, see Peter Galison, *Image and Logic: A Material Culture of Microphysics* (University of Chicago Press, 1997); and Harry Collins, Robert Evans, and Mike Gorman, "Trading Zones and Interactional Expertise," *Studies in History and Philosophy of Science Part A* 38, no. 4 (2007): 657–66. For an application to research in the computational era, see Daniel A. McFarland, Kevin Lewis, and Amir Goldberg, "Sociology in the Era of Big Data: The Ascent of Forensic Social Science," *American Sociologist* 47, no. 1 (2016): 12–35.

2. E.g., Harry M. Collins, "The Meaning of Data: Open and Closed Evidential Cultures in the Search for Gravitational Waves," *American Journal of Sociology* 104, no. 2 (1998): 293–338; Gil Eyal, Brendan Hart, Emine Onculer, Neta Oren, and Natasha Rossi, *The Autism Matrix: The Social Origins of the Autism Epidemic* (Polity, 2010); Karine Knorr-Cetina, *The Manufacture of Knowledge: An Essay on the Constructivist and Contextual Nature of Science* (Elsevier, 2013); Bruno Latour, *Science in Action: How to Follow Scientists and Engineers Through Society* (Harvard University Press, 1987).

3. E.g., Joseph Ben-David, *The Scientist's Role in Society: A Comparative Study* (Prentice Hall, 1971); Erin Leahey, "Alphas and Asterisks: The Development of Statistical Significance Testing Standards in Sociology," *Social Forces* 84, no. 1 (2005): 1–24; Robert K. Merton, *The Sociology of Science: Theoretical and Empirical Investigations* (University of Chicago Press, 1973); Harriet Zuckerman, "Nobel Laureates in Science: Patterns of Productivity, Collaboration, and Authorship," *American Sociological Review* 32, no. 3 (1967): 391–403.

4. Erving Goffman, *Behavior in Public Places: Notes on the Social Organization of Gatherings* (Free Press, 1963), 18.

5. Goffman, *Behavior in Public Places*, chap. 4.
6. Margret Archer's theoretical framework rests on this idea that people "consider themselves in relation to their (social) contexts": Margaret S. Archer, *Making Our Way Through the World: Human Reflexivity and Social Mobility* (Cambridge University Press, 2007), 4.
7. Randall Collins, *Interaction Ritual Chains* (Princeton University Press, 2004).
8. Collins, *Interaction Ritual Chains*, xiv.
9. Collins, *Interaction Ritual Chains*, 47–49. Many intellectuals may spend "much time in solitary bookish pursuits; but both the stars and the followers are highly socialized by the intellectual community" (378). See also 190–96.
10. Ivan Ermakoff, "The Structure of Contingency," *American Journal of Sociology* 121, no. 1 (2015): 67, 82.
11. This jump from data science to the French Revolution could seem like an excessive stretch. But Vaughan and more recently Krause have argued for the utility of "analogical theorizing" and considering the larger diversity in the world. Monika Krause, "On Sociological Reflexivity," *Sociological Theory* 39, no. 1 (2021): 3–18; Diane Vaughan, "NASA Revisited: Theory, Analogy, and Public Sociology," *American Journal of Sociology* 112, no. 2 (2006): 353–93.
12. Philipp Brandt, "Sociology's Stake in Data Science," *Sociologica* 16, no. 2 (2022): 149–66.
13. Rather than developing each observation as a full presentation of the speaker, in this chapter I will do that only for a few, but I will also use more voices from the field to make the argument. This speaker was Jeroen, who worked for a data science consultancy and wrote about data science methods. I am using his real name because he has taken a public role beyond the meetup: Jeroen Janssens, *Data Science at the Command Line: Facing the Future with Time-Tested Tools* (O'Reilly Media, 2014).
14. JSON files were one of the data storage formats I used for the data science exercise in chapter 2.
15. William H. Sewell, "A Theory of Structure: Duality, Agency, and Transformation," *American Journal of Sociology* 98, no. 1 (1992): 1–29.

16. I call this presenter Connor, which was not his real name. Connor worked for a database company and had an advanced academic background.

17. I included this contribution on the basis of my field notes, but they did not quote the speaker in full. Since the exact technical words are relevant in this context, I obtained them from a recording available online of a shorter version of the talk on the same topic from the following year.

18. This phrase could indicate a subtle "everyone who's anyone knows what this is" power move. However, against the backdrop of the performance and atmosphere at these events, the more likely interpretation would be the humble version: The presenter feared the audience would question his competence if he thought such basics required explanation.

19. Research in psychology regularly uses public speaking tasks to induce stress, and studies have shown that presenters get sweaty hands, feel negative emotions, and show cardiovascular responses during these activities even when they prepare for them. Pamela J. Feldman, Sheldon Cohen, Natalie Hamrick, and Stephen J. Lepore, "Psychological Stress, Appraisal, Emotion and Cardiovascular Response in a Public Speaking Task," *Psychology & Health* 19, no. 3 (2004): 353–68; P. Michiel Westenberg, Caroline L. Bokhorst, et al., "A Prepared Speech in Front of a Pre-Recorded Audience: Subjective, Physiological, and Neuroendocrine Responses to the Leiden Public Speaking Task," *Biological Psychology* 82, no. 2 (2009): 116–24.

20. John F. Padgett and Christopher K. Ansell, "Robust Action and the Rise of the Medici, 1400–1434," *American Journal of Sociology* 98, no. 6 (1993): 1259–319.

21. Modern quantitative models process the majority of all trades and have replaced the brokers from older images; Donald MacKenzie, "Material Signals: A Historical Sociology of High-Frequency Trading," *American Journal of Sociology* 123, no. 6 (2018): 1635–83.

22. O'Neil explains how problems that are less quantitative to begin with can experience greater damage from data scientific perspectives. Here, I'm focusing on the presentation. Cathy O'Neil, *Weapons of Math*

Destruction: How Big Data Increases Inequality and Threatens Democracy (Crown, 2016), chap. 1.

23. See John Dewey, *Logic: The Theory of Inquiry* (Henry Holt, 1938), 105, proposed discourse as one type of means; Ermakoff, "The Structure of Contingency."

24. Stephen L. Morgan and Christopher Winship, *Counterfactuals and Causal Inference: Methods and Principles for Social Research* (Cambridge University Press, 2007); Judea Pearl, *Causality* (Cambridge University Press, 2009).

25. Ermakoff, "The Structure of Contingency."

26. As Erving Goffman pointed out, performers could be sincere, but they could be cynical as well and conform to their audiences' expectations. They often dramatize, idealize, or mystify themselves or their work. Erving Goffman, *The Presentation of Self in Everyday Life* (Doubleday, 1959), 17–21, 30, 34, 67.

27. Customer support teams are the most grinding activities in social media organizations. Catherine J. Turco, *The Conversational Firm: Rethinking Bureaucracy in the Age of Social Media* (Columbia University Press, 2016).

28. Eviatar Zerubavel, *Social Mindscapes: An Invitation to Cognitive Sociology* (Harvard University Press, 1997), 48–49.

29. Zerubavel, *Social Mindscapes*, 42, stressed that it is the "professional community that usually rewards academics for restricting their academic concerns to the inevitable parochial confines of their 'field' of scholarship."

30. Eyal's idea of "spaces between fields" fits here: Gil Eyal, "Spaces Between Fields," in *Bourdieu and Historical Analysis*, ed. Philip S. Gorski (Duke University Press, 2013).

31. Benedict Anderson, *Imagined Communities: Reflections on the Origin and Spread of Nationalism* (Verso, 1983), 14.

32. Zerubavel, *Social Mindscapes*, 9.

33. Ludwik Fleck, *Genesis and Development of a Scientific Fact* (University of Chicago Press, 1979), 45.

34. Collins, *Interaction Ritual Chains*.

35. Ermakoff, "The Structure of Contingency," 67.

36. Anderson, *Imagined Communities*, 14.

5. RELATIONS

1. For an overview, see Erin Leahey, "Methodological Memes and Mores: Toward a Sociology of Social Research," *Annual Review of Sociology* 34 (2008): 33–53.

2. E.g., John P. Heinz, *Urban Lawyers: The New Social Structure of the Bar* (University of Chicago Press, 2005); Lauren A. Rivera, *Pedigree: How Elite Students Get Elite Jobs* (Princeton University Press, 2015); Lauren A. Rivera, "When Two Bodies Are (Not) a Problem: Gender and Relationship Status Discrimination in Academic Hiring," *American Sociological Review* 82, no. 6 (2017): 1111–38. But science as an institution also offers opportunities to remediate the influence of sociodemographic factors on scientific activities, e.g., for gender or relations. Flaminio Squazzoni, Giangiacomo Bravo, Mike Farjam, et al., "Peer Review and Gender Bias: A Study on 145 Scholarly Journals," *Science Advances* 7, no. 2 (2021).

3. Matthew Desmond, "Disposable Ties and the Urban Poor," *American Journal of Sociology* 117, no. 5 (2012): 1295–335; Mark S. Granovetter, "The Strength of Weak Ties," *American Journal of Sociology* 78, no. 6 (1973): 1360–80; Alejandro Portes, "Social Capital: Its Origins and Applications in Modern Sociology," *Annual Review of Sociology* 24 (1998): 1.

4. Jan A. Fuhse, *Social Networks of Meaning and Communication* (Oxford University Press, 2021); Jan A. Fuhse, "The Meaning Structure of Social Networks," *Sociological Theory* 27, no. 1 (2009): 51–73; Jan A. Fuhse and Neha Gondal, "Networks from Culture: Mechanisms of Tie-Formation Follow Institutionalized Rules in Social Fields," *Social Networks* 77 (2024); Omar Lizardo, "How Cultural Tastes Shape Personal Networks," *American Sociological Review* 71, no. 5 (2006): 778–807.

5. Michel Foucault, *Discipline and Punish: The Birth of the Prison* (Vintage, 1995); Philip S. Gorski, *The Disciplinary Revolution* (University of Chicago Press, 2003).

6. White proposed "interface," "council," and "arena" as technical terms for these three types of discipline. Harrison C. White, *Identity and*

Control: How Social Formations Emerge, 2nd ed. (Princeton University Press, 2008), chap. 3.

7. This is the conceptual idea of a role structure with the structural equivalence operationalization. Scott A. Boorman and Harrison C. White, "Social Structure from Multiple Networks. II. Role Structures," *American Journal of Sociology* 81, no. 6 (1976): 1384–446; Harrison C. White, Scott A. Boorman, and Ronald Breiger, "Social Structure from Multiple Networks. I. Blockmodels of Roles and Positions," *American Journal of Sociology* 81, no. 4 (1976): 730–80.

8. Ann Swidler, *Talk of Love: How Culture Matters* (University of Chicago Press, 2001).

9. Swidler distinguishes between settled and unsettled situations, highlighting that while in the latter actors fall back on ideologies, structural opportunities still give them agency to pick from a range of ideologies. Swidler, *Talk of Love*; Ann Swidler, "Culture in Action: Symbols and Strategies," *American Sociological Review* 51, no. 2 (1986): 273–86.

10. Frederick Winslow Taylor, *The Principles of Scientific Management* (Harper & Brothers, 1919).

11. A. Goldberg, S. B. Srivastava, V. G. Manian, et al., "Fitting In or Standing Out? The Tradeoffs of Structural and Cultural Embeddedness," *American Sociological Review* 81, no. 6 (2016): 1190–222; Gideon Kunda, *Engineering Culture: Control and Commitment in a High-Tech Corporation* (Temple University Press, 2009); Catherine J. Turco, *The Conversational Firm: Rethinking Bureaucracy in the Age of Social Media* (Columbia University Press, 2016).

12. Andrew Abbott, *The System of Professions: An Essay on the Division of Expert Labor* (University of Chicago Press, 1988), chap. 9; Roger V. Gould, *Insurgent Identities: Class, Community, and Protest in Paris from 1848 to the Commune* (University of Chicago Press, 1995); Charles Tilly, *The Vendée*, 2nd ed. (Harvard University Press, 1976).

13. This is the most generic name in my anonymization choices because it was an anonymous audience member whose appearance fit that of the proverbial Tom, Dick, and Harry.

14. Quinn worked for an accommodation platform.

15. Recall the LinkedIn software engineers who made the work difficult for the new data scientist until the CEO intervened: Thomas H. Davenport and DJ Patil, "Data Scientist: The Sexiest Job of the 21st Century," *Harvard Business Review* 90, no. 10 (2012): 70–76.

16. Rebecca worked for a news organization she had recently joined.

17. This speaker was Toby, who discussed his experiences at an earlier workplace, a social media platform.

18. Beth A. Bechky, "Sharing Meaning Across Occupational Communities: The Transformation of Understanding on a Production Floor," *Organization Science* 14, no. 3 (2003): 312–30.

19. E.g., Bruce G. Carruthers and Wendy Nelson Espeland, "Accounting for Rationality: Double-Entry Bookkeeping and the Rhetoric of Economic Rationality," *American Journal of Sociology* 97, no. 1 (1991): 31–69; Peter S. Dodds, Duncan J. Watts, and Charles F. Sabel, "Information Exchange and the Robustness of Organizational Networks," *Proceedings of the National Academy of Sciences of the United States of America* 100, no. 21 (2003): 12516–21; Arthur L. Stinchcombe, "Bureaucratic and Craft Administration of Production: A Comparative Study," *Administrative Science Quarterly* 4, no. 2 (1959): 168–87. These all go back to Max Weber, *Writschaft und Gesellschaft*, 5th ed. (1925; Mohr Siebeck, 1976); see H. H. Gerth and C. Wright Mills, *From Max Weber: Essays in Sociology* (Routledge, 2009).

20. See Stinchcombe, "Bureaucratic and Craft Administration of Production," on different information processing arrangements in different areas of work.

21. Kunda, *Engineering Culture*.

22. Turco, *The Conversational Firm*.

23. For the story of how economics started, see Emily Erikson and Mark Hamilton, "Companies and the Rise of Economic Thought: The Institutional Foundations of Early Economics in England, 1550–1720," *American Journal of Sociology* 124, no. 1 (2018): 111–49; Emily Erikson, *Trade and Nation: How Companies and Politics Reshaped Economic Thought* (Columbia University Press, 2021).

24. Eliot Freidson, *Profession of Medicine: A Study of the Sociology of Applied Knowledge* (University of Chicago Press, 1988); Daniel A. Menchik,

"Decisions About Knowledge in Medical Practice: The Effect of Temporal Features of a Task," *American Journal of Sociology* 120, no. 3 (2014): 701–49; Damon J. Phillips, Catherine J. Turco, and Ezra W. Zuckerman, "Betrayal as Market Barrier: Identity-Based Limits to Diversification Among High-Status Corporate Law Firms," *American Journal of Sociology* 118, no. 4 (2013): 1023–54.

25. Herminia Ibarra, "Provisional Selves: Experimenting with Image and Identity in Professional Adaptation," *Administrative Science Quarterly* 44, no. 4 (1999): 764–91.

26. Alex worked for a small firm that offered access to datasets of social media platforms.

27. Joshua also ran a meetup group.

28. Even states employ vastly different approaches when it comes to collecting statistics on poverty. Luciana de Souza Leão, "Optics of the State: The Politics of Making Poverty Visible in Brazil and Mexico," *American Journal of Sociology* 128, no. 1 (2022): 1–46.

29. E.g., Junsol Kim and Byungkyu Lee, "AI-Augmented Surveys: Leveraging Large Language Models for Opinion Prediction in Nationally Representative Surveys," *arXiv* preprint (2023), arXiv:2305.09620; Matthew J. Salganik and Karen E. C. Levy, "Wiki Surveys: Open and Quantifiable Social Data Collection," *PLOS One* 10, no. 5 (2015): e0123483.

30. Claudia is the speaker's real name, which I left here because she was a prominent member of the community with a prominent public profile. She also appears as a reference in a discussion in the next chapter.

31. All experiments on living organisms raise ethical questions. Experiments on humans raise those questions and also analytic questions because they are not grown for experimental purposes. Luciana de Souza Leão and Gil Eyal, "The Rise of Randomized Controlled Trials (RCTs) in International Development in Historical Perspective," *Theory and Society* 48 (2019): 383–418.

32. White, *Identity and Control*, chap. 3.

33. These observations respond to White's relational view of discipline. Access is a question of status, or prestige, and producing useful output is a question of quality. White, *Identity and Control*, chap. 3.

34. Virginia Eubanks. *Automating Inequality: How High-Tech Tools Profile, Police, and Punish the Poor* (St. Martin's, 2018); Cathy O'Neil, *Weapons of Math Destruction: How Big Data Increases Inequality and Threatens Democracy* (Crown, 2016).

35. Swidler, *Talk of Love*.

36. Thomas S. Kuhn, *The Structure of Scientific Revolutions*, 2nd ed. (University of Chicago Press, 1970).

37. Data scientists and data science groups often show their work at conferences and publish them as working papers and in academic journals. But among all data scientists, this knowledge sharing is less of a requirement or convention, compared to academic researchers. Philipp Brandt, "Sociology's Stake in Data Science," *Sociologica* 16, no. 2 (2022): 149–66.

38. Lucas discussed his experience at a microblogging platform.

39. Peter McMahan and Daniel A. McFarland, "Creative Destruction: The Structural Consequences of Scientific Curation," *American Sociological Review* 86, no. 2 (2021): 341–76; Robert K. Merton, "The Matthew Effect in Science," *Science* 159, no. 3810 (1968): 56–63; Etienne Ollion and Andrew Abbott, "French Connections: The Reception of French Sociologists in the USA (1970–2012)," *Archives Européennes de Sociologie* 57, no. 2 (2016): 331; Arthur L. Stinchcombe, "Should Sociologists Forget Their Mothers and Fathers?," *American Sociologist* 17, no. 1 (1982): 2–11.

40. Bruno Latour and Steve Woolgar, *Laboratory Life: The Construction of Scientific Facts* (Princeton University Press, 1986).

41. Herminia Ibarra, "Provisional Selves: Experimenting with Image and Identity in Professional Adaptation," *Administrative Science Quarterly* 44, no. 4 (1999): 764–91.

42. And scientists from disciplines other than his have still advanced our understanding of those choices. In return, and in line with the purists' positions from chapter 2, they, too, have concerns that make them overlook his specific problems. Andrew Abbott, *Chaos of Disciplines* (University of Chicago Press, 2001), chap. 1; Brandt, "Sociology's Stake."

43. Chapter 3 showed a slice of the scholarship that has uncovered this discrepancy.

44. Yann is the speaker's real name. His last name is LeCun. I left it unchanged because Yann was a speaker with a large public profile.

45. The statistical approach is the dominant approach today. Decades ago, a more mechanical approach that Feigenbaum and McCorduck described dominated. Edward A. Feigenbaum and Pamela McCorduck, *The Fifth Generation: Artificial Intelligence and Japan's Computer Challenge to the World* (Addison-Wesley, 1983).

46. Scholars of science know that science has become less and less innovative and that important scientific innovations involve outside partners. James A. Evans, "Industry Induces Academic Science to Know Less About More," *American Journal of Sociology* 116, no. 2 (2010): 389–452; Jason Owen-Smith and Walter W. Powell, "Careers and Contradictions: Faculty Responses to the Transformation of Knowledge and Its Uses in the Life Sciences," *Research in the Sociology of Work* 10 (2001); Michael Park, Erin Leahey, and Russell J. Funk, "Papers and Patents Are Becoming Less Disruptive Over Time," *Nature* 613, no. 7942 (2023): 138–44.

47. Scott Frickel and Neil Gross, "A General Theory of Scientific/ Intellectual Movements," *American Sociological Review* 70, no. 2 (2005): 210.

48. These were the words of no one less central in this community than Jeff Hammerbacher, the author of one of the first data science definitions. Jeff Hammerbacher, "Information Platforms and the Rise of the Data Scientist," in *Beautiful Data: The Stories Behind Elegant Data Solutions*, ed. Toby Segaran and Jeff Hammerbacher (O'Reilly Media, 2009).

49. Andrew Abbott, "Things of Boundaries," *Social Research* 62, no. 4 (1995): 857.

50. See Abbott, *The System of Professions*, on "jurisdictions."

6. IDENTITY

1. Peter L. Berger and Thomas Luckmann, *The Social Construction of Reality: A Treatise in the Sociology of Knowledge* (Doubleday, 1966); Eliot Freidson, *Professionalism: The Third Logic* (University of Chicago Press, 2001); Daniel A. Menchik, "Decisions About Knowledge in Medical

Practice: The Effect of Temporal Features of a Task," *American Journal of Sociology* 120, no. 3 (2014): 701–49; Lauren A. Rivera, *Pedigree: How Elite Students Get Elite Jobs* (Princeton University Press, 2015).

2. Herminia Ibarra, "Provisional Selves: Experimenting with Image and Identity in Professional Adaptation," *Administrative Science Quarterly* 44, no. 4 (1999): 764–91.

3. For some recent studies that focus on identity specifically in the workplace, consider Frans Bévort and Roy Suddaby, "Scripting Professional Identities: How Individuals Make Sense of Contradictory Institutional Logics," *Journal of Professions and Organization* 3, no. 1 (2016): 17–38; Masashi Goto, "Collective Professional Role Identity in the Age of Artificial Intelligence," *Journal of Professions and Organization* 8, no. 1 (2021): 86–107.

4. As a nonexhaustive list of examples, for morality see Jan E. Stets and Michael J. Carter, "A Theory of the Self for the Sociology of Morality," *American Sociological Review* 77, no. 1 (2012): 120–40; for religion and ethnicity, Lars Leszczensky, Sebastian Pink, David Kretschmer, and Frank Kalter, "Studying Youth Group Identities, Intergroup Relations, and Friendship Networks: The Friendship and Identity in School Data," *European Sociological Review* 38, no. 3 (2022): 493–506; and for class Margaret R. Somers, "Narrativity, Narrative Identity, and Social Action: Rethinking English Working-Class Formation," *Social Science History* 16, no. 4 (1992): 591–630.

5. Harrison C. White, *Identity and Control: How Social Formations Emerge*, 2nd ed. (Princeton University Press, 2008).

6. Harrison White, Scott Boorman, and Ronald Breiger, "Social Structure from Multiple Networks. I. Blockmodels of Roles and Positions," *American Journal of Sociology* 81, no. 4 (1976): 730–80.

7. Rogers Brubaker and Frederick Cooper, "Beyond 'Identity,'" *Theory and Society* 29, no. 1 (2000): 15.

8. Brubaker and Cooper, "Beyond 'Identity,'" 14–17, considers self-understanding as a psychodynamic and emotional process, which they trace to Sigmund Freud.

9. Brubaker and Cooper, "Beyond 'Identity,'" 17–19, considers social location as a source of identity.

10. The *New York Times* reported in 2016 on changes in hiring policies; Claire Cain Miller, "Is Blind Hiring the Best Hiring?," *New York Times Magazine*, February 25, 2016.

11. Bol et al. analyze the extent and variability of transitions into jobs in the United States, France, and Germany and find considerable variability in the first two. Thijs Bol, Christina Ciocca Eller, Herman G. Van De Werfhorst, and Thomas A. DiPrete, "School-to-Work Linkages, Educational Mismatches, and Labor Market Outcomes," *American Sociological Review* 84, no. 2 (2019): 275–307.

12. Ibarra, "Provisional Selves."

13. E.g., Carl Shan, Henry Wang, William Chen, and Max Song, *The Data Science Handbook: Advice and Insights from 25 Amazing Data Scientists.* (n.p., 2015).

14. The presenter later revealed that his data science implementation of the technical two-sided market idea from economics had backfired in practice.

15. Jeff Hammerbacher, "Information Platforms and the Rise of the Data Scientist," in *Beautiful Data: The Stories Behind Elegant Data Solutions*, ed. Toby Segaran and Jeff Hammerbacher (O'Reilly Media, 2009), 74.

16. For consistent observations of similar workplaces, see David Stark, *The Sense of Dissonance: Accounts of Worth in Economic Life* (Princeton University Press, 2009), chap. 3; and Catherine J. Turco, *The Conversational Firm: Rethinking Bureaucracy in the Age of Social Media* (Columbia University Press, 2016).

17. Max Besbris and Caitlin Petre, "Professionalizing Contingency: How Journalism Schools Adapt to Deprofessionalization," *Social Forces* 98, no. 4 (2020): 1524–47; Angèle Christin, "Counting Clicks: Quantification and Variation in Web Journalism in the United States and France," *American Journal of Sociology* 123, no. 5 (2018): 1382–415.

18. While men are more likely to enroll in and complete STEM degrees then women, they are less likely to enroll in college in the first place. As a result, even the enrollment of 18 percent for men and 7.9 percent for women overstates the tendency to pursue advanced technical training among high school graduates: Kim A. Weeden, Dafna Gelbgiser, and Stephen L. Morgan, "Pipeline Dreams: Occupational Plans and

Gender Differences in Stem Major Persistence and Completion," *Sociology of Education* 93, no. 4 (2020): 297–314.

19. Colleen M. Ganley, Casey E. George, Joseph R. Cimpian, and Martha B. Makowski, "Gender Equity in College Majors: Looking Beyond the Stem/Non-Stem Dichotomy for Answers Regarding Female Participation," *American Educational Research Journal* 55, no. 3 (2018): 453–87.

20. Andrew Abbott, "Mechanisms and Relations," *Sociologica* 2 (2007).

21. E.g., Limor Gabay-Egozi, Yossi Shavit, and Meir Yaish, "Gender Differences in Fields of Study: The Role of Significant Others and Rational Choice Motivations," *European Sociological Review* 31, no. 3 (2015): 284–97; Stephen L. Morgan, "Adolescent Educational Expectations: Rationalized, Fantasized, or Both?," *Rationality and Society* 10, no. 2 (1998): 131–62.

22. Turco, *The Conversational Firm*, 77.

23. The classic example here is corporate consulting and investment banking. The situation has changed more recently with the rise of UX jobs. Lauren A. Rivera, *Pedigree: How Elite Students Get Elite Jobs* (Princeton University Press, 2015).

24. Settled in the sense of Swider's distinction between settled and unsettled situations; A. Swidler, "Culture in Action: Symbols and Strategies," *American Sociological Review* 51, no. 2 (April 1986): 273–86.

25. For an account of this expertise in the banking industry, see Donald MacKenzie, "Material Signals: A Historical Sociology of High-Frequency Trading," *American Journal of Sociology* 123, no. 6 (2018): 1635–83.

26. The general theoretical idea here is the isomorphism argument: Paul DiMaggio and Walter Powell, "The Iron Cage Revisited: Institutional Isomorphism and Collective Rationality in Organizational Fields," *American Sociological Review* 48, no. 2 (1983): 147–60.

27. I'm using real names here because both Hilary and Chris maintained a prominent profile inside and outside of the community.

28. I'm using Jeff's real name because he maintained a popular profile far beyond the community.

29. This was Rebecca, whose conflict with data warehouse colleagues featured in the previous chapter.

30. In line with Swidler's thinking about unsettled situations; Swidler, "Culture in Action."

31. The *New York Times Magazine* reported in 2016 that Google had also changed its hiring practices toward avoiding brainteasers; Miller, "Is Blind Hiring the Best Hiring?"

32. Benedict Anderson, *Imagined Communities: Reflections on the Origin and Spread of Nationalism* (Verso, 1983); Berger and Luckmann, *The Social Construction of Reality*; Eviatar Zerubavel, *Social Mindscapes: An Invitation to Cognitive Sociology* (Harvard University Press, 1997).

33. Etienne Ollion and Andrew Abbott, "French Connections: The Reception of French Sociologists in the USA (1970–2012)," *Archives Européennes de Sociologie* 57, no. 2 (2016): 331; Arthur L. Stinchcombe, "Should Sociologists Forget Their Mothers and Fathers?," *American Sociologist* 17, no. 1 (1982): 2–11.

34. The language in question was MapReduce.

35. He didn't say that Jeff agreed with the specific thinking about the programming language. He construed another point Jeff had made in a personal conversation to support this point. The conversation was about how a simple programming language added to a more technical one made more people use a database.

36. Although we find something new to remember often enough, or maybe that we don't want to remember.

37. Such a focus may seem more obvious today with the rise of LLMs and their applications to coding problems. Back then, they were on the horizon, but more often as a project for data scientists than as a threat to their existence.

38. I'm using Hannah's real name because she maintained a prominent profile outside of the community and has been quoted in the same context elsewhere: Chris Wiggins and Matthew L. Jones, *How Data Happened: A History from the Age of Reason to the Age of Algorithms* (Norton, 2023).

39. Wiggins and Jones, *How Data Happened*.

CONCLUSION

1. This idea builds on Breiger's discussion of the duality between person and groups and Sewell's duality of structure and agency. Several chapters also discussed these issues in terms of Swidler's settled and unsettled lives. Ronald L. Breiger, "The Duality of Persons and Groups,"

Social Forces 53, no. 2 (1974): 181–90; Sophie Mützel and Ronald Breiger, "Duality Beyond Persons and Groups," in *The Oxford Handbook of Social Networks* (Oxford University Press, 2020), 392; William H. Sewell, "A Theory of Structure: Duality, Agency, and Transformation," *American Journal of Sociology* 98, no. 1 (1992): 1–29; A. Swidler, "Culture in Action: Symbols and Strategies," *American Sociological Review* 51, no. 2 (April 1986): 273–86.

2. E.g., Netta Avnoon, "Data Scientists' Identity Work: Omnivorous Symbolic Boundaries in Skills Acquisition," *Work, Employment, and Society* 35, no. 2 (2021): 332–49; Netta Avnoon, "The Gates to the Profession Are Open: The Alternative Institutionalization of Data Science," *Theory and Society* 53, no. 2 (2024): 239–71; Philippe Saner, "Envisioning Higher Education: How Imagining the Future Shapes the Implementation of a New Field in Higher Education," *Swiss Journal of Sociology* 45, no. 3 (2019): 359–81; Shoshana Zuboff, *The Age of Surveillance Capitalism: The Fight for a Human Future at the New Frontier of Power* (Profile, 2019).

3. Several of the accounts that were the basis of the analysis had contributed to the popular definitions of data science, including during work stints on the West Coast.

4. Though see Robert Dorschel and Philipp Brandt, "Professionalization Via Ambiguity. The Discursive Construction of Data Scientists in Higher Education and the Labor Market," *Zeitschrift für Soziologie* 50, no. 3–4 (2021): 193–210.

5. Another area where this divide has become salient is the biotech sector. James A. Evans, "Industry Induces Academic Science to Know Less About More," *American Journal of Sociology* 116, no. 2 (2010): 389–452; Jason Owen-Smith and Walter W. Powell, "Careers and Contradictions: Faculty Responses to the Transformation of Knowledge and Its Uses in the Life Sciences," *Research in the Sociology of Work* 10 (2001).

6. E.g., Avnoon, "The Gates to the Profession Are Open"; Daniel DellaPosta and Victor Nee, "Emergence of Diverse and Specialized Knowledge in a Metropolitan Tech Cluster," *Social Science Research* 86 (2020): 102377.

7. E.g., LinkedIn, "Emerging Jobs Report," https://economicgraph.linkedin.com/research/linkedin-2018-emerging-jobs-report.

8. E.g., for Switzerland, Saner, "Envisioning Higher Education"; for Israel, Avnoon, "Data Scientists' Identity Work."

9. In 2002, the Committee on Data for Science and Technology (CODATA) began publishing the *Data Science Journal*, introducing "data science as an academic discipline" in a 2006 issue: F. Jack Smith, "Data Science as an Academic Discipline," *Data Science Journal* 5 (2006): 163–64. DJ Patil, Hilary Mason, and Mike Loukides, *Ethics and Data Science* (O'Reilly Media, 2018), wrote about ethics for data scientists. For thorough analyses of data science in higher education institutions, see Dorschel and Brandt, "Professionalization Via Ambiguity"; Philippe Saner, *Datenwissenschaften und Gesellschaft. Die Genese eines transversalen Wissensfeldes* (transcript, 2022).

10. John P. Heinz, *Urban Lawyers: The New Social Structure of the Bar* (University of Chicago Press, 2005).

11. The organization is DataKind.

12. Ann Swidler, *Talk of Love: How Culture Matters* (University of Chicago Press, 2001); Josh Whitford and Francesco Zirpoli, "Pragmatism, Practice, and the Boundaries of Organization," *Organization Science* 25, no. 6 (2014): 1823–39.

13. For changes in occupational boundaries, see Siwei Cheng and Barum Park, "Flows and Boundaries: A Network Approach to Studying Occupational Mobility in the Labor Market," *American Journal of Sociology* 126, no. 3 (2020): 577–631; Ken-Hou Lin and Koit Hung, "The Network Structure of Occupations: Fragmentation, Differentiation, and Contagion," *American Journal of Sociology* 127, no. 5 (2022): 1551–601; Jonas Toubøl and Anton Grau Larsen, "Mapping the Social Class Structure: From Occupational Mobility to Social Class Categories Using Network Analysis," *Sociology* 51, no. 6 (2017): 1257–76.

14. The same studies show new patterns that are partly even more stable than formal occupational categories.

15. David Stark and Ivana Pais, "Algorithmic Management in the Platform Economy," *Sociologica* 14, no. 3 (2020): 47–72; Zeynep Tufekci, *Twitter and Tear Gas: The Power and Fragility of Networked Protest* (Yale University Press, 2017).

.

BIBLIOGRAPHY

Abbott, Andrew. *Chaos of Disciplines*. University of Chicago Press, 2001.

——. "Mechanisms and Relations." *Sociologica* 2 (2007).

——. "Status and Status Strain in the Professions." *American Journal of Sociology* 86, no. 4 (1981): 819–35.

——. *The System of Professions: An Essay on the Division of Expert Labor*. University of Chicago Press, 1988.

——. "Things of Boundaries." *Social Research* 62, no. 4 (1995): 857.

Anderson, Benedict. *Imagined Communities: Reflections on the Origin and Spread of Nationalism*. Verso, 1983.

Aral, Sinan, and Marshall Van Alstyne. "The Diversity-Bandwidth Trade-off." *American Journal of Sociology* 117, no. 1 (2011): 90–171.

Archer, Margaret S. *Making Our Way Through The World: Human Reflexivity and Social Mobility*. New York: Cambridge University Press.

Arseniev-Koehler, Alina. "Theoretical Foundations and Limits of Word Embeddings: What Types of Meaning Can They Capture?" *Sociological Methods & Research* 53, no. 4 (2022): 1753–93.

Autor, David H. "Wiring the Labor Market." *Journal of Economic Perspectives* 15, no. 1 (2001): 25–40.

Avnoon, Netta. "Data Scientists' Identity Work: Omnivorous Symbolic Boundaries in Skills Acquisition." *Work, Employment, and Society* 35, no. 2 (2021): 332–49.

——. "The Gates to the Profession Are Open: The Alternative Institutionalization of Data Science." *Theory and Society* 53, no. 2 (2024): 239–71.

Azoulay, Pierre, Joshua S. Graff Zivin, and Gustavo Manso. "Incentives and Creativity: Evidence from the Academic Life Sciences." *RAND Journal of Economics* 42, no. 3 (2011): 527–54.

Baldassarri, Delia, and Mario Diani. "The Integrative Power of Civic Networks." *American Journal of Sociology* 113, no. 3 (2007): 735–80.

Barabási, Albert-Laszlo, Hawoong Jeong, Zoltan Néda, Erzsebet Ravasz, Andras Schubert, and Tamas Vicsek. "Evolution of the Social Network of Scientific Collaborations." *Physica A: Statistical Mechanics and Its Applications* 311, no. 3–4 (2002): 590–614.

Bearman, Peter S. *Relations Into Rhetorics: Local Elite Structure in Norfolk, England, 1540–1640*. Rutgers University Press, 1993.

Bearman, Peter S., and Katherine Stovel. "Becoming a Nazi: A Model for Narrative Networks." *Poetics* 27, no. 2–3 (2000): 69–90.

Bechky, Beth A. "Object Lessons: Workplace Artifacts as Representations of Occupational Jurisdiction." *American Journal of Sociology* 109, no. 3 (2003): 720–52.

——. "Sharing Meaning Across Occupational Communities: The Transformation of Understanding on a Production Floor." *Organization Science* 14, no. 3 (2003): 312–30.

Ben-David, Joseph. *The Scientist's Role in Society: A Comparative Study*. Prentice Hall, 1971.

Berger, Peter L., and Thomas Luckmann. *The Social Construction of Reality: A Treatise in the Sociology of Knowledge*. Doubleday, 1966.

Besbris, Max, and Caitlin Petre. "Professionalizing Contingency: How Journalism Schools Adapt to Deprofessionalization." *Social Forces* 98, no. 4 (2020): 1524–47.

Beunza, Daniel, and David Stark. "Tools of the Trade: The Socio-Technology of Arbitrage in a Wall Street Trading Room." *Industrial and Corporate Change* 13, no. 2 (2004): 369–400.

Bhowmick, Ayan Kumar, Soumajit Pramanik, Sayan Pathak, and Bivas Mitra. "On the Splitting Dynamics of Meetup Social Groups." Proceedings of the International AAAI Conference on Web and Social Media, 2020.

Blei, David M., and John D. Lafferty. "Topic Models." In *Text Mining: Classification, Clustering, and Applications*, ed. Ashok N. Srivastava and Mehran Sahami, 101–24. Chapman & Hall/CRC, 2009.

Bol, Thijs, Christina Ciocca Eller, Herman G. Van De Werfhorst, and Thomas A. DiPrete. "School-to-Work Linkages, Educational Mismatches, and Labor Market Outcomes." *American Sociological Review* 84, no. 2 (2019): 275–307.

Boorman, Scott A., and Harrison C. White. "Social Structure from Multiple Networks. II. Role Structures." *American Journal of Sociology* 81, no. 6 (1976): 1384–1446.

Börner, Katy, Olga Scrivner, Mike Gallant, et al. "Skill Discrepancies Between Research, Education, and Jobs Reveal the Critical Need to Supply Soft Skills for the Data Economy." *Proceedings of the National Academy of Sciences* 115, no. 50 (2018): 12630–37.

Brandt, Philipp. "Sociology's Stake in Data Science." *Sociologica* 16, no. 2 (2022): 149–66.

Brandt, Philipp, and Sean Safford. "La globalisation à la croisée des stratégies organisationnelles et des institutions nationales." In *La société des organisations*, ed. Olivier Borraz. Presses de Sciences Po, 2022.

Brandt, Philipp, and Stefan Timmermans. "Abductive Logic of Inquiry for Quantitative Research in the Digital Age." *Sociological Science* 8 (2021): 191–210.

Bravo, Giangiacomo, Mike Farjam, Francisco Grimaldo Moreno, Aliaksandr Birukou, and Flaminio Squazzoni. "Hidden Connections: Network Effects on Editorial Decisions in Four Computer Science Journals." *Journal of Informetrics* 12, no. 1 (2018): 101–12.

Breiger, Ronald L. "The Duality of Persons and Groups." *Social Forces* 53, no. 2 (1974): 181–90.

Breiman, Leo. "Statistical Modeling: The Two Cultures (with Comments and a Rejoinder by the Author)." *Statistical Science* 16, no. 3 (2001): 199–231.

Briscoe, Forrest, and Sean Safford. "The Nixon-in-China Effect: Activism, Imitation, and the Institutionalization of Contentious Practices." *Administrative Science Quarterly* 53, no. 3 (2008): 460–91.

Brubaker, Rogers. *Citizenship and Nationhood in France and Germany.* Harvard University Press, 2009.

Brubaker, Rogers, and Frederick Cooper. "Beyond 'Identity.'" *Theory and Society* 29, no. 1 (2000): 1–47.

Brunet, Ferran. "The Great Recession and the American and European Economic Governance Challenges." *Europe en Formation* 360, no. 2 (2011): 59–78.

Bucher, Rue, and Anselm Strauss. "Professions in Process." *American Journal of Sociology* 66, no. 4 (1961): 325–34.

Burt, Ronald S. *Brokerage and Closure: An Introduction to Social Capital.* Oxford University Press, 2005.

——. "Social Contagion and Innovation: Cohesion Versus Structural Equivalence." *American Journal of Sociology* 92, no. 6 (1987): 1287–1335.

Bévort, Frans, and Roy Suddaby. "Scripting Professional Identities: How Individuals Make Sense of Contradictory Institutional Logics." *Journal of Professions and Organization* 3, no. 1 (2016): 17–38.

Börner, Katy, Olga Scrivner, Mike Gallant, Shutian Ma, Xiaozhong Liu, Keith Chewning, Lingfei Wu, and James A. Evans. "Skill Discrepancies Between Research, Education, and Jobs Reveal the Critical Need to Supply Soft Skills for the Data Economy." *Proceedings of the National Academy of Sciences* 115, no. 50 (2018): 12630–37.

Camic, Charles, and Yu Xie. "The Statistical Turn in American Social Science: Columbia University, 1890 to 1915." *American Sociological Review* 59, no. 5 (1994): 773–805.

Carruthers, Bruce G., and Wendy Nelson Espeland. "Accounting for Rationality: Double-Entry Bookkeeping and the Rhetoric of Economic Rationality." *American Journal of Sociology* 97, no. 1 (1991): 31–69.

Caza, Brianna Barker, and Stephanie Creary. "The Construction of Professional Identity." In *Perspectives on Contemporary Professional Work*, ed. Adrian Wilkinson, Donal Hislop, and Christine Coupland, 259–85. Edward Elgar, 2016.

Chen, Jiawei, Xiying Wang, Jordan Beck, Chuqing Wu, and John M. Carroll. "Beyond Leaders and Followers: Understanding Participation Dynamics in Event-Based Social Networks." *International Journal of Human–Computer Interaction* 35, no. 20 (2019): 1892–1905.

Cheng, Siwei, and Barum Park. "Flows and Boundaries: A Network Approach to Studying Occupational Mobility in the Labor Market." *American Journal of Sociology* 126, no. 3 (2020): 577–631.

Christin, Angèle. 2018. "Counting Clicks: Quantification and Variation in Web Journalism in the United States and France." *American Journal of Sociology* 123, no. 5 (2020): 1382–1415.

Cleveland, William S. "Data Science: An Action Plan for Expanding the Technical Areas of the Field of Statistics." *International Statistical Review* 69, no. 1 (2001): 21–26.

Coleman, E. Gabriella. *Coding Freedom: The Ethics and Aesthetics of Hacking*. Princeton University Press, 2013.

Coleman, James Samuel. *Foundations of Social Theory*. Belknap Press of Harvard University Press, 1990.

Collins, Harry. *Gravity's Ghost: Scientific Discovery in the Twenty-First Century*. University of Chicago Press, 2011.

——. "The Meaning of Data: Open and Closed Evidential Cultures in the Search for Gravitational Waves." *American Journal of Sociology* 104, no. 2 (1998): 293–338.

Collins, Harry, and Robert Evans. *Rethinking Expertise*. University of Chicago Press, 2007.

Collins, Harry, Robert Evans, and Mike Gorman. "Trading Zones and Interactional Expertise." *Studies in History and Philosophy of Science Part A* 38, no. 4 (2007): 657–66.

Collins, Randall. *Interaction Ritual Chains*. Princeton University Press, 2004.

Cowles, Henry M. *The Scientific Method*. Harvard University Press, 2020.

Cox, David R. "[Statistical Modeling: The Two Cultures]: Comment." *Statistical Science* 16, no. 3 (2001): 216–18.

Craig, Allen T. "Our Silver Anniversary." *Annals of Mathematical Statistics* 31, no. 4 (1960): 835–37.

Davenport, Thomas H., and DJ Patil. "Data Scientist: The Sexiest Job of the 21st Century." *Harvard Business Review* 90, no. 10 (2012): 70–76.

de Souza Leão, Luciana. "Optics of the State: The Politics of Making Poverty Visible in Brazil and Mexico." *American Journal of Sociology* 128, no. 1 (2022): 1–46.

de Souza Leão, Luciana, and Gil Eyal. "The Rise of Randomized Controlled Trials (RCTs) in International Development in Historical Perspective." *Theory and Society* 48 (2019): 383–418.

DellaPosta, Daniel, and Victor Nee. "Emergence of Diverse and Specialized Knowledge in a Metropolitan Tech Cluster." *Social Science Research* 86 (2020): 102377.

DellaPosta, D., Y. Shi, and M. Macy. "Why Do Liberals Drink Lattes?" *American Journal of Sociology* 120, no. 5 (2015): 1473–1511.

Desmond, Matthew. "Disposable Ties and the Urban Poor." *American Journal of Sociology* 117, no. 5 (2012): 1295–1335.

Desrosières, Alain. *The Politics of Large Numbers: A History of Statistical Reasoning*. Harvard University Press, 1998.

Dewey, John. *Human Nature and Conduct*. Modern Library, 1922.

——. *Logic: The Theory of Inquiry*. Henry Holt, 1938.

DiMaggio, Paul, and Walter Powell. "The Iron Cage Revisited: Institutional Isomorphism and Collective Rationality in Organizational Fields." *American Sociological Review* 48, no. 2 (1983): 147–60.

Dodds, Peter S., Duncan J. Watts, and Charles F. Sabel. "Information Exchange and the Robustness of Organizational Networks." *Proceedings of the National Academy of Sciences of the United States of America* 100, no. 21 (2003): 12516–21.

Donoho, David. "Fifty Years of Data Science." Paper presented at the Tukey Centennial workshop, Princeton, New Jersey, 2015.

Dorschel, Robert, and Philipp Brandt. "Professionalization Via Ambiguity: The Discursive Construction of Data Scientists in Higher Education and the Labor Market." *Zeitschrift für Soziologie* 50, no. 3–4 (2021): 193–210.

Epstein, Steven. *Impure Science: AIDS, Activism, and the Politics of Knowledge*. University of California Press, 1996.

Erikson, Emily. *Between Monopoly and Free Trade: The English East India Company, 1600–1757*. Princeton University Press, 2014.

——. *Trade and Nation: How Companies and Politics Reshaped Economic Thought*. Columbia University Press, 2021.

Erikson, Emily, and Peter Bearman. "Malfeasance and the Foundations for Global Trade: The Structure of English Trade in the East Indies, 1601–1833." *American Journal of Sociology* 112, no. 1 (2006): 195–230.

Erikson, Emily, and Mark Hamilton. "Companies and the Rise of Economic Thought: The Institutional Foundations of Early Economics in England, 1550–1720." *American Journal of Sociology* 124, no. 1 (2018): 111–49.

Ermakoff, Ivan. *Ruling Oneself Out: A Theory of Collective Abdications*. Duke University Press, 2008.

——. "The Structure of Contingency." *American Journal of Sociology* 121, no. 1 (2015): 64–125.

Espeland, Wendy Nelson, and Michael Sauder. "Rankings and Reactivity: How Public Measures Recreate Social Worlds." *American Journal of Sociology* 113, no. 1 (2007): 1–40.

Eubanks, Virginia. *Automating Inequality: How High-Tech Tools Profile, Police, and Punish the Poor.* St. Martin's, 2018.

Evans, James A. "Industry Induces Academic Science to Know Less About More." *American Journal of Sociology* 116, no. 2 (2010): 389–452.

Eyal, Gil. "For a Sociology of Expertise: The Social Origins of the Autism Epidemic." *American Journal of Sociology* 118, no. 4 (2013): 863–907.

——. "Spaces Between Fields." In *Bourdieu and Historical Analysis*, ed. Philip S. Gorski, 158–82. Duke University Press, 2013.

Eyal, Gil, Brendan Hart, Emine Onculer, Neta Oren, and Natasha Rossi. *The Autism Matrix: The Social Origins of the Autism Epidemic.* Polity, 2010.

Feigenbaum, Edward A., and Pamela McCorduck. *The Fifth Generation: Artificial Intelligence and Japan's Computer Challenge to the World.* Addison-Wesley, 1983.

Feldman, Pamela J., Sheldon Cohen, Natalie Hamrick, and Stephen J. Lepore. "Psychological Stress, Appraisal, Emotion, and Cardiovascular Response in a Public Speaking Task." *Psychology & Health* 19, no. 3 (2004): 353–68.

Fincham, Robin. "Knowledge Work as Occupational Strategy: Comparing IT and Management Consulting." *New Technology, Work, and Employment* 21, no. 1 (2006): 16–28.

Fleck, Ludwik. *Genesis and Development of a Scientific Fact.* University of Chicago Press, 1979.

Foster, Jacob G., Andrey Rzhetsky, and James A. Evans. "Tradition and Innovation in Scientists' Research Strategies." *American Sociological Review* 80, no. 5 (2015): 875–908.

Foucault, Michel. *Discipline and Punish: The Birth of the Prison.* Vintage, 1995.

Foucault, Michel, and François Ewald. *Dispositive der Macht: Über Sexualität, Wissen und Wahrheit.* Merve Verlag, 1978.

Fourcade, Marion. *Economists and Societies: Discipline and Profession in the United States, Britain, and France, 1890s to 1990s.* Princeton University Press, 2009.

Franzosi, Roberto. "From Words to Numbers: A Generalized and Linguistics-Based Coding Procedure for Collecting Textual Data." *Sociological Methodology* 19 (1989): 263–98.

Freidson, Eliot. *Profession of Medicine: A Study of the Sociology of Applied Knowledge*. University of Chicago Press, 1988.

———. *Professional Powers: A Study of the Institutionalization of Formal Knowledge*. University of Chicago Press, 1986.

———. *Professionalism Reborn: Theory, Prophecy, and Policy*. University of Chicago Press, 1994.

———. *Professionalism: The Third Logic*. University of Chicago Press, 2001.

Frickel, Scott, and Neil Gross. "A General Theory of Scientific/Intellectual Movements." *American Sociological Review* 70, no. 2 (2005): 204–32.

Fuhse, Jan. "The Meaning Structure of Social Networks." *Sociological Theory* 27, no. 1 (2009): 51–73.

———. *Social Networks of Meaning and Communication*. Oxford University Press, 2021.

Fuhse, Jan, and Neha Gondal. "Networks from Culture: Mechanisms of Tie-Formation Follow Institutionalized Rules in Social Fields." *Social Networks* 77 (2024): 43–55.

Gabay-Egozi, Limor, Yossi Shavit, and Meir Yaish. "Gender Differences in Fields of Study: The Role of Significant Others and Rational Choice Motivations." *European Sociological Review* 31, no. 3 (2015): 284–97.

Galison, Peter. *Image and Logic: A Material Culture of Microphysics*. University of Chicago Press, 1997.

Galton, Francis. "Kinship and Correlation." *North American Review* 150, no. 401 (1890): 419–31.

Ganley, Colleen M, Casey E. George, Joseph R. Cimpian, and Martha B. Makowski. "Gender Equity in College Majors: Looking Beyond the STEM/Non-STEM Dichotomy for Answers Regarding Female Participation." *American Educational Research Journal* 55, no. 3 (2018): 453–87.

Garfinkel, Harold. "The Rational Properties of Scientific and Common Sense Activities." *Behavioral Science* 5, no. 1 (1960): 72–83.

Gerth, H. H., and C. Wright Mills. *From Max Weber: Essays in Sociology*. Routledge, 2009.

Gibson, David R. "Taking Turns and Talking Ties: Networks and Conversational Interaction." *American Journal of Sociology* 110, no. 6 (2005): 1561–97.

Giddings, Franklin H. "The Concepts and Methods of Sociology." *Science* 20, no. 515 (1904): 624–34.

——. *Exact Methods in Sociology*. 1899.

Gieryn, Thomas F. "Boundary-Work and the Demarcation of Science from Non-science: Strains and Interests in Professional Ideologies of Scientists." *American Sociological Review* 46, no. 6 (1983): 781–95.

Goel, Vindu. 2014. "Facebook Tinkers With Users' Emotions in News Feed Experiment, Stirring Outcry." *New York Times*, June 29, 2014.

Goffman, Erving. *Behavior in Public Places: Notes on the Social Organization of Gatherings*. Free Press, 1963.

——. *The Presentation of Self in Everyday Life*. Doubleday, 1959.

Goldberg, Amir, Sameer B. Srivastava, V. Govind Manian, William Monroe, and Christopher Potts. "Fitting In or Standing Out? The Tradeoffs of Structural and Cultural Embeddedness." *American Sociological Review* 81, no. 6 (2016): 1190–222.

González-Bailón, Sandra. *Decoding the Social World: Data Science and the Unintended Consequences of Communication*. MIT Press, 2017.

Goode, William J. "Community Within a Community: The Professions." *American Sociological Review* 22, no. 2 (1957): 194–200.

Gorman, Elizabeth H., and Rebecca L. Sandefur. "'Golden Age,' Quiescence, and Revival: How the Sociology of Professions Became the Study of Knowledge-Based Work." *Work and Occupations* 38, no. 3 (2011): 275–302.

Gorski, Philip S. *The Disciplinary Revolution*. University of Chicago Press, 2003.

Goto, Masashi. "Collective Professional Role Identity in the Age of Artificial Intelligence." *Journal of Professions and Organization* 8, no. 1 (2021): 86–107.

Gould, Roger V. *Insurgent Identities: Class, Community, and Protest in Paris from 1848 to the Commune*. University of Chicago Press, 1995.

Granovetter, Mark S. *Getting a Job: A Study of Contacts and Careers*. 2nd ed. University of Chicago Press, 1995.

——. "The Strength of Weak Ties." *American Journal of Sociology* 78, no. 6 (1973): 1360–80.

Grimmer, Justin, Margaret E. Roberts, and Brandon M. Stewart. *Text as Data: A New Framework for Machine Learning and the Social Sciences.* Princeton University Press, 2022.

Guler, Isin, Mauro F. Guillén, and John Muir Macpherson. "Global Competition, Institutions, and the Diffusion of Organizational Practices: The International Spread of ISO 9000 Quality Certificates." *Administrative Science Quarterly* 47, no. 2 (2002): 207–32.

Hammerbacher, Jeff. "Information Platforms and the Rise of the Data Scientist." In *Beautiful Data: The Stories Behind Elegant Data Solutions*, ed. Toby Segaran and Jeff Hammerbacher. O'Reilly Media, 2009.

Hayashi, Chikio. "What Is Data Science? Fundamental Concepts and a Heuristic Example." Proceedings of the Fifth Conference of the International Federation of Classification societies (IFCS-96), Kobe, Japan, 1996.

Hedström, Peter, Rickard Sandell, and Charlotta Stern. "Mesolevel Networks and the Diffusion of Social Movements: The Case of the Swedish Social Democratic Party." *American Journal of Sociology* 106, no. 1 (2000): 145–72.

Heinz, John P., and Edward O. Laumann. *Chicago Lawyers: The Social Structure of the Bar.* Russell Sage Foundation/American Bar Foundation, 1982.

Heinz, John P., Robert L. Nelson, Rebecca L. Sander, and Edward O. Laumann. *Urban Lawyers: The New Social Structure of the Bar.* University of Chicago Press, 2005.

Hénaut, Léonie, Jennifer C. Lena, and Fabien Accominotti. "Polyoccupationalism: Expertise Stretch and Status Stretch in the Postindustrial Era." *American Sociological Review* 88, no. 5 (2023): 872–900.

Hendrikx, Wiljan. "Priced Not Praised: Professional Identity of GPs Within Market-Oriented Healthcare Reform." *Journal of Professions and Organization* 5, no. 1 (2018): 12–27.

Hillmann, Henning. *The Corsairs of Saint-Malo: Network Organization of a Merchant Elite Under the Ancien Régime.* Columbia University Press, 2021.

Hoffman, Mark Anthony, Jean-Philippe Cointet, Philipp Brandt, Newton Key, and Peter Bearman. "The (Protestant) Bible, the (Printed) Sermon, and the Word(s): The Semantic Structure of the Conformist and Dissenting Bible, 1660–1780." *Poetics* 68 (2018): 89–103.

Hughes, Everett C. "Professions." *Daedalus* 92, no. 4 (1963): 655–68.

Ibarra, Herminia. "Provisional Selves: Experimenting with Image and Identity in Professional Adaptation." *Administrative Science Quarterly* 44, no. 4 (1999): 764–91.

Janssens, Jeroen. *Data Science at the Command Line: Facing the Future with Time-Tested Tools.* O'Reilly Media, 2014.

Joas, Hans. *Die Kreativität des Handelns.* Suhrkamp, 1992.

Kelty, Christopher M. *Two Bits: The Cultural Significance of Free Software.* Duke University Press, 2008.

Kim, Junsol, and Byungkyu Lee. "AI-Augmented Surveys: Leveraging Large Language Models for Opinion Prediction in Nationally Representative Surveys." *arXiv preprint* (2023): 2305.09620.

Knorr-Cetina, Karine. *The Manufacture of Knowledge: An Essay on the Constructivist and Contextual Nature of Science.* Pergamon, 1981.

Kossinets, Gueorgi, and Duncan J. Watts. "Origins of Homophily in an Evolving Social Network." *American Journal of Sociology* 115, no. 2 (2009): 405–50.

Kraft, Philip. *Programmers and Managers: The Routinization of Computer Programming in the United States.* Springer-Verlag, 1977.

Krause, Monika. "On Sociological Reflexivity." *Sociological Theory* 39, no. 1 (2021): 3–18.

Kuhn, Thomas S. *The Structure of Scientific Revolutions.* 2nd ed. University of Chicago Press, 1970.

Kunda, Gideon. *Engineering Culture: Control and Commitment in a High-Tech Corporation.* Temple University Press, 2009.

Larson, Magali Sarfatti. *The Rise of Professionalism: A Sociological Analysis.* University of California Press, 1977.

Latour, Bruno. *Science in Action: How to Follow Scientists and Engineers Through Society.* Harvard University Press, 1987.

Latour, Bruno, and Steve Woolgar. *Laboratory Life: The Construction of Scientific Facts.* Princeton University Press, 1986.

Lazega, Emmanuel. "Networks and Institutionalization: A Neo-structural Approach." *Connections* 37, no. 1–2 (2018): 7–22.

Lazer, David, Alex Pentland, Lada Adamic, Sinan Aral, Albert-László Barabasi, Devon Brewer, et al. "Social Science: Computational Social Science." *Science* 323, no. 5915 (2009): 721–23.

Lazer, David, Alex Pentland, Duncan J. Watts, Sinan Aral, Susan Athey, Noshir Contractor, et al. "Computational Social Science: Obstacles and Opportunities." *Science* 369, no. 6507 (2020): 1060–62.

Leahey, Erin. "Alphas and Asterisks: The Development of Statistical Significance Testing Standards in Sociology." *Social Forces* 84, no. 1 (2005): 1–24.

——. "Methodological Memes and Mores: Toward a Sociology of Social Research." *Annual Review of Sociology* 34 (2008): 33–53.

Leahey, Erin, Christine M. Beckman, and Taryn L. Stanko. "Prominent but Less Productive: The Impact of Interdisciplinarity on Scientists' Research." *Administrative Science Quarterly* 62, no. 1 (2017): 105–39.

Lee, Byungkyu, and Peter Shawn Bearman. "Important Matters in Political Context." *Sociological Science* 4 (2017): 1–30.

Leicht, Kevin T., and Mary L. Fennell. "The Changing Organizational Context of Professional Work." *Annual Review of Sociology* 23 (1997): 215–31.

Leifer, Eric M. "Interaction Preludes to Role Setting: Exploratory Local Action." *American Sociological Review* 53, no. 6 (1988): 865–78.

Leszczensky, Lars, Sebastian Pink, David Kretschmer, and Frank Kalter. "Studying Youth Group Identities, Intergroup Relations, and Friendship Networks: The Friendship and Identity in School Data." *European Sociological Review* 38, no. 3 (2022): 493–506.

Lifshitz-Assaf, Hila. 2018. "Dismantling Knowledge Boundaries at NASA: The Critical Role of Professional Identity in Open Innovation." *Administrative Science Quarterly* 63, no. 4 (2022): 746–82.

Lin, Ken-Hou, and Koit Hung. "The Network Structure of Occupations: Fragmentation, Differentiation, and Contagion." *American Journal of Sociology* 127, no. 5 (2022): 1551–1601.

Liu, Sida. "Boundaries and Professions: Toward a Processual Theory of Action." *Journal of Professions and Organization* 5, no. 1 (2018): 45–57.

Lizardo, Omar. "How Cultural Tastes Shape Personal Networks." *American Sociological Review* 71, no. 5 (2006): 778–807.

Lohr, Steve. *Data-ism: The Revolution Transforming Decision Making, Consumer Behavior, and Almost Everything Else.* HarperCollins, 2015.

Loukides, M. *What Is Data Science?* O'Reilly Media, 2011.

Lynn, Freda B. "Diffusing Through Disciplines: Insiders, Outsiders, and Socially Influenced Citation Behavior." *Social Forces* 93, no. 1 (2014): 355–82.

MacKenzie, Donald A. "Material Signals: A Historical Sociology of High-Frequency Trading." *American Journal of Sociology* 123, no. 6 (2018): 1635–83.

——. "Statistical Theory and Social Interests: A Case-Study." *Social Studies of Science* 8, no. 1 (1978): 35–83.

——. *Statistics in Britain, 1865–1930: The Social Construction of Scientific Knowledge.* Edinburgh University Press, 1981.

Manyika, James, Michael Chui, Brad Brown, Jaques Bughin, Richard Dobbs, Charles Roxburgh, and Angela Hung Byers. *Big Data: The Next Frontier for Innovation, Competition, and Productivity.* McKinsey & Company (McKinsey Global Institute), 2011. http://www.mckinsey.com/insights/mgi/research/technology_and_innovation/big_data_the_next_frontier_for_innovation.

Marchal, Emmanuelle, Kevin Mellet, and Géraldine Rieucau. "Job Board Toolkits: Internet Matchmaking and Changes in Job Advertisements." *Human Relations* 60, no. 7 (2007): 1091–113.

Marres, Noortje. *Digital Sociology: The Reinvention of Social Research.* Wiley, 2017.

Marwell, Gerald, and Pamela Oliver. *The Critical Mass in Collective Action.* Cambridge University Press, 1993.

Mason, Hilary, and Chris Wiggins. "A Taxonomy of Data Science." *dataists.com*, April 22, 2010. https://web.archive.org/web/20160220042455/dataists.com/2010/09/a-taxonomy-of-data-science/.

Mau, Steffen. *Das metrische Wir: über die Quantifizierung des Sozialen.* Suhrkamp, 2017.

McCloskey, Deirdre N. *The Rhetoric of Economics.* University of Wisconsin Press, 1998.

McFarland, Daniel A., Kevin Lewis, and Amir Goldberg. "Sociology in the Era of Big Data: The Ascent of Forensic Social Science." *American Sociologist* 47, no. 1 (2016): 12–35.

McMahan, Peter, and Daniel A. McFarland. "Creative Destruction: The Structural Consequences of Scientific Curation." *American Sociological Review* 86, no. 2 (2021): 341–76.

Menchik, Daniel A. "Decisions About Knowledge in Medical Practice: The Effect of Temporal Features of a Task." *American Journal of Sociology* 120, no. 3 (2014): 701–49.

Merton, Robert K. "The Matthew Effect in Science." *Science* 159, no. 3810 (1968): 56–63.

——. "Priorities in Scientific Discovery: A Chapter in the Sociology of Science." *American Sociological Review* 22, no. 6 (1957): 635–59.

——. "Science, Technology and Society in Seventeenth Century England." *Osiris* 4 (1938): 360–632.

——. *The Sociology of Science: Theoretical and Empirical Investigations.* University of Chicago Press, 1973.

Meyer, John W., and Brian Rowan. "Institutionalized Organizations: Formal Structure as Myth and Ceremony." *American Journal of Sociology* 83, no. 2 (1977): 340–63.

Miller, Claire Cain. "Is Blind Hiring the Best Hiring?" *New York Times Magazine*, February 25, 2016.

Mohr, John W. "Soldiers, Mothers, Tramps, and Others: Discourse Roles in the 1907 New York City Charity Directory." *Poetics* 22, no. 4 (1994): 327–57.

Mohr, John W., and Petko Bogdanov. "Introduction—Topic Models: What They Are and Why They Matter." *Poetics* 41, no. 6 (2013): 545–69.

Moody, James. "The Structure of a Social Science Collaboration Network: Disciplinary Cohesion from 1963 to 1999." *American Sociological Review* 69, no. 2 (2004): 213–38.

Morgan, Stephen L. "Adolescent Educational Expectations: Rationalized, Fantasized, or Both?" *Rationality and Society* 10, no. 2 (1998): 131–62.

Morgan, Stephen L., and Christopher Winship. *Counterfactuals and Causal Inference: Methods and Principles for Social Research.* Cambridge University Press, 2007.

Musselin, Christine. "University Governance in Meso and Macro Perspectives." *Annual Review of Sociology* 47 (2021).

Mützel, Sophie, and Ronald Breiger. "Duality Beyond Persons and Groups: Culture and Affiliation." In *The Oxford Handbook of Social Networks*, ed. Ryan Light and James Moody, 392. Oxford University Press, 2020.

Muzio, Daniel, Stephen Ackroyd, and J. Chanlat. "Introduction: Lawyers, Doctors and Business Consultants." In *Redirections in the Study of Expert*

Labour: Established Professions and New Expert Occupations, ed. Daniel Muzio, Stephen Ackroyd, and J. Chanlat. Palgrave Macmillan, 2008.

Navon, Daniel, and Uri Shwed. "The Chromosome 22q11.2 Deletion: From the Unification of Biomedical Fields to a New Kind of Genetic Condition." *Social Science & Medicine* 75, no. 9 (2012): 1633–41.

Nelson, Laura K. "Computational Grounded Theory: A Methodological Framework." *Sociological Methods & Research* 49, no. 1 (2020): 3–42.

Newman, M. E. J., and M. Girvan. "Finding and Evaluating Community Structure in Networks." *Phys. Rev. E* 69, no. 2 (2004): 026113.

Noble, Safiya Umoja. *Algorithms of Oppression: How Search Engines Reinforce Racism*. New York University Press, 2018.

Noordegraaf, Mirko. "Hybrid Professionalism and Beyond: (New) Forms of Public Professionalism in Changing Organizational and Societal Contexts." *Journal of Professions and Organization* 2, no. 2 (2015): 187–206.

O'Neil, Cathy. *Weapons of Math Destruction: How Big Data Increases Inequality and Threatens Democracy*. Crown, 2016.

Ollion, Etienne, and Andrew Abbott. "French Connections: The Reception of French Sociologists in the USA (1970–2012)." *Archives Européennes de Sociologie* 57, no. 2 (2016): 331.

Owen-Smith, Jason, and Walter W. Powell. "Careers and Contradictions: Faculty Responses to the Transformation of Knowledge and Its Uses in the Life Sciences." *Research in the Sociology of Work* 10 (2001).

Pachucki, Mark A., and Ronald L. Breiger. "Cultural Holes: Beyond Relationality in Social Networks and Culture." *Annual Review of Sociology* 36 (2010): 205–24.

Padgett, John F., and Christopher K. Ansell. "Robust Action and the Rise of the Medici, 1400–1434." *American Journal of Sociology* 98, no. 6 (1993): 1259–1319.

Park, Michael, Erin Leahey, and Russell J. Funk. "Papers and Patents Are Becoming Less Disruptive Over Time." *Nature* 613, no. 7942 (2023): 138–44.

Parzen, Emanuel. "[Statistical Modeling: The Two Cultures]: Comment." *Statistical Science* 16, no. 3 (2001): 224–26.

Patil, DJ, Hilary Mason, and Mike Loukides. *Ethics and Data Science*. O'Reilly Media, 2018.

Pearl, Judea. *Causality*. Cambridge University Press, 2009.

Phillips, Damon J., Catherine J. Turco, and Ezra W. Zuckerman. "Betrayal as Market Barrier: Identity-Based Limits to Diversification Among High-Status Corporate Law Firms." *American Journal of Sociology* 118, no. 4 (2013): 1023–54.

Plackett, Robin L. "Studies in the History of Probability and Statistics. XXIX: The Discovery of the Method of Least Squares." *Biometrika* 59, no. 2 (1972): 239–51.

Polanyi, Karl. *The Great Transformation: The Political and Economic Origins of Our Time.* Beacon, 2001.

Porter, Theodore M. *The Rise of Statistical Thinking, 1820–1900.* Princeton University Press, 1986.

——. *Trust in Numbers: The Pursuit of Objectivity in Science and Public Life.* Princeton University Press, 1995.

Portes, Alejandro. "Social Capital: Its Origins and Applications in Modern Sociology." *Annual Review of Sociology* 24 (1998): 1.

Pramanik, Soumajit, Midhun Gundapuneni, Sayan Pathak, and Bivas Mitra. "Can I Foresee the Success of My Meetup Group?" 2016 IEEE/ACM International Conference on Advances in Social Networks Analysis and Mining (ASONAM), 2016.

Pratt, Michael G., Kevin W. Rockmann, and Jeffrey B. Kaufmann. "Constructing Professional Identity: The Role of Work and Identity Learning Cycles in the Customization of Identity Among Medical Residents." *Academy of Management Journal* 49, no. 2 (2006): 235–62.

Putnam, Robert. "Bowling Alone." *Journal of Democracy* 6, no. 1 (1995): 65–78.

——. *Bowling Alone: The Collapse and Revival of American Community.* Simon & Schuster, 2000.

Restrepo-Echavarría, Paulina, and Maria A. Arias. "U.S., European Economies and the Great Recession." Federal Reserve Bank of St. Louis, April 21, 2017.

Ribes, David. "STS, Meet Data Science, Once Again." *Science, Technology, & Human Values* 44, no. 3 (2019): 514–39.

Ricken, Stephen, Louise Barkhuus, and Quentin Jones. "Going Online to Meet Offline: Organizational Practices of Social Activities Through Meetup." Proceedings of the 8th International Conference on Communities and Technologies, 2017.

Rivera, Lauren A. *Pedigree: How Elite Students Get Elite Jobs*. Princeton University Press, 2015.

——. "When Two Bodies Are (Not) a Problem: Gender and Relationship Status Discrimination in Academic Hiring." *American Sociological Review* 82, no. 6 (2017): 1111–38.

Rosenberg, Matthew, Nicholas Confessore, and Carole Cadwalladr. "How Trump Consultants Exploited the Facebook Data of Millions." *New York Times*, March 17, 2018.

Rueschemeyer, Dietrich. *Lawyers and Their Society: A Comparative Study of the Legal Profession in Germany and in the United States*. Harvard University Press, 1973.

Rule, Alix, Jean-Philippe Cointet, and Peter S. Bearman. "Lexical Shifts, Substantive Changes, and Continuity in State of the Union Discourse, 1790–2014." *Proceedings of the National Academy of Sciences* 112, no. 35 (2015): 10837–44.

Rule, Alix, and Philipp Brandt. "Dynamic Art Objects: The Evolving Structural Composition of the Global Art Scene." SUNBELT International Social Networks Research Association Conference, Hamburg, Germany, 2013.

Rule, Alix, Zhongyu Wang, Rupayan Basu, Mohamed AlTantawy, and Owen Rambow. "Using Simple NLP Tools to Trace the Globalization of the Art World." *Proceedings of the ACL 2014 Workshop on Language Technologies and Computational Social Science, Baltimore, Maryland, USA* (2014), 66–70.

Salganik, Matthew J. *Bit by Bit: Social Research in the Digital Age*. Princeton University Press, 2018.

Salganik, Matthew J., and Karen E. C. Levy. "Wiki Surveys: Open and Quantifiable Social Data Collection." *PLOS One* 10, no. 5 (2015): e0123483.

Sandefur, Rebecca L. "Elements of Professional Expertise: Understanding Relational and Substantive Expertise Through Lawyers' Impact." *American Sociological Review* 80, no. 5 (2015): 909–33.

Saner, Philippe. *Datenwissenschaften und Gesellschaft. Die Genese eines transversalen Wissensfeldes*. transcript, 2022.

——. "Envisioning Higher Education: How Imagining the Future Shapes the Implementation of a New Field in Higher Education." *Swiss Journal of Sociology* 45, no. 3 (2019): 359–81.

Sauder, Michael, and Wendy Nelson Espeland. "The Discipline of Rankings: Tight Coupling and Organizational Change." *American Sociological Review* 74, no. 1 (2009): 63–82.

Saxenian, AnnaLee. *Regional Advantage: Culture and Competition in Silicon Valley and Route 128.* Harvard University Press, 1996.

Schader, Martin, Wolfgang A. Gaul, and Maurizio Vichi. "Between Data Science and Applied Data Analysis." Proceedings of the 26th Annual Conference of the Gesellschaft Für Klassifikation EV, University of Mannheim, July 22–24, 2002.

Schofer, Evan, and John W. Meyer. "The Worldwide Expansion of Higher Education in the Twentieth Century." *American Sociological Review* 70, no. 6 (2005): 898–920.

Schutt, Rachel, and Cathy O'Neil. *Doing Data Science.* O'Reilly Media, 2013.

Schweber, Libby. *Disciplining Statistics: Demography and Vital Statistics in France and England, 1830–1885.* Duke University Press, 2006.

Sewell, William H. "A Theory of Structure: Duality, Agency, and Transformation." *American Journal of Sociology* 98, no. 1 (1992): 1–29.

Shan, Carl, Henry Wang, William Chen, and Max Song. *The Data Science Handbook: Advice and Insights from 25 Amazing Data Scientists.* Self-published, 2015.

Shapin, Steven. "'A Scholar and a Gentleman': The Problematic Identity of the Scientific Practitioner in Early Modern England." *History of Science* 29, no. 3 (1991): 279–327.

——. *The Scientific Life: A Moral History of a Late Modern Vocation.* University of Chicago Press, 2008.

Shwed, Uri, and Peter S. Bearman. "The Temporal Structure of Scientific Consensus Formation." *American Sociological Review* 75, no. 6 (2010): 817–40.

Smith, F. Jack. "Data Science as an Academic Discipline." *Data Science Journal* 5 (2006): 163–64.

Somers, Margaret R. "Narrativity, Narrative Identity, and Social Action: Rethinking English Working-Class Formation." *Social Science History* 16, no. 4 (1992): 591–630.

Squazzoni, Flaminio, Giangiacomo Bravo, Mike Farjam, Ana Marusic, Bahar Mehmani, Michael Willis, et al. "Peer Review and Gender Bias:

A Study on 145 Scholarly Journals." *Science Advances* 7, no. 2 (2021): eabdo299.

Star, Susan Leigh. *Ecologies of Knowledge: Work and Politics in Science and Technology.* State University of New York Press, 1995.

Star, Susan Leigh, and James R. Griesemer. "Institutional Ecology, Translations, and Boundary Objects: Amateurs and Professionals in Berkeley's Museum of Vertebrate Zoology, 1907–39." *Social Studies of Science* 19, no. 3 (1989): 387–420.

Stark, David. *The Sense of Dissonance: Accounts of Worth in Economic Life.* Princeton University Press, 2009.

Stark, David, and Ivana Pais. "Algorithmic Management in the Platform Economy." *Sociologica* 14, no. 3 (2020): 47–72.

Stark, Tobias, J. Rambaran, and Daniel McFarland. "The Meeting of Minds: Forging Social and Intellectual Networks Within Universities." *Sociological Science* 7 (2020).

Stets, Jan E., and Michael J. Carter. "A Theory of the Self for the Sociology of Morality." *American Sociological Review* 77, no. 1 (2012): 120–40.

Stevenson, Angus. "Data Scientist." In *Oxford English Dictionary.* Oxford University Press, 2010.

Stigler, Stephen M. *The History of Statistics.* Harvard University Press, 1990.

Stinchcombe, Arthur L. 1959. "Bureaucratic and Craft Administration of Production: A Comparative Study." *Administrative Science Quarterly* 4, no. 2 (1990): 168–87.

——. "Should Sociologists Forget Their Mothers and Fathers?" *American Sociologist* 17, no. 1 (1982): 2–11.

——. *Theoretical Methods in Social History.* Studies in social discontinuity. Academic Press, 1978.

——. *When Formality Works: Authority and Abstraction in Law and Organizations.* University of Chicago Press, 2001.

Swartz, Aaron. *The Boy Who Could Change the World: The Writings of Aaron Swartz.* New Press, 2016.

Swidler, Ann. "Culture in Action: Symbols and Strategies." *American Sociological Review* 51, no. 2 (1986): 273–86.

——. *Talk of Love: How Culture Matters.* University of Chicago Press, 2001.

Tavory, Iddo, and Stefan Timmermans. *Abductive Analysis: Theorizing Qualitative Research.* University of Chicago Press, 2014.

——. "A Pragmatist Approach to Causality in Ethnography." *American Journal of Sociology* 119, no. 3 (2013): 682–714.

Taylor, Frederick Winslow. *The Principles of Scientific Management.* Harper & Brothers, 1919.

Tilly, Charles. *Coercion, Capital, and European States, AD 990–1992.* Blackwell, 1992.

——. *The Vendée.* 2nd ed. Harvard University Press, 1976.

Tocqueville, Alexis de, Eduardo Nolla, and James T. Schleifer. *Democracy in America.* 2 vols. Liberty Fund, 2012.

Toubøl, Jonas, and Anton Grau Larsen. "Mapping the Social Class Structure: From Occupational Mobility to Social Class Categories Using Network Analysis." *Sociology* 51, no. 6 (2017): 1257–76.

Trompette, Pascale, and Dominique Vinck. "Revisiting the Notion of Boundary Object." *Revue d'Anthropologie des Connaissances* 3 (2009).

Tufekci, Zeynep. *Twitter and Tear Gas: The Power and Fragility of Networked Protest.* Yale University Press, 2017.

Turco, Catherine J. *The Conversational Firm: Rethinking Bureaucracy in the Age of Social Media.* Columbia University Press, 2016.

Vallas, Steven P. "The Concept of Skill—a Critical Review." *Work and Occupations* 17, no. 4 (1990): 379–98.

Vaughan, Diane. "NASA Revisited: Theory, Analogy, and Public Sociology." *American Journal of Sociology* 112, no. 2 (2006): 353–93.

——. "Theorizing Disaster: Analogy, Historical Ethnography, and the *Challenger* Accident." *Ethnography* 5, no. 3 (2004): 315–47.

Weber, Max. *Writschaft und Gesellschaft.* 5th ed. Mohr Siebeck, 1976.

Weeden, Kim A. "Why Do Some Occupations Pay More Than Others? Social Closure and Earnings Inequality in the United States." *American Journal of Sociology* 108, no. 1 (2002): 55–101.

Weeden, Kim A., Dafna Gelbgiser, and Stephen L. Morgan. "Pipeline Dreams: Occupational Plans and Gender Differences in STEM Major Persistence and Completion." *Sociology of Education* 93, no. 4 (2020): 297–314.

Weinberg, Bruce D., and Christine B. Williams. "The 2004 US Presidential Campaign: Impact of Hybrid Offline and Online 'Meetup' Communities." *Journal of Direct, Data and Digital Marketing Practice* 8 (2006): 46–57.

Westenberg, P. Michiel, Caroline L. Bokhorst, Anne C. Miers, Sindy R. Sumter, Victor L. Kallen, Johannes van Pelt, and Anke W. Blöte. "A Prepared Speech in Front of a Pre-recorded Audience: Subjective, Physiological, and Neuroendocrine Responses to the Leiden Public Speaking Task." *Biological Psychology* 82, no. 2 (2009): 116–24.

White, Harrison, Scott Boorman, and Ronald Breiger. "Social Structure from Multiple Networks. I. Blockmodels of Roles and Positions." *American Journal of Sociology* 81, no. 4 (1976): 730–80.

White, Harrison C. *Identity and Control: How Social Formations Emerge.* 2nd ed. Princeton University Press, 2008.

Whitford, Josh, and Francesco Zirpoli. "Pragmatism, Practice, and the Boundaries of Organization." *Organization Science* 25, no. 6 (2014): 1823–39.

Wiggins, Chris, and Matthew L. Jones. *How Data Happened: A History from the Age of Reason to the Age of Algorithms.* Norton, 2023.

Wilensky, Harold L. "The Professionalization of Everyone." *American Journal of Sociology* 70, no. 2 (1964): 137–58.

Williams, Sarah. *Data Action: Using Data for Public Good.* MIT Press, 2020.

Wu, Jeff C. F. "Statistics = Data Science?" Lecture slides, 1997.

Wynne, Brian. "Misunderstood Misunderstanding: Social Identities and Public Uptake of Science." *Public Understanding of Science* 1, no. 3 (1992): 281–304.

Zerubavel, Eviatar. *Social Mindscapes: An Invitation to Cognitive Sociology.* Harvard University Press, 1997.

Zuboff, Shoshana. *The Age of Surveillance Capitalism: The Fight for a Human Future at the New Frontier of Power.* Profile, 2019.

Zuckerman, Harriet. "Nobel Laureates in Science: Patterns of Productivity, Collaboration, and Authorship." *American Sociological Review* 32, no. 3 (1967): 391–403.

INDEX

Abbott, Andrew, 5–8, 173, 207, 252–54
abduction, 15–17, 32, 269, 277
abstract knowledge, 8, 33, 81. *See also* stock of knowledge
accommodation services. *See* data science applications, accommodation services
advertising. *See* data science applications, advertising
AI. *See* artificial intelligence
algorithms, 79; in data science, 8; example, 92. *See also* data pipeline; machine learning
ambiguity: as mechanism, 276; in roles, 4, 123, 204, 249; in social world, 228; strategic effect of, 123; in tasks, 146, 228, 249
analogical theorizing: as mechanism, 91; as method, 313n11. *See also* Vaughan, Diane
Anderson, Benedict, 170–71, 233
application programming interface, 61. *See also* data pipeline
applied mathematics, 21, 97, 197, 248

Archer, Margaret, 20, 137
artificial intelligence: data science and, 2, 10, 106, 201, 250; society and, 23, 106. *See also* machine learning

Bayes, Thomas, 237
Bayesian statistics, 77
Bearman, Peter, 300n17, 302–3n35
Bechky, Beth, 7
Ben-David, Joseph, 103, 126
big data: data science and, 25, 149, 196; era 2; science and, 219; trend, 10, 149, 238
Big Tech, 4, 97, 114, 136. *See also* big data
bipartite networks: in application, 87; at meetups, 143, 152–53. *See also* networks
blogging platform. *See* data science applications, blogging platform
Bloomberg, Michael 12, 46. *See also* New York City
boundary objects, 124
boundary work, 305n4

Harvard Business Review, 25
Harvard University, 50
Hayashi, Chikio, 104–5
Hughes, Everett C., 5

identity, 7–10, 277–78; categorical understanding, 209; construction of, 245, 269, 278; relational understanding, 210. *See also* professional identity
image sharing platform. *See* data science applications: image sharing platform
imagined communities, 170, 233, 244. *See also* Anderson, Benedict
indecision, 163, 169. *See also* Ermakoff, Ivan
informal dynamics. *See* relational explanations
informal theory. *See* relational explanations
interaction ritual chains, 137
isomorphism, 218

Japan, 104–5
Java. *See* programming languages
Joas, Hans, 279, 291n48. *See also* creativity
JSON, 66–68, 143–45. *See also* data structures
jurisdiction, 7, 208; conflicts over, 229, 288, 298. *See also* Abbott, Andrew

Kaggle, 35, 273
Krause, Monika, 313n11
Kuhn, Thomas S., 108, 196

labor markets, 20–21, 58, 65, 216, 255
Larson, Magali S., 6, 254
LeCun, Yann, 201–2
Legendre, Adrien-Marie, 118–22
linear algebra, 147–48, 273
LinkedIn: data science and, 8, 25, 28, 30, 46, 180, 183, 242; research site, 62–64, 73
logistic regression: application of, 85; as technique, 77, 92, 273

machine learning: application of, 79, 87; applied math and, 147; classification, 85; competitions, 235; critique of, 243; data science definition, 2; history of, 240; prediction, 76; science and, 219; standard errors and, 204–5; statistics and, 204–5; technological change, 10; training, 32, unsupervised, 77, 87
MacKenzie, Donald, history of quantitative thought, 110–14
Marx, Karl, 4
Mason, Hilary, 223, 225, 240
Matlab. *See* programming languages
Mayer, Tobias, 116–18
meetups: history, 40; political campaigning: 40; spread, 42; organization, 42–43; data science, 41; field site, 13, 139
Meetup.com. *See* meetups
Menchik, Dan, 7, 40
Merton, Robert K., 4, 107
methodology. *See* abduction

GPSR Authorized Representative: Easy Access System Europe, Mustamäe tee 50, 10621 Tallinn, Estonia, gpsr.requests@easproject.com

www.ingramcontent.com/pod-product-compliance
Lightning Source LLC
Chambersburg PA
CBHW022133020426
42334CB00015B/883